WORDS TO EAT BY

WORDS
TO EAT BY

FIVE FOODS
and the
CULINARY HISTORY
of the
ENGLISH LANGUAGE

Ina Lipkowitz

ST. MARTIN'S PRESS

NEW YORK

Recipe and illustration credits on pages 289–291 represent an extension of the copyright page.

www.stmartins.com

Book design by Jonathan Bennett

Library of Congress Cataloging-in-Publication Data

Lipkowitz, Ina.
    Words to eat by : five foods and the culinary history of the English language / Ina Lipkowitz.—1st ed.
        p. cm.
    ISBN 978-0-312-66218-9
    1. English language—Etymology.   2. English language—Terms and phrases.
3. Food—Terminology.   I. Title.
    PE1574.L57 2011
    422—dc22

                                                                2011006361

FIRST EDITION: July 2011

10 9 8 7 6 5 4 3 2 1

For

Natt and Camilla

Noah and Dylan

Gary

CONTENTS

Who the first inhabitants of Britain were, whether natives or immigrants, is open to question: one must remember we are dealing with barbarians.

—Tacitus, *The Agricola* (98 CE)

Hengist, leader of the Saxons, made grand entertainments for king Vortigern, but no particulars have come down to us; and certainly little exquisite can be expected from a people then so extremely barbarous as not to be able either to read or write.

—*The Forme of Cury: A Roll of Ancient English Cookery* (1390)

Every country possesses, it seems, the sort of cuisine it deserves, which is to say the sort of cuisine it is appreciative enough to want. I used to think that the notoriously bad cooking of England was an example to the contrary, and that the English cook the way they do because, through sheer technical deficiency, they had not been able to master the art of cooking. I have discovered to my stupefaction that the English cook that way because that is the way they like it. This leaves nothing to be said, as I suppose the rule that there can be no argument about matters of taste applies to absence of taste—in the literal sense—as well.

—Waverley Root, *The Food of France* (1958)

WORDS TO EAT BY

Pig-Pickin's, Prunes, and Häagen-Dazs

"What's in a Name?"

A nd we hope y'all can join us for our annual Welcome-to-North-Carolina-Labor-Day-Pig-Pickin'." A pig-pickin'? Were they kidding? What was a pig-pickin' in the first place and, in the second place, no thank you. Visions of ravenous hyenas scavenging on wildebeest carcasses flashed through my mind. Needless to say, I was no hyena roaming about on the vast plains of the Serengeti. I was from New York City, the land of Zabar's, H & H bagels, Korean greengrocers, and matchbox-sized kitchens. Where dinner was likely to be cold sesame noodles, ta-chien chicken, and broccoli in garlic sauce that arrived at your apartment door in little white cardboard boxes with metal handles, or, when you decided to eat out (which you did as often as possible, especially on hot summer nights), sturdy white oversized plates of *insalata caprese* and *risotto con gli asparagi* to be lingered over with a bottle of Pinot Grigio or a Vernaccia in the colorfully lit back garden of an Italian *ristorante* in the West Village. If I ever ate pig at all—and to be honest, I ate it as little as possible—I never thought of it as pig, but as *pork*, or better still, as prosciutto, pancetta, mortadella, or one of the many other wonderful cured or

smoked Italian cold cuts that go by the collective name of *salume.*
After all, they don't sell pig loins, pig tenderloins, and pig chops
in the meat section of the supermarket. Pigs are the short-legged,
stout-bodied, even-toed ungulates that waddle around in sties,
rooting their muddy snouts into garbage-filled troughs and snort-
ing with delight. Pork, on the other hand, is what you eat. Or
ham. But even then, it's all too easy to think of your own pulled
hamstring and once you've realized that it's not only pigs who
have hams—how else could you have a hamstring?—you're no
longer in the world of the edible, but of the living.

I'm sure I'm not the only one who wants to distinguish what I
eat from what it was when it was alive and kicking. An entire
language shares my viewpoint. In Spanish, the word for fish is
pez—the fish that swims in the water, that is. The word for the
fish you eat is *pescado,* which literally means "the fish that was
fished" or "the fish that is no more." A lot of other languages
make the same distinction, if not as tidily. Thus, a French pig is a
cochon, but once it's been slaughtered, butchered, and sautéed
with Calvados and cream, the resulting dish is called *porc à la
normande.* An Italian cow is a *vacca,* but thinly sliced beefsteaks
pan-broiled with tomatoes and olives are called *fettine di manzo
alla sorrentina.* In English, it's cows that graze contentedly out in
the meadows, but *roast beef* that we serve *au jus.* And why else
would it be calves that suckle at their mothers' udders, but milk-fed
veal that we pound ever so thin and sauté as quickly as possible
with lemon and capers? How many of us would relish sitting
down to a dinner of *roast cow* or *calf cutlets*?

But back to the pig-pickin'. There I was, a born and bred New
Yorker about to move to North Carolina for a year because my
husband had won an academic fellowship that carried with it a
residency requirement. The pickin' was the brainchild of a Southern gentleman by the name of Corbett Capps, an engineer by trade

who was in charge of the building in which all the serious academic research was to be conducted, and a pit master by avocation who regularly drove up to points north, pig and all necessary accoutrements in the back of his pickup truck, in his tireless quest to introduce curious Yankees to the gustatory pleasures of the Tar Heel State. "Put a little South in yo' mouth" might well have been the clarion call of Corbett Capps's mission to spread the taste of barbecue to those not lucky enough to have been born south of the Mason-Dixon line. Like me, for instance.

Now, my husband might have been most concerned with finishing the book he was working on (he did), but I, not as highminded, was more interested in the food of the region—and what I very quickly discovered was that eastern North Carolina's claim to culinary fame is, hands down, barbecue. Not what we Northerners call barbecue, which is dismissively shrugged off down there as no more than grilled hamburgers and hot dogs, and not what they call barbecue in Texas, which tends to be beef ribs or beef brisket slathered in a spicy tomato-based sauce, but *real* barbecue, which, in North Carolina, can only mean pig. More specifically, a pig somewhere between sixty and a hundred pounds, beheaded, betailed, and befooted, splayed open and gutted, cooked over hickory wood for anywhere from eight to eighteen hours, mopped from time to time with a hot red peppery vinegar, and served with cole slaw and hush puppies, those deep-fried little corn bread fritters that, rumor has it, were tossed to the hungry dogs yapping around the campfire in order to keep them quiet, hence their name.

A splayed-open and gutted pig may be a thing of beauty to a North Carolinian, but it wasn't to me. What I saw on that sticky September late afternoon was a big dead animal sprawled belly up across a huge metal barrel drum. What I smelled, however, wasn't bad. In fact, it smelled good. Very good. So, determined not to be the snobby New Yorker that I so clearly was, I steeled myself to do just as the natives did. I picked. With my fork, not my fingers. From the middle of the carcass—avoiding those areas that only a day or two before had abutted the head, feet, or tail, as though the degree of unadulterated pigginess somehow mysteriously increased the farther one traveled from the relatively innocuous torso, if one can speak of a pig's torso, that is. With not the slightest bit of resistance whatsoever, the meat came off in shreds and chunks, and the instant I brought those shreds and chunks to my lips, I saw the light, just as surely as Paul did on the road to Damascus almost two millennia ago. I was instantly and irrevocably converted. Barbecue suddenly made complete and total sense to me. This was, hands down, the best meat I'd ever tasted in my entire life. Sweet, salty, succulent, with tender fleshy bits alternating with burnt crispy ones. I couldn't stop picking and eating, and I'm sure that I made quite a pig of myself on that hot September day in the woods, with banjos playing, sweet tea flowing, banana pudding waiting for dessert, and more "y'alls" and "darlin's" than I'd ever heard.

In an 1822 essay called "A Dissertation upon Roast Pig," the English writer Charles Lamb imagined the very first time anyone ever tasted roasted pig meat. The story he concocted, ostensibly related in an ancient Chinese manuscript, goes something like this: left to take care of the family's pigs, a young swineherd named Bo-bo began to amuse himself by playing with fire. Fire being what it is, sparks quickly flew to the cottage where the prized sow had recently given birth to nine piglets. The cottage burned down and the pigs were all killed, which would have been an utter and complete catastrophe except that "an odour assailed his nostrils, unlike any scent which he had before experienced. What could it proceed from?" Guilty and afraid of the punishment his father would certainly wreak on him, Bo-bo looked everywhere for signs of life, hoping against hope that at least one of the piglets had survived the conflagration. He felt for a heartbeat but succeeded only in burning his fingers on the scorched skin. And so he did what anyone does when he burns his fingers: he put them in his mouth. As he stood there, licking his fingers and gazing at the roasted carcasses lying in a smoking heap at his feet, "the truth at length broke into his slow understanding, that it was the pig that smelt so, and the pig that tasted so delicious; and, surrendering himself up to the new-born pleasure, he fell to tearing up whole handfuls of the scorched skin with the flesh next it." Thus was discovered, quite by accident, the world's first pig-pickin'—without the hallmark North Carolinian slow cooking and peppery vinegar, but a pig-pickin' nonetheless.

Very clearly, Lamb must have loved his roast pork, but what may be less immediately apparent is that he also loved his words (he was a writer, after all) and knew how to get the most mileage out of them. He knew that it was *pig* Bo-bo was eating, not *pork,* just as he knew that it was *flesh,* not *meat,* that the young Chinese swineherd couldn't stop cramming down his throat. When you think about it, *flesh* is to *meat* as *pig* is to *pork*—or as living is to edible. Bo-bo was eating what had minutes ago been alive and was still more flesh than meat, more pig than pork. And it was unspeakably good, in an unabashedly carnivorous way.

I was reminded of Lamb's essay when I came across another description of what can only be called a pig-pickin' that took place almost two hundred years later, not in a rural Chinese village but in a trendy Manhattan restaurant. I don't know whether the *New York Times* restaurant critic Frank Bruni has ever read Lamb's essay, but judging from his review of Momofuku Ssäm Bar, I think he must have. Read for yourself his description of the meal at which he and five of his friends metamorphosed from the sophisticated urban cosmopolitans they were by day into the scavenging wild animals they became that night and note how in the process of their transformation, *pork* shifts to *pig* and *meat* to *flesh*:

> I'm not sure it's possible to behave with much dignity around seven glistening pounds of *pork* butt, but on a recent night at Momofuku Ssäm Bar, five friends and I weren't even encouraged to try.
>
> Servers didn't bother to carve the mountain of *meat* . . . They just popped it in the center of the table, handed out sets of tongs, left us to our own devices and let the *pig* scatter where it may. . . .
>
> We lunged at the *flesh*. Tore at it. Yanked it toward ourselves in dripping, jagged hunks . . . so we could stuff it straight into our mouths. We looked, I realized like hyenas at an all-you-can-eat buffet on the veldt.[1]

As I sat at my kitchen table reading the newspaper's restaurant review that morning, two not entirely unrelated thoughts went through my mind. First, I wondered if I would ever be up to ordering the *bo ssäm* (a whole butt, a dozen oysters, kimchi, rice, and Bibb lettuce, to be reserved in advance for parties of six to ten, the menu specifies) at Momofuku Ssäm, and I had a hunch that if I ever did rise to the occasion, I'd be likely to have the same reaction I had to my North Carolina pig-pickin': a guilty pleasure. Guilty, because we're supposed to be above such base hyenalike appetites, and pleasure, because those insistent bestial appetites are being so completely and utterly gratified.

Second, I wondered at the identical word choice that two such talented writers—one from early-nineteenth-century England and the other from early-twenty-first-century New York—used to convey the undeniably animalistic act of lunging at roasted pig, of tearing flesh from bone. Much as the blunt alliterative name of the pig-pickin' did on that other morning when I held the phone to my ear, their words refused to allow me to blithely ignore the corporeal reality of the animal, of the flesh in the meat, of the pig in the pork. And this made me pause.

Perhaps I'm overstating my case. After all, I know there are plenty of people who don't seem to mind peering into the large tanks of water at the entrance of seafood restaurants to choose the lobster they want boiled for their dinner, and I have a clear memory of my sister's gazing out placidly at the teals and mallards paddling about on the pond which the restaurant we were eating in overlooked and calmly ordering *duck à l'orange*. When I was a child, on the other hand, I refused to eat anything that at all resembled what it had looked like before it became my dinner. Drumsticks, wings, and ribs of any kind were out of the question, as were whole birds, fish, and, obviously, anything like a lobster or a shrimp. Once I came home from school, opened the refrigerator for a snack, and saw a whole beef tongue resting on a plate. The memory stays with me to this day. I wasn't, however, a vegetarian, which would have been the more consistent and certainly less hypocritical way to go, so much as an eater who consciously and willfully chose to deny the reality of what she was putting into her mouth. I'd eat hamburgers and chicken breasts because the leap required to visualize a Hereford, Angus, or Texas Longhorn from a patty of chopped meat or a feathered and combed Chantecler or Jersey Giant from a skinless white oval was too vast for my imagination to traverse. As far as I was concerned, eating was truly a feat of mind over matter.

My childhood eating restrictions might have been a bit extreme, but I know now that I'm hardly alone in not wanting to dwell on the fact that the thing I'm eating was once alive or even to know too precisely what it is that I'm eating. Hence, words like *sweetbread*. We don't mind eating a thymus gland, which is what a sweetbread is, but we don't want to see the words on a menu or we're likely to start thinking of the human immune system and the production of infection-fighting cells. And why else would celebrity chef Mario Batali have had to hoodwink his customers into ordering the *lardo bruschetta* he'd created for his Otto Enoteca Pizzeria? "I knew that they wouldn't eat it if I just said, 'This is the fat of a pig melted onto toast,'" Batali confided to restaurant reviewer Frank Bruni, and so he invented the nonsense phrase "white prosciutto."[2] The dish soon became one of the signature items on his menu. Clearly it wasn't the cholesterol-laden calories that were putting people off, but the wording. Of course we all know precisely where pork fat comes from, but somehow we just don't want to have the words thrust down our throats, as though we were force-fed geese whose livers were being readied for the slaughter. On that sticky hot September evening in North Carolina, though, there was no denying exactly where the pork, fat and all, had come from and not a soul could have gotten away with calling the festivity anything other than what it was: a pig-pickin'.

The whole business of pig-pickin's, porcine nomenclature, and meat eating in general got me thinking. What was I reacting to more viscerally as I stood there in my New York City apartment, holding the phone to my ear and listening to that oh-so-hospitable Southern voice invite me to eat a pig? The mental image of a big dead animal splayed wide open or the no-holds-barred name *pig-pickin'*? Would I have had the same immediate stomach-clenching reaction if that drawling voice on the telephone had invited me to a Labor Day *pork roast*? Perhaps, I thought, it was more the name than the thing that sent such a spasm of nausea straight through me. And the longer I thought about that possibility, the more I realized that our tendency to strategically rename organ meats and pig fat is extended to many other foods as well—not simply to those we have to kill and butcher. What about the prune, after all? Mocked and derided as no more than a shriveled-up high-fiber fruit to be endured by old people who suffer from irregularity (itself a bit of a euphemism), the prune—qua prune, that is—is no more. In 2000, after the California Prune Board successfully lobbied the Food and Drug Administration to allow the fruit to be renamed, it officially became a *dried plum*. The result? Sales among young people skyrocketed and the Prune Board itself is now known as the California Dried Plum Board.

Even foods that need no name change whatsoever to make our mouths water nonetheless benefit from clever marketing. Think ice cream. Arguably most people's favorite dessert, whether hard or soft-serve, whether Mocha Chip, White Chocolate Raspberry Truffle, or Toasted Coconut Sesame Brittle. But readers of a certain age will remember a time when flavors such as these didn't yet exist, when going out for ice cream meant vanilla, chocolate, strawberry, or maybe butter pecan at Carvel's, Howard Johnson's, or Dairy Queen, and when the only ice cream to be bought at the supermarket had names like Breyers and Sealtest. And then came Häagen-Dazs, with its Scandinavian-looking name that in fact isn't Scandinavian at all, but a complete invention of the Nestlé Corporation, which wanted to market a super-premium (read: higher fat content) ice cream and knew an American name just wouldn't cut it. The Nordic name, however, conjuring up images of icy fjords and midnight suns, was a runaway success—until it was challenged by another less longlived Scandinavian-sounding competitor: Frusen Glädjé. I remember being stopped on the sidewalk shortly after these ice creams had become the household items they are today. A young man clad in a spotless white uniform, clipboard in hand, was conducting an informal poll of passersby. "What is your favorite flavor?" "Do you prefer ice cream or sorbet?" "What, in your opinion, is the single most determining factor in the choice of which ice cream to purchase?" To the latter question I answered as honestly as I could: an umlaut. For those of you who haven't studied one of the Germanic languages, an umlaut is the diacritical symbol represented by those two dots over the "a" in Häagen and Glädjé. The young man stared blankly at me for a moment, thanked me, and turned to the next passerby. Obviously he had decided not to record my response, but this many years later, I continue to maintain that mine was the correct answer. If you want to sell as much premium ice cream as possible, be sure that your brand name has a Nordic-looking umlaut.

So, what do pig-pickin's and Häagen-Dazs have in common? Each, in its different way, awakened me to the power of food words. Sometimes these words stir our desire, sometimes they make us queasy, and sometimes they all but eclipse the very things they refer to, the foods themselves. And they awakened me to something else as well: the hierarchy of languages. The more you look at the matter, all languages were created equal, but some languages have become more equal than others. We English speakers seem to prefer it when our food names come to us from somewhere else. Certainly this is the case when we want to forget that what we're eating is, for example, the fat liver of a force-fed goose. And so we call it *foie gras,* which means just that, fat liver, but sounds a whole lot more appetizing. Fried squid tentacles don't sound as tempting as *calamari fritti* either, do they? But if it were just the foreignness of the names that won us over, we'd be equally likely to order *Leberwurst* or *Tintenfisch.* The fact that we're not suggests that in the cases of *foie gras* and *calamari fritti,* we prefer the sounds of some languages to others. Certain languages seem to appeal to us and sound more refined, more cultured, more sophisticated than others. Generally speaking (ice cream aside), we like it best of all when our food sounds French or Italian, and we're much less inclined to eat things that sound too German—with the notable exceptions of hamburgers and frankfurters, neither of which answer to our idea of gourmet fare anyway. Just think of the difference between *osso buco* and *geschmorte Kalbshaxe*. Braised veal shanks both, but one gets our mouths watering with the thought of its accompanying saffron-scented *risotto alla milanese,* while my guess is that very few of us even know what *Kalbshaxe* is, whether *geschmorte* or *gebräunt* (braised or browned). By the same token, nutritionally speaking, ham-and-cheese croissants may be no better than cheeseburgers, but they've never been the target of a documentary such as Morgan Spurlock's *Super Size Me* or a book such as Eric Schlosser's *Fast Food Nation.* Why is all our scorn heaped on McDonald's and Burger King while no such offensive has been launched against popular lunch franchises with the Euro-sounding names of Au Bon Pain and Panera? Because the food is better and healthier? Or because we simply like the names more and assume that if it's French or Italian, it's got to be better?

The story is much the same with our more upscale restaurants. We English speakers have a long-standing and unrequited love for Italian and French foods—whoever heard of a Milanese preferring mushy peas to *rici e bisi* or a Parisian choosing bangers and mash over a slow-cooked *cassoulet?*—so it's hardly surprising that when we go out to eat, we gravitate to almost any awning displaying the words *trattoria, osteria, brasserie,* or *bistro.*

Our culinary language is positively saturated with French and Italian words, from *à la carte* to *zabaglione.* And yet when we stay at home—or down home, as the case may be in North Carolina—the foods we cook and eat most often, as well as the names we know them by, are neither French nor Italian. We don't eat *polpettone* at home, but meat loaf; we don't bake a *tarte aux pommes* for the Thanksgiving table, but apple pie. On the feast days that we celebrate at home, we serve traditional English-style standing rib roasts, hams, and legs of lamb, or that true-blue American specialty, the gargantuan roast turkey, and yet when our taste buds dream, it's of the meal we ate on vacation in a little bistro on Paris's Rive Gauche or in a trattoria on Florence's Oltrarno. If it had been a pork roast I'd been invited to, I might have had a much different reaction. Pork, after all, is not all that different from the French *porc,* or roast from *rôtir.* But a pig-pickin'? Nothing French or Italian about those words. *Picg* was what medieval Germanic tribes would have called baby swine and *pician* was what they would have done to that baby swine's carcass—hardly an image of elegant gourmets sitting down to dine.

When it comes to culinary matters, I have come to conclude, we English speakers suffer from a profound insecurity complex. We might even call it a collective split personality. With the outward sophistication and respectability of a Dr. Jekyll, we prefer French and Italian foods and their names; but with the lustful appetites of a Mr. Hyde, we long for and feel most comfortable and even happiest with our traditional foods and their German-sounding names, even as our proper Dr. Jekylls consistently denigrate them. We may not be terribly proud of our inner culinary Mr. Hyde, but we can no more deny his appetites than we can any other desire, compulsion, or fetish. When it comes to the matter of our bodily appetites—whether for food or sex—our minds don't stand a chance, which is precisely why we greedily devour in the privacy of our own homes what we'd be embarrassed to be caught enjoying in public, whether it's glasses of milk before bedtime, individually wrapped slices of American cheese on buttered Wonder bread, peanut butter on Ritz crackers, or the green bean casserole with french-fried onion rings without which many a Thanksgiving table would be woefully incomplete.

Granted, few of us have either the time or the ability to prepare the *primi* and *secondi piatti* of a complete Italian dinner, not to mention the *béchamels, veloutés,* and *demi-glâces* necessary to classical French haute cuisine, and so on one level, it's easy to understand why we so often eat quickly assembled familiar meals at home and why we choose to dine out where we do. Yet our split culinary personality expresses itself in more than just restaurant preference. The closer we look at the difference between our attitudes toward French and Italian food, on the one hand, and English and American on the other, the more we learn something very revealing about our idea of what food should be—*real* food, that is.

When you think about it, almost everything we eat or drink is a balancing act between nature and nurture. Everyone knows, for instance, that vegetables would grow naturally without any intervention from us, but how many of us are aware that virtually every vegetable we buy at the supermarket today has been drastically reengineered from its long-ago forebear, sometimes to the point at which even the faintest family resemblance is almost impossible to perceive? The large-kerneled sugary sweet corn on the cob we enjoy at backyard cookouts has little resemblance to the fifty-six-hundred-year-old corncobs found at an archaeological dig in New Mexico that were the size of a human finger—and I'm not referring to the individual kernels, but to the entire cob. By the same token, the apples we eat today still grow on trees, but they're a far cry from the hard little sour *Malus sieversii* that once grew (and still do) in the immense primeval forests of modern-day Kazakhstan and that are believed to be the ancestor of all modern apples. Milk obviously would emerge from cows, sheep, goats, and other mammals with or without us there to drink it, but only people can transform it into cheese, yogurt, butter, ice cream, and all the other hundreds of dairy products found the world over. Bread is the clearest example of a food that brings together nature and nurture: made from wheat or any number of grains from wild grasses, bread simply wouldn't *be* without people who do the work of reaping, threshing, parching, hulling, grinding, combining with water, shaping, and baking. And meat? Well, just think of my reaction to the pig-pickin'. We like to think we have evolved if only a little bit from our Stone Age ancestors who tore their prey limb from limb. There's the simple matter of cooking, after all, that separates us from the rest of the animal kingdom. In other words, we nurture the foods that we find in nature—sometimes to the point that it's quite a stretch to call the results of our nurturing natural.

So what does it say about us English speakers that so many of us still like to drink our milk pure and simple (and, perhaps regrettably, still like the good old American cheese of our school lunch boxes), even as we put on pedestals the sophisticated artisanal cheeses of the French and Italians, who have historically turned their noses up at the untransformed raw beverage? That we're known for our hamburgers, our Angus and Omaha steaks, our roast beef, our barbecue, and our pig-pickin's, whereas signature French dishes such as *boeuf en daube* and *coq au vin* are as much as, if not more, about the preparation as they are about the meat itself? That both the native leeks of the British Isles and the wild leeks, or ramps, of the mid-Atlantic states look a lot more like weeds than the horticulturally improved varieties of the Mediterranean? That, although the reengineered sweet and juicy apples we eat today are worlds removed from the sour little wild crab apples that our forebears knew, we nonetheless still call them by an ancient name that originally referred to any old wild fruit that grew on a tree? Or that our *bread,* unlike *pain, pane,* and *panini,* might very well derive its name from the same unpredictable and wild yeasts that cause malted barley and hops to ferment into beer?

What, I wonder, does the striking disparity between our foods and words and those of the French and Italians say about us?

To my mind, it says that the fairly relentless denigration of English and American food and the accompanying glorification of French and Italian are as much about attitude as they are about taste—perhaps much more so, in the final analysis. We might prefer French food to English, but there's nothing inherently superior about a *boeuf à la bourguignon* to a roast beef with Yorkshire pudding. It's simply that we've grown accustomed to think that the former is a more sophisticated gourmet offering than the latter. But why have we been bred to think that the more elaborate presentation is the better one? Where do these attitudes come from? Why do things sound so much better when they're in French or Italian? Why do we English speakers have such a split personality?

The more I thought about this, the more I realized how very deep-seated our split personality is and how far back in time it goes. Back to the very first encounter between Mediterranean and English food—to the year 55 BC, which was when Julius Caesar left Rome to conquer the island at the westernmost end of the known world. The island he knew as Britannia. Of all the things he could have commented on when he first caught sight of those wild northern savages who painted their skin blue, it was their appalling dietary habits that most struck him—appalling to a Roman who thrived on olives, wine, and fresh fruits and vegetables, that is. "Inland, the people for the most part do not plant corn-crops, but live on milk and meat," he wrote. Except he wrote not in English, but in Latin—the ancestor, of course, of today's French and Italian—and the exact words he used to conclude his reflection about these strange eating practices were *lacte et carne vivunt.* The more I reflected on the at once horrified and patronizing attitude dripping out of his Latin words, the more I came to realize that our contemporary scorn for English foods and their blunt, often monosyllabic names echoes Caesar's disdain for those long-ago blue-skinned non-Latin-speaking barbarians and their foraged foods. He had come from Rome and spoke the language of the empire that to this day is known for its aqueducts, dams, bridges, plumbing, domes, and arches. In short, Rome was an awful lot more sophisticated than northern Europe in the first century BC.

And it remained more sophisticated several centuries later when the Romans, by then turned Christian, came once again to the island, determined to convert the Angles and Saxons who in the intervening years had invaded the island from their home in north-western Germany. It was those savage northern heathens, who found their food in the wild and called it by Germanic names that they refused to replace with Latin counterparts, who bequeathed to us the words we use to this day: *apple, garlic, leek, milk, butter, meat, chicken, broth, loaf, bread, bean, beer, water*—the list could go on and on. Which is why so many of our most everyday food words still sound a lot more like their German cousins than they do their Italian equivalents: *Apfel, Lauch, Milch, Fleisch,* and *Brot* look much more familiar to an English speaker than do *mela, perro, latte, carne,* and *pane.*

Or *pomme, poireau, lait, viande,* and *pain*—the food words that arrived on the island with the aristocratic and French-speaking Duke William who landed at Hastings in 1066 and summarily defeated the Old English–speaking troops of King Harold, re-sulting in what has gone down in history as the Norman Con-quest of England. Much like the Romans who had brought their Mediterranean foods and food names with them a millennium earlier, the Normans too brought exotic new herbs, spices, fruits, and vegetables, calling them by French names that can still be understood today, with only a slight expenditure of effort: *gingem-bre, safran, cardamome, clou de girofle, pêche, cerise, prune, abricot, orange, limon*—ginger, saffron, cardamom, clove, peach, cherry, plum, apricot, orange, lemon.★ And thus was born the English language, one parent Germanic and the other French. Thus was born, as well, our national split personality. Even though today the language of gourmet cuisine is francophile through and through (*gourmet* and *cuisine* being two perfect examples), the words of the everyday home kitchen—*cook* and *bake,* for instance—have remained true to their Germanic parentage.

But as my reaction to that North Carolina Labor Day pig-pickin' made painfully clear to me, food words are never neutral. In one way or another, we react to them. They make our mouths water, they make our stomachs twinge, and—no less importantly—they convey attitude. When today we imagine that food instantly becomes more refined when called by a French or Italian name—think *pâté de foie gras* as compared to chopped liver or *osso buco* as compared to hollow bones—we are keeping alive the ancient attitudes of the Romans who ventured up into the barbarian north, the Christians who sought to convert the Germanic heathens, and the aristocratic Normans who defeated the Angles and Saxons in that fateful battle of 1066. By the same token, when we continue to call our apples *apples* and our milk *milk,* we are still conveying the attitudes held by those foraging hunter-gatherers of so long ago: that real food is supposed to be as unprocessed and untransformed as possible, that it should have more to do with nature than with nurture.

In recent years, in fact, a new generation of cooks and foodies is beginning to put these attitudes into practice, and they're doing so by reversing the preferences that have reigned since Caesar first landed on the shores of Britannia. Openly preferring foods

---

★There are two French words spelled *limon:* one, from the Latin *limonis,* is usually translated as "silt" or "alluvial deposit"; the other, from the Persian *limun,* refers to citrus fruit—more specifically, to the lemon, also called *citron* in today's French.

that have not been transformed and reengineered, they're using age-old Germanic words to state their case. Poetically named heirloom apples that would never be seen in our large chain supermarkets regularly appear at small local farm stands even though they lack the polish of the ubiquitous Red Delicious. "By modern commercial standards," writes Edward Behr, "the old varieties often have shortcomings. They may bruise easily, store poorly, be plain-looking or outright ugly. . . . An orchardist who still has some Wolf River trees told me, 'It's probably about the poorest apple I grow.'"[3] And yet Wolf River apples, as big as grapefruits or small cantaloupes (they often weigh more than a pound each) with dull red skin, coarsely textured flesh, and a tart flavor, have become so popular that hundred of Web sites sell seeds and offer such cooking tips as "One apple, one pie."

Or just think of the entire Wild Food Movement. Not so long ago, "farm-fresh" was synonymous with "wholesome" and "natural." Today it's more likely to make us think "agribusiness." Who really believes that there's a farm named Pepperidge anyway? Now it's no longer "farm-fresh" but "wild" that gets people going. Granted, wild mushrooms have been around forever, but now there are wild green vegetables as well. Wild green vegetables? Weeds, in other words. Edible weeds. There's a movement afoot to reintroduce into our diets plants that we're far more likely to think of as garden pests; "If you can't beat 'em, eat 'em" is its mantra. What is purslane, for instance, that perennial weed with the rubbery leaves and the little yellow flowers that springs up out of the cracks in your driveway? Gardening books tell you that it's one of the hardest weeds to get rid of, but Rhode Island chef Champe Speidel so likes cooking with it that he considered naming his restaurant after the weed (he didn't—it's called Persimmon instead). He serves a warm salad of purslane with artichokes and mussels as an appetizer and a cold purslane salad to accompany his pan-roasted glazed squab. Boston's Gordon Hamersley adds the weed to his spring vegetable risotto, and still another chef uses it to flavor his cured slow-cooked pork belly with pineapple taco sauce. So which is it? Invasive weed or summer treat?

Then there's milk, that most natural of beverages. Or is it? Can it still be natural after it's been pasteurized to kill off the salmonella and *E. coli* bacteria and homogenized to prevent the cream from rising to the top as nature intended it to? Is it still natural when it's been pumped from the udders of cows treated with recombinant bovine growth hormones (rBGH) designed to maximize the production of milk? No, says the Campaign for Real (or raw) Milk, whose members resort to such loopholes as "cow-sharing" so that they can legally drink raw milk, which the law allows only from cows that one personally owns.

By the same token, meat seems to be making a comeback these days, and I don't mean elegantly plated veal scaloppine pounded paper-thin between pieces of waxed paper or tiny baby lamb chops broiled until just pink inside and then festooned with paper frills and served with mint sauce. No, I mean *real* meat. Great big pieces of it—what they used to call joints or haunches. Grilled or roasted, without fuss or fanfare, those hunks of well-marbled beef and pork, moist and glistening with fat, arrive at tables in restaurants such as Momofuku Ssäm Bar, chasing away all thoughts of the grain- and vegetable-based Mediterranean diet. Perhaps we can thank the Atkins and all those other low-carbohydrate diets for meat's renaissance, but maybe it's really the other way around. Maybe all these animal protein diets are so popular because they allow us to eat guilt-free what we've been wanting to eat for years and years anyway. Or at least, according to the "Refined Meathead" school of cooking, we have. The mostly male, pork- and offal-obsessed cooks, who include among their ranks David Chang, chef-owner of Momofuku Ssäm, and

Mario Batali, who repeatedly dismisses the haute cuisine of "the faggotty French," prefer parts of animals that not too many of us have willingly eaten for years. Highly touted new cookbooks like Hugh Fearnley-Whittingstall's *The River Cottage Meat Book* and Fergus Henderson's *The Whole Beast: Nose to Tail Eating* give us recipes entirely lacking from *The Joy of Cooking,* which devotes a brief seven of its over a thousand pages to what it euphemistically calls "variety meats." In Henderson's book, something of a cult classic, we learn how to cook "Rolled Pig's Spleen," "Deep-Fried Lamb's Brains," "Crispy Pig's Tails," "Sorrel, Chicory, and Crispy Ear Salad," and many more such dishes that conjure up images of carnivorous barbarians ripping whole beasts apart more than they do sophisticated twenty-first-century restaurant goers out for a new and exciting dining experience.

There's even a contemporary trend to make bread—that most unnatural of foods—as little engineered as possible. The artisanal breads on display at independently owned and waftingly inviting bakeries across the country, from California's Acme Bread Company and La Brea Bakery to New York's Sullivan Street Bakery, are as different as can be from the industrially manufactured presliced white loaves awaiting purchase at supermarkets everywhere: lovingly crafted according to age-old techniques from natural ingredients rather than mass-produced from refined flours enriched with vitamins and minerals; shaped and baked individually rather than conveyed down an assembly line like a Ford Model T; brown-bagged upon purchase rather than prepackaged in polyethylene. No bread can be entirely natural, but some breads can be more natural than others.

All these new trends have two things in common: they all make it okay for food not to be engineered, not to be transformed, not to be "improved"; and they all return us to the attitudes still evoked by some of the oldest English food words we have: apple, leek, milk, meat, and bread. It was these five every-day foods and the names we know them by—one for each major section of the Surgeon General's nutritional pyramid—that inspired the writing of this book and that remain at its core. Tracing their unlikely histories, *Words to Eat By* highlights the inextricable interweaving of what we put into our mouths and the sounds that come out of them. In the process it reveals something distinctive about us as well: turns out that when it comes down to our default understanding of what food is supposed to be, we're a lot more like those long-ago northern Europeans who hunted and gathered their food from nature than we are like the Mediterranean people who believed it their business in life to transform the raw ingredients they found into civilized products. To us, food—*real* food—is far more a matter of nature than nurture. As much as we may have been civilized over the centuries, we English speakers still eat with barbarian appetite.

CHAPTER ONE

Fruit and Apples

"Dare to Say What You Call Apple"[1]

Infants sought the mother's nipple as soon as born; and when grown, and able to feed themselves, run naturally to fruit.

—John Evelyn, *Acetaria: A Discourse of Sallets* (1699)

The Apple. This useful fruit is mentioned in Holy Writ; and Homer describes it as valuable in his time. It was brought from the East by the Romans, who held it in the highest estimation. . . . The best varieties are natives of Asia, and have, by grafting them upon others, been introduced into Europe. The crab, found in our hedges, is the only variety indigenous to Britain; therefore, for the introduction of other kinds we are, no doubt, indebted to the Romans.

—*Beeton's Book of Household Management* (1861)

England, you see, is much too far north for fruits to come to fullest flavor. Her grapes are anticlimaxes. Her apricots, apologies. So the British, long ago, learned to add the lost sun to her fruits through fire and coals. Hence she has given the world its best jams.

—Robert P. Tristram Coffin, "British Breakfast" (1948)

Proto-Indo-European: *abel, melon*

GERMANIC: *apalaz*   CELTIC: *aballo*   LATIN: *malum; pomum*   GREEK: *mílon*

Norwegian: *eple*   Irish: *abal*   Italian: *mela*

Swedish: *äpple*   Scottish: *ubhal*   French: *pomme*

Danish: *æble*   Welsh: *afal*   Spanish: *manzana*

Dutch: *appel*   Cornish: *aval*   Romanian: *mar*

German: *Apfel*   Breton: *aval*

Old English: *æppel*

English: *apple*

In one of the books I used to read to my children when they were still young enough to be read aloud to, a little girl enlists the help of a wise but prodigal rabbit in choosing a birthday gift for her mother. When she confesses that she can't possibly afford the emeralds and rubies he suggested, he turns to Plan B: peas and spinach. " 'No,' said the little girl. 'We have those for dinner all the time.' " At last they resolve on a basket of fruit. "So she took her basket," the story ends, "and she filled it with the green pears and the yellow bananas and the red apples and the blue grapes. It made a lovely present."[2] Obviously the story is meant to teach children about colors: rubies and apples are red, emeralds and pears are green. To my mind, though, it teaches another, equally important lesson. Fruit makes a better gift than vegetables. The book doesn't have to tell us why because we already know. We like fruit better than vegetables. It's sweeter. We don't have to work for it. We don't have to cook it. All we have to do is pick and eat. Fruit promises and delivers immediate gratification—how many things in life can that be said of? Even a child knows that fruit gives us a happiness all the cauliflowers, peas, spinach, and turnips in the world can never hope to match.

What neither the rabbit nor the little girl in the children's book can possibly know, however, is that the very word they use to name all those pears, bananas, apples, and grapes had its origins in happiness. The Latin *fructus*, from which our own word gradually evolved, came to refer to fruit as years went by, but it began life as a form of the verb *fruor,* which meant "to have pleasure" or "to enjoy." How appropriate is that? And fruit's origins in happiness go further back still. Long before the Romans were around to enjoy their *fructi* and long before the Greeks who preceded them, there were people who spoke a language believed today to be the mother of somewhere between a third and a half of all the world's languages. Greek, Latin, the Romance, Germanic, and Celtic languages, not to mention the Baltic, Slavic, Indian, and Iranian ones and many more, all trace back to that ancient tongue that linguists have painstakingly reconstructed and christened Proto-Indo-European.

Somewhere between 6000 and 4500 BC, linguists infer, these Proto-Indo-European-speaking people lived in a cold northern landlocked world, probably somewhere in the Eurasian steppes north of the Black Sea and as far east as Kazakhstan. Thus it was that they had a word for snow (*sneig^wh*), but no name for the ocean. Of trees they knew the beech and the birch (*bhāgo* and *bherəg*); of animals, the wolf and the bear (*wlk^wo* and *bher*); of fruits, the apple and cherry (*abel* and *ker*). Just about the only sweetness (*swād*) these ancient people would have known would have come from honey or from fruit that was ripe and juicy. Lacking sugar—which wasn't to become available until many centuries later—they would have early learned to treasure sweetness as a rare joy in a way that we Americans can hardly imagine today with our estimated average sugar consumption of more than 150 pounds per year. Who can be surprised, then, that *bhrug,* the Proto-Indo-European root word that lies behind *fructus,* and, consequently, behind *fruit,* referred to both agricultural produce and enjoyment? In its almost forgotten harvest metaphor, our modern phrase "to reap the benefits" suggests the same idea of fruitful enjoyment. Apparently, to both the early Proto-Indo-European peoples and to those of us who speak a language derived from theirs, fruit provides such an unsurpassable pleasure that its very name evokes happiness.

However much we may enjoy our eggplants, string beans, and rutabagas, they simply don't give us the same effortless delight. Since the gustatory pleasure that beets and cabbages offer is far and away outstripped by their sheer ability to grow and even thrive under the toughest conditions, they received their name from the Latin *vegere,* "to animate," which, in turn, traces back to the Proto-Indo-European *weg,* "to be strong, lively, or vigilant." Our English *wake up* comes from that same ancient root. For centuries parents have been coaxing children to eat their peas and carrots so that they will grow up to be big and strong, but few of those parents realized that the very word *vegetable* is as closely related to *vigilance* as peas and carrots are to bodily vigor.

As parents have long realized, though, it's a lot more fun to be happy than it is to be vigilant, and it's a lot easier to get children to eat watermelon than spinach. No Popeye is needed to make them eat fruit.[3] As the English writer and gardener John Evelyn astutely observed more than three centuries ago, children are naturally drawn to fruit. More recently, scientists have determined that we're born preferring the sweetness of berries, grapes, and nectarines to turnips, radishes, and brussel sprouts because more often than not sweet foods provide the vitamin-rich nutrients and

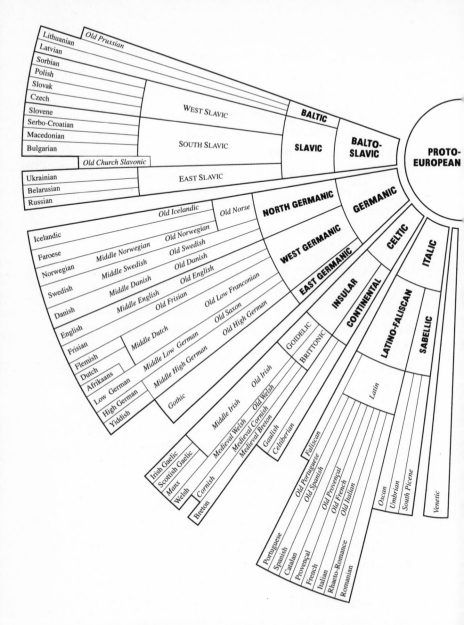

A chart of Indo-European languages.

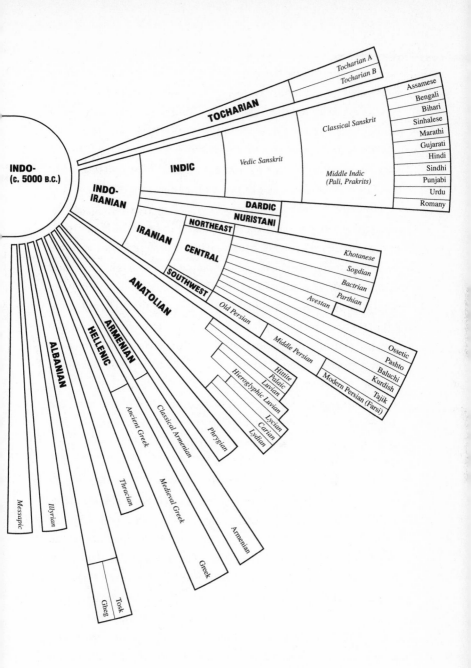

carbohydrates our bodies require without the bitterness that our species has been bred to associate with poison. But parents don't need scientists to tell them why their children eat fruit. They eat it not because it's good for them, but because it tastes so good.

I'm not as concerned with nutrition or the physiology of taste, however, as I am with the connections between our foods and the names we know them by, so it's inevitable I would be struck by how wonderfully appropriate it is that our feelings about the sweet and savory plants we eat should be so beautifully mirrored in these names. I know of course that our preference for fruit has long been shared by people whose names for it don't express their delight quite as neatly as our English one does. All you have to do is think of one of the first stories in the Bible. There's absolutely no relationship in Hebrew between the words for fruit and pleasure, but it's clear nonetheless that whoever wrote the story of the Garden of Eden liked fruit a whole lot more than vegetables: it's not about forbidden vegetables, after all. There was no need to prevent Adam and Eve from eating the herbs of the field, but the writer knew just what he was up to when he had God test them by putting a particularly alluring fruit within easy arm's reach and then telling them *not* to eat it.

The writer knew something else as well. Unlike fruit, most vegetables require work. Although we may fantasize about a seemingly endless succession of lazy days in Eden, vegetables needed to be tended even there. We might forget this fact, but it's no fault of the fruit-loving writer who made it abundantly clear that even in Eden, the vegetable beds had to be nurtured: "The Lord God took the man and put him in the garden of Eden to till it and keep it." Curious, then, that we so rarely see tidy rows of lettuces, leeks, and fennel in the thousands of Renaissance paintings depicting the flora of Eden. You have to look long and hard for a single image of a broad bean or a lettuce, but our museums

A detail from Hieronymus Bosch's *The Garden of Earthly Delights.*

are bursting at the seams with paintings of grapes, berries, figs, pomegranates, and apples. Obviously writers and painters over the centuries have long known what the wise rabbit and the little girl from the children's book came to realize as they assembled their basket of bananas and pears. Not too many of us would risk expulsion and death for a cabbage and it's a lot easier to believe that the wily serpent tempted Eve not with a rutabaga but with a juicy red apple ripe for the plucking from a low-hanging branch.

It's for this reason that so many of our poems and paintings of paradise feature fruit rather than labor-intensive vegetables.

There's not a single turnip, beet, or other vegetable in Hierony-mus Bosch's masterpiece, *The Garden of Earthly Delights,* but the Dutch master sure filled his canvas with fruit, most notably, gar-gantuan strawberries. In fact, the painting was originally regis-tered under the title "The Picture with the Strawberry-Tree Fruits." In an equally fruit-filled vision of Eden, the seventeenth-century English poet Andrew Marvell conjured up an omni-ripe paradise in which there was no need to even pick the apples, the grapes exploded themselves on the tongue, nectarines and peaches dangled from laden tree boughs, and fragrantly perfumed melons littered the landscape. Note that there's not a single mention of a bean or a cabbage in this stanza from "The Garden":

> *What wondrous life is this I lead!*
> *Ripe apples drop about my head;*
> *The luscious clusters of the vine*
> *Upon my mouth do crush their wine;*
> *The nectarene, and curious peach,*
> *Into my hands themselves do reach;*
> *Stumbling on melons, as I pass,*
> *Ensnared with flowers, I fall on grass.*

Whether their fruit words are etymologically related to happi-ness or not, people have just always seemed to prefer nectarines and peaches to lima beans and parsnips. The Bible certainly didn't need the linguistic correspondence to know that fruit would be a lot harder to resist than herbs.

But the author of the Eden story had something very important in common with the Romans whose *fructus* so perfectly ex-pressed their delight in dates and figs: they were both from the Mediterranean where the sun shines and all manner of fruit grows easily. Grapes, pomegranates, figs, citron, mulberries, elderberries, peaches, pears, quinces, and apricots are all featured in the oldest known cookbook, the first-century Roman gourmet Apicius' *De re coquinaria* (On the subject of cooking).[4] Many of the same fruits appear in the Bible as well. From the fig leaves that God sews into loincloths to cover the suddenly modest Adam and Eve to the grapes of wrath that will be trampled in the apocalyptic days to come, the biblical stories are veritable cornucopias of fruit.

When those fruit-obsessed Mediterranean peoples headed north, however—first the Romans to conquer the known world and later the Christians to convert that same known world—they brought with them not only their words but their sweet tooth as well. What even they, powerful as they were, weren't able to bring was their balmy southern weather and bright meridian sunshine. If they wanted to dine the way they were used to dining or bless the way they were used to blessing, they had to bring their prized foods with them—or at least the knowledge of how to grow those foods so far up north—because when they arrived at the bleak and windswept shores at the very end of the world, what they discovered was a far cry from the cultivated gardens and orchards back home. About the only fruit they found was what botanists today call the *Malus sylvestris*—the humble little wild crab apple that existed before any grafting or horticultural improvement had transformed it into the large, sweet, juicy fruit that comes to mind today when we hear the word *apple*.

THE APPLE-FRUIT

It is striking that of all the fruits Andrew Marvell named in his ode to Eden—apples, grapes (the less poetic way of saying "the luscious clusters of the vine"), nectarines, peaches, melons—only one is native to Britain: the apple. Perhaps it's because of England's lack of fruit that he had to imagine, rather than actually eat, those more exotically scented nectarines and peaches. One doesn't need to be much of an expert to know that most fruits hail from sunny climates. The apricot, peach, plum, nectarine, cherry, and citrus all originated in the East. None of the fruits we so enjoy today—with two notable exceptions—is native to either England or its language. All owe their existence on British soil and their English names to other peoples, whether conquerors, traders, gardeners, or missionaries. Behind each of the names, then, lies a story of immigration.

Consider, for instance, the story of how the apricot made it to England and into our language. In Latin, it was a *praecocum,* literally, "the precocious one," on account of its tendency to ripen before the peach or the plum. The Byzantine Greeks adapted the word as *berikokken* and the Arabs as *birquq.* By the time the Moors arrived in Spain, it had acquired the definite article *al*—thus, *albirquq*—and it is from the resulting Spanish *albaricoque* that the other European languages derive their names for the precocious fruit. In 1542, Henry VIII's gardener, Jean Le Loup, introduced the fruit to England from Italy where it was called *albercocco*; its earliest English name, *abrecock*, was used into the eighteenth century. The modern *-cot* ending, finally, was borrowed from the French *abricot,* and the *ap-* beginning probably resulted from the mistaken belief that the word derived from the Latin *apricus*, "sunny."[5]

Similarly meandering histories lie behind so many of the fruits we eat every day. The orange that provides the juice most of us drink each morning traces back through the French *orange* to the Spanish *naranja* to the Arabic *naranj* to the Persian *narang* and ultimately to the Sanskrit *naranga*. The lemon was brought to Europe in the thirteenth century by Crusaders on their return from the Holy Land, where it was called *limah* in Arabic. The quince comes to us from the Old French *cooin,* the Latin *cotoneum* and, more remotely still, from the Greek *melon Kudonion,* literally, "apple of Cydonia," which is today's Chania, a town in Crete known for its quince.

India, the Persian Gulf, the Greek Isles—sunny locations all. But as everyone knows, from the first-century Roman historian Tacitus, who described the typical English weather as "wretched, with its frequent rains and mists," to the present-day tourist, the British Isles would be hard put to boast of cloudless climes and sunny skies.[6] Neither, consequently, can they boast of fruit. Although its mild climate and rich soil were ideal for wheat—to such a degree that in the fourth century, Britain was known as the breadbasket of the Roman Empire—the island is rarely sunny enough to grow much fruit other than crab apples and wild berries. It stands to reason, then, that our word for the entire class of sweet plant foods should have come to us from Latin. In the first centuries of the Common Era, the Romans planted vineyards in southern England, thus inaugurating the British wine industry, which is still four hundred vineyards strong today. They even managed to get peach, plum, and fig trees to grow in enclosed gardens. No wonder that our names for these imported fruits echo Latin nomenclature: *peach* is a late adaptation of *malum persicum,* *plum* derives from *prunum,* and *fig* from *ficus.* The Romans were masterful gardeners, and they looked down imperiously at those unhorticultural northerners who, as Tacitus noted in his treatise on the tribes north of the Rhine, "do not plant orchards, fence meadows, or irrigate gardens."[7] Apparently the people who lived in Britain before the Romans arrived—the Celts— were content enough with their wild apples and berries, or at least they couldn't have missed what they never knew. The Germanic people who took over the island from the Celts were similarly northern and consequently didn't have much fruit either. They did have a word that referred to fruit, but it was entirely ousted by its Latin counterpart *fructus* and it has no contemporary English descendants whatsoever. Who today can even pronounce the strange-looking *wæstm*? On the other hand, we still use Anglo-Saxon names for the two fruits indigenous to England: the apple and the berry, barely changed from *æppel* and *berie* of more than fifteen hundred years ago.

Yet although the names look familiar, it isn't entirely clear what they once referred to. *Berie* could have meant any small round juicy fruit. Grapes, for instance, which the Romans introduced to Britain, were known in Old English as *winberige,* literally, "wineberries." And while *æppel* seems a straightforward enough word today, it very well might have been closer in meaning to our general term *fruit* than to the more specific designation *apple*; if one's only tree fruit is the apple, one hardly needs to be very precise. Precision is a tricky word to use in the context of apples anyway, since unlike most other fruits and vegetables, they do not necessarily resemble their parents. Because apple blossoms can be fertilized only by the pollen of other apple varieties, wild apple trees (ones that have grown from seeds, that is) do not share the genetic structure of the mother tree. You simply never know what you're going to get if you plant an apple seed and let nature run its course. Geneticists refer to this unpredictability as heterozygosity. Cultivated apple trees, on the other hand, are the result of the grafting process first developed by the ancient Chinese, who figured out how to replicate the features they most liked from a given fruit. The knowledge spread to the Greeks and later to the Romans, who concocted hundreds of varieties not originally found in nature. Today, apple blossoms are intentionally fertilized with selected pollen to produce fruit with exactly the qualities we like the most: sweetness and juiciness, size and color. Without such human intervention, "each tree would constitute its own distinct variety," notes food writer Edward Behr.[8] A millennium and a half ago in northern Europe, there was no human intervention whatsoever. Wild apples would have grown freely, and consequently there would have been an almost infinite variety of apples of all different sizes, colors, shapes, and tastes. What would have allowed a person who lived back then and who obviously knew nothing about genetics or binomial nomenclature the understanding to lump together under a single name this pingpong-ball-sized hard green fruit with that grapefruit-sized soft red one? Short of some Platonic idea of apple, what could have accounted for the ability to recognize that two differently colored and sized tree fruits were one and the same species? No wonder the Old English *æppel* was such an ambiguous word, either exclusively designating members of the genus *malus* or, more largely, referring to any tree fruit at all.

But the word can be traced further back still; in fact, it has one of the most ancient fruit names in existence today. The region that is usually identified as the primordial home of the oldest known apple trees, modern-day Kazakhstan, is the same region linguists believe to be the home of those long-ago Proto-Indo-European peoples who brought their words with them as they dispersed to places as far-flung as India and Iceland. One such word sounds remarkably familiar to modern ears: *abel*. It lives on in many of today's apple words: the German *Apfel*, the Danish *æble*, the Dutch *appel*, the Russian *iablokaa*, the Polish *jablko*, the Welsh *afal*, the Irish *abal*, the Cornish *aval*, and, of course, our own English *apple*. In many of the European languages, whether living or dead, apple words share the root letters *ap, ab, af,* or *av* from so many eons ago. Many, but not all—not those derived from Greek or Latin.

In the Mediterranean, apple words lack the *a*'s, *b*'s, *p*'s, and *v*'s of northern Europe. Instead, *m* and *l* dominate, as in the Greek *melon*, Latin *malum*, Italian *mela,* and Albanian *molle*. The southern names trace back to a different Proto-Indo-European root: *melon*. It's easy for us to confuse the ancient *melon* with our modern word for cantaloupes, honeydews, and crenshaws, but all those millennia ago, it seems to have referred either to what we know as the apple, or, on the other hand, to any seed- or pit-bearing fruit. Ultimately we may never know precisely what *melon* once designated any more than we know what *abel* once referred to. Whether derived from the southern *m* and *l* sounds or from the northern *ap*, *ab*, *af*, and *av* sounds, apple words have always been fuzzy terms, virtually indistinguishable from the entire class of fruit. Fuzziness aside, however, they are and apparently always have been inextricably bound up with what we might call "fruit-ness." Studies have shown that when asked to draw a picture of a house, most children will sketch a center-entrance, two-story colonial, even if they live in a ranch, a split-level, or a Cape Cod house. Apples are the colonials of the fruit world, so to speak, whether in the Mediterranean, where almost any new fruit was regarded as a type of *melon*, or in northern Europe, where the apple was about the only fruit able to survive. Without apples, we would of course have our other fruits, but we wouldn't be calling them by the names we do. We'd still be eating melons, peaches, pomegranates, and pineapples, but we'd be calling them something else. I'll explain.

One of the earliest written mentions of apples appears in Homer's *Odyssey,* in the description of an island orchard on which the Greek hero Odysseus is washed ashore. The epic hav-ing been written in Greek, the word used was *melon,* which is usually translated as apple, but it might equally have referred to any other kind of tree fruit. It's our historical vantage point that understands *melon* to mean apple. We know what the word evolved into—*milon* is apple in modern Greek—and so we transplant our own understanding back to Homer's time. But we don't really know what the blind bard had in mind. Nor do we know whether the legendary golden apples of the Hesperides were apples, at all, or whether it might have been oranges or quinces that waylaid the fleet-footed Atalanta as she raced to preserve her virginity. Perhaps the best we can do is think of the ancient Greek *melon* as an "apple-fruit" and call it a day.

The fuzziness of the Mediterranean *m* and *l* words explains why so many strange new fruits—and even sometimes vegetables— were given names based on them. In both Greek and Latin, for instance, melons were *melopepon*, literally, "ripe apple-fruit." The Romans called the pomegranate a *malum punicum,* or Punic apple-fruit, and the peach a *malum persicum*, or Persian apple-fruit. As the centuries rolled by, *malum persicum* was shortened to *persica*, from which Italian derived its *pesca*, French its *pêche*, and English its *peach*—all traces of *malum* virtually invisible to the naked eye but still detectable with a powerful enough lens.

The same haziness applied to a later fruit word that entered Latin most likely from the language of the mysterious Etruscan people who lived in the area of today's Tuscany. *Pomum,* obviously related to Pomona, the goddess of fruit trees, gardens, and orchards, entered the language after *malum* had already been firmly established as a leading fruit word.[9] Once again, it's easy to assume the word meant apple; after all, in today's French *pomme* means precisely that and it's clear where the French got their word. But originally, *pomum* had no such tidy reference. Pomona derived her name from *all* the fruits in the gardens and orchards she tended so lovingly, not from any one in particular. It was only later, after the fall of the Roman Empire, as we will see, that words shifted in meaning, with *fructus* becoming the general term, *malum* the more specific word used in southern Europe, and *pomum* the term favored up north. This is why today's French *pomme* refers only to apples, rather than to peaches, plums, figs, apricots, and the like. No one today would expect a *tarte aux pommes* to be filled with anything else.

Centuries after this shift in meaning, unfamiliar fruits and vegetables were still being considered a type of apple-fruit and thus featured a *malum, pomum,* or *apple* somewhere in their names. When the Spanish encountered the Aztec vegetable-that-is-really-a-fruit, they shortened the indigenous name from the hard-to-pronounce *xitomatl* to *tomate.* When tomatoes arrived in Italy in 1544, they were hailed by the Italian herbalist Mattioli as *mala aurea,* golden apples.[10] To the Italians today, tomatoes are still *pomodori,* golden apples, as eggplants are *melanzana,* apples of insanity, from the Latin *mala insana.* In English as well, the eggplant was once called a *madde apple:* folk wisdom held that the eggplant, a member of the very poisonous nightshade family of plants, would make the eater go mad. A French potato is a *pomme de terre,* "earth apple," which is also the literal meaning of the Dutch *aardappel,* Icelandic *jardepli,* and *Erdapfel,* the name the Germans used before it was ousted by *Kartoffel,* based on the tuber's fancied resemblance to a truffle, *Trüffel* or *Tartuffel,* derived from the Italian *tartufolo.* The Germans still call oranges *Apfelsine,* literally, "Chinese apples." Or consider the *pineapple,* which has no botanical relationship whatsoever to the apple: when the exotic tropical fruit called *anana* in the Guarani language of Bolivia and southern Brazil arrived in Europe in the seventeenth century, the English fancied a resemblance to a pinecone and so dubbed the prickly thing a pineapple. Similarly, although the pomegranate is an entirely distinct species from the apple, the word literally means "seeded apple"; the Spanish name, *granada,* also refers to the fruit's many seeds, or grains.

It's often remarked that in Chinese, rice is such a staff of life that the word used to refer to it, *fan,* also means food. Everything else, whether chicken, pork, vegetables, or tofu is *cai,* literally, flavor or variety, but it's *fan* that remains the indispensable necessity and primary sustenance of over a billion of the earth's people. The same double reference applies to apple, and for the very same reason. It is all but impossible to distinguish the apple from our idea of fruitness.

THE *MALUM* HEADS NORTH

Because the apple has for so long reigned supreme in the world of fruit, it has not only been planted more often than other species, but it's been written about more often as well. As early as the second century BC, Cato the Elder's *De agri cultura* (On farming) had detailed how to graft desirable cuttings onto hardy rootstock, thus ensuring that the resulting apples would be predictably and consistently larger, sweeter, and juicier than their wild forebears. The Romans loved few things as much as they did agriculture, but when they ventured north and west, they found a land that was uncultivated and where the only fruit that grew at all was just as nature intended it to be: wild. Enterprising and industrious as ever, they set to work clearing the land, enclosing gardens, and grafting their favorite imported species onto native roots. Thus it was that the Roman *Malus pumila*, the domesticated Mediterranean apple, was grafted onto *M. sylvestris*, the wild apple native to the British Isles, more like a hard little crab apple than anything we'd find at the store today. But of course *M. sylvestris* wasn't called that at the time. It was known then by the same name (more or less) that it's known by today in the Celtic regions of the country: *aballo*.

What happened when the two names ran headlong into one another? It wasn't just a matter of two separate but equal fruits merging into a new entity, although merge they certainly did— into the forerunners of the apples we eat today. The tiny little blush-colored Lady Apples sometimes found in farmers' markets date back to the ancient Romans, who engineered them in their quest to improve upon the vagaries of capricious nature by producing consistently sweet flesh. Now, it would be foolish to argue that food isn't there to satisfy our hunger and please our taste buds, but it's obviously about something more as well. What we eat says a lot about who we are. The Romans, for instance, were at their happiest transforming what they found in nature. Thanks be to whichever god or goddess it was who caused nature to yield its bounty, but it was the Romans who *improved* upon that bounty by their careful planting, grafting, tending, irrigating, and preserving. Wild fruit was made sweet and juicy, and, as we'll see in later chapters, weeds were transformed into vegetables, raw milk was preserved into the wonders of cheese, and animal flesh became edible meat by the eminently civilizing rituals of sacrifice. The northerners, on the other hand, ate what they found—just as they found it. "They do not plant orchards, fence off meadows, or irrigate gardens," Tacitus had written derisively in the first century. What could the food of such savages be but entirely natural—and it would be our mistake to assume "all natural" was the positive attribute in the world of the Romans that it is to us today. We may pay extra for "all natural" breakfast cereals and granola bars, but back then, "natural" was more or less on par with "uncivilized." Northern food was thus both natural and uncivilized. "Their food is plain," Tacitus summed up, "wild fruit, fresh game, and curdled milk. They satisfy their hunger without any elaborate cuisine or appetizers." Tacitus didn't write in English, however, but in Latin and the words he used for "wild fruit" were *agrestia poma*. *Agresti* meant wild, savage, or uncultivated, and *poma*, as I've explained, was a Latin word for fruit before *fructus* took over several centuries later. To a Roman, though, *poma* didn't grow in the wild, but in *pomaria*, orchards, which were precisely what Tacitus noted the northerners knew nothing of ("they do not plant orchards [*pomaria*]"). The only thing those savage people, whether

Celts or Germans, knew was the unimproved, uncivilized wild apple.

So what happened when the Mediterranean *malum* traveled to the apple-eating lands of the north and west? What happened when culture and nature collided?

In what is today's France, the dialects that were spoken were gradually ousted by Latin, which is why today the French eat *pommes* and refer to their apples, pears, and cherries collectively as *fruit*. Surely it's no coincidence that French food is almost universally acclaimed as the most sophisticated—read: transformed—cuisine in the world and the French language deemed resonantly beautiful. East of the Rhine and north of the Danube, on the other hand, the Germans remained by and large immune to Roman influence, clinging—again in the words of Tacitus—to their "forbidding landscapes and unpleasant climate—a country that is thankless to till." For the most part, they clung to their native words as well, despite the Roman historian's rather smug assurance that "instead of loathing the Latin language, they became eager to speak it effectively."[11] Thus in today's Germany an apple is an *Apfel* as it was two millennia ago, and fruit has remained the equally Teutonic *Obst*.[12] Again, it's no coincidence that German cuisine has for so long suffered from comparison with France's and that we're so ready to caricature the language as a harsh and guttural cacophony of *ich*'s and *ach*'s.

It's only in English, our resiliently healthy mutt of a language, that we hear both northern European and Latin words, *apple* and *fruit*. The story of why we hear both is the story of our linguistic and culinary inferiority complex as well, and it can be summed up in a single sentence: we English speakers may envy the French their *tartes aux pommes*, but we feel far cozier about our home-baked *apple pies*. When we dine out, we order *tartes*, *galettes*, and *mille-feuilles*, but when we celebrate our national holidays at home, the desserts we serve our friends and family are pies, whether, pumpkin, pecan, sweet potato, blueberry, or, of course, apple— and *pie* is a word that appears in no language other than English. Our split culinary personality is nothing new. It stretches back through the centuries, way back to the time those superior-in-every-way Romans first landed on the wild shores of the misty island known as Britannia.

THE APPLE IN AVALON

When the Romans crossed into Britain, they had truly come to the end of the world. Beyond, in the words of Tacitus, was "nothing but waves and rocks . . . here where the world and all created things come to an end." What could be expected of the savage people who painted their skin blue and lived in such a godforsaken place? The Greeks had called them *Keltoi,* which literally means "others," and so they must have seemed to their Roman conquerors as well. Northern Europeans that they were, they subsisted on milk and meat and must have seemed utterly barbaric to Caesar and his legionnaires, who were used to feasting on delicacies such as *minutal matianum,* the oldest known recipe featuring apples. From Apicius's first-century *De re coquinaria,* the dish features pork stewed with leeks, coriander, herbs, and spices in a sweet-and-sour broth, the sweetness coming from Matian apples, named after Gaius Matius, author of three cookbooks and a friend of Julius Caesar himself. The Celts wouldn't even have recognized many of these ingredients—certainly not coriander or cumin, which were both native to the Mediterranean and weren't introduced to Britain until the arrival of the Romans. Apples, though, even the blue-skinned warriors would have known very well.

In fact they so revered their indigenous wild *aballos* that their myths and legends were chock-full of them. Irish sagas frequently feature apples as the food that confers eternal youth. The people

Minutal Matianum

Put in a saucepan oil, broth, finely chopped leeks, coriander, small tid-bits, cooked pork shoulder, cut into long strips including the skin, have everything equally half done. Add Matian apples cleaned, the core removed, slice lengthwise and cook them together: meanwhile crush pepper, cumin, green coriander, or seeds, mint, laser root, moistened with vinegar, honey and broth and a little reduced must, add to this the broth of the above morsels, vinegar to taste, boil, skim, bind strain over the morsels sprinkle with pepper and serve.[13]

Note: *Laser* seems to have been another name for the herb known to the Greeks as *sylphium* and to us as *asafetida; must* was freshly pressed fruit juice.

of the Sid, the legendary original inhabitants of Ireland, were recognized by the branches of apple trees they carried with them when they ushered the newly deceased to the Land of Eternal Youth. The most well known Celtic hero of them all, the legendary King Arthur himself, awaits his return to his ancestral kingdom on the Isle of Avalon, which means the Place of Apples. The Welsh poem *Yr Afallenau,* "The Apple Tree," depicts the wizard Merlin standing in an apple orchard as he delivers his prophecies of the impending druidical overthrow of the Romans. "Sweet apple tree, sweet its branches, bearing precious fruit, famed as mine," the first stanza opens. One of the most important days of the Celtic year was Samhain, literally, "summer's end," and many of its rituals involved apples. One in particular was the ancestor of our modern apple-bobbing contest. Today it's all fun and games for costumed children at Halloween parties, but then, it was serious business: capturing a bobbing apple with one's teeth symbolized the journey across the seas to the magic apple tree at the heart of the Celtic otherworld. Sagas told of heroes crossing the western sea to find this wondrous country, known in Britain as Avalon and in Ireland as Emhain Abhlach, similarly, the Place of Apples.

The classical mythology of the Mediterranean was as obsessed with the *malum* as the Celts were with their *aballos*, but with a notable difference. Down south, apples (for so, as we have seen, those *malums* have traditionally been identified over the centuries) were alluring and often fatal. The golden apples of the Hesperides, for instance, lured many would-be eaters to their death. Believed to confer immortality, they were hidden in a secret orchard guarded over by a never-sleeping, hundred-headed serpentine dragon twined around the base of the central apple tree. It was a golden apple that Eris, the goddess of strife and discord, tossed into a wedding to which she had not been invited. The words inscribed on it, "For the fairest," led to the decadelong war in which untold thousands of Greeks and Trojans were hurled into Hades. It was a golden apple that caused the fleet-footed Atalanta to lose her race against her lusty suitor, not to mention her virginity, when she paused to pick up the distractingly alluring fruit he threw alongside their racecourse. In the south, the *malum* had long been a desired, but enticingly dangerous fruit.

When the Mediterranean *malum* traveled north with the Roman legions to the *aballo*-eating lands, the fruit was cultivated and improved in enclosed orchards into the *Malus domesticus* that we enjoy to this day, but the name that resulting new fruit was known by remained unchanged. However much the Celts must have enjoyed the sweeter and juicier *malum*, they were reluctant to relinquish their *aballo*, conjuring up, as it did, the rituals and festivities of Samhain and the misty island of Avalon. When the Romans abandoned the island in order to defend their capital, which was fast being overrun by the Huns, their apple nomenclature went with them, and so in the north and west of Britain—those far-lying outreaches where the return of Arthur from the mists of Avalon is still awaited—the ancient Celtic name for the legendary fruit has survived. In Cornish to this day, it's called an *aval*, in Irish *abal*, in Welsh *afal*, in Gaelic *ubhal*, and in Breton *aval*.

As with so many foods, an apple by any other name simply did not taste the same.

THE APPLE IN EDEN

It was only a few centuries later that the *malum*, rebaptized the *pomum*, traveled north once again, this time with the missionaries of the late fifth and early sixth centuries who sought to convert a confirmed apple-eating people to their own Mediterranean religion based on the olive and the grape. During those few centuries, the Germanic tribes had taken advantage of the Romans' sudden departure to colonize the lushly fertile land for themselves. Their name for one of the few fruits they knew had evolved from the same Proto-Indo-European root as the Celtic *aballo*, and like their predecessors on the island, the Angles and Saxons held the fruit in enormous esteem. In their legends as well, the apple is the food of enlightenment and divine blessing. Their gods remained immortal only so long as they ate the apples of the goddess Idun; without them, even they would wither and die. One of the myths recounted in the Icelandic *Prose Edda* tells of the giant Thiazi who descended in the form of an eagle and stole away both Idun and her apples, after which the pantheon of Nordic gods was "much dismayed at Idun's disappearance, and they soon grew old and grey-haired."[14] Aged and feeble they remained until they roused the energy needed to slay the giant and win back their apples of immortality. In Germanic epic poetry as well, apples guaranteed fertility. When Odin's grandson King Rerir prayed for a son, the sign that his wish was about to be fulfilled was an apple dropped into his lap. The child born grew up to be Völsung, the ancestor of the heroes whose deeds are recounted in the Norse *Völsungasaga* and the Old German *Nibelungenlied*. In the middle of the great hall Völsung built for himself, he planted—what else?—a large apple tree.

It was these apple-loving Germanic people who forced the Celts to the outermost fringes of the island and who planted themselves firmly in the midst of the country, and it was these people whose language took root and flourished as Latin never had, despite the more than four centuries that the Romans had remained in control of Britannia. And so it is that today's English speaker bites into an *apple* rather than a *malum* or a *pomum*. But an apple is not quite the same as its Mediterranean counterpart, at least not in imaginative association. The one is wild and uncultivated and confers fertility, immortality, and blessings of all sorts; the other is grafted, tended, and improved—not to mention sweet, tempting, and dangerous.

It was at just this time that the forbidden fruit of Eden was at last identified. Turned out that it was none other than the apple.

And yet not a single apple ever appears in the Genesis story, nor was the apple implicated in the Fall of Man before the southern religion moved north. It seems far more logical that Eve would have been tempted by a fig, a pomegranate, a quince, or some other fruit native to Mesopotamia. The clothing our first parents hastily stitched together to cover their nakedness is clearly identified as having been made from fig leaves, but on the far more important matter of the forbidden fruit, the biblical story remains oddly silent. We can't even blame our confusion on ambiguity, because Hebrew had two distinct words for fruit and apple—*p'ri* and *tapuach*—and the word used in the Eden story is clearly *p'ri*.

> The woman said to the serpent, "We may eat of the fruit
> [*p'ri*] of the trees in the garden; but God said, "You shall
> not eat of the fruit [*p'ri*] of the tree that is in the middle
> of the garden, nor shall you touch it, or you shall die."

For no obvious reason whatsoever, millions of people the world over have automatically assumed the forbidden fruit of Eden to have been an apple. In this, they are aided and abetted by thousands of paintings in which the biblical garden is more apple orchard than anything else. Hugo van der Goes's *The Fall of Man* (c. 1470), for instance, shows an alabaster-skinned Eve, flanked by a scrawny-looking Adam and a four-limbed serpent with human face, reaching up to pluck a fruit that can in no way be confused with fig, pomegranate, or quince.

On the one hand, the assumption is easy to account for. When people think fruit, they all but invariably envision apples, which is why so many exotic new species have historically been considered a type of apple. It's certainly possible to imagine that the same apple-fruit confusion that gave the pineapple, the *pomme de terre*, and the *Apfelsine* their names was responsible for pinning the blame for the Fall of Man on the blushingly innocent apple.

On the other hand, *malum,* one of the Latin names for apple, had an almost exact homonym. Pronounced with a long ā, *malum* means apple; when the vowel is short, it means evil. It is from the short-voweled *malum* that we derive many of our nastiest English words, like malice, malevolent, malady, and malignant. Suddenly we're in a better position to understand the connection between malice and apples and to appreciate all the myths and stories in which the apple's apparent sweetness is used to tempt, seduce, and destroy. It's no accident that the vainly jealous queen chooses an irresistible yet poisonous apple to tempt her too beautiful stepdaughter Snow White. The biblical story is

Hugo van der Goes's *The Fall of Man*.

by no means the only one in which the pleasure that the fruit promises comes with a hefty price tag. The Fall of Man, the fall of Troy, and the fall of Snow White can all be pinned on those nasty little apples.

Neither theory explains, however, why it was only after the Mediterranean *malum* had been shipped north, just about the time that Pope Gregory the Great was sending missionaries to England to convert the northern heathens to the Roman religion, that Eden's fruit was at last declared to be the beloved northern apple. Why then?

In the early sixth century, a Roman poet living in the area then called Gaul used the Latin word *pomum,* which had traditionally meant "fruit," in a far more restricted sense, apparently for the first time in print. The work was *The Fall of Man*, a poetic rendition of the Eden story, and in it Alcimus Ecdicius Avitus identified the precise fruit it was that grew in the middle of the garden.[15] He called it a *pomum*:

> But when the doomed woman's fatal judgment settled
> on indulging that eternal hunger with the fruit of sin
> [*criminis escam*] and of satisfying the serpent by eating the
> food she took from him, she gave in to his treachery and,
> herself consumed, bit into the apple [*pomum*].[16]

Avitus was not only a poet but also an archbishop in Gaul. Today he's remembered for his biblical epic, but back then he was better known for his tireless battle against the heresies that were threatening Christian orthodoxy. Seen in this light, Avitus's poetic work takes on the same missionary zeal that inspired his prose. How better to convert the pagans than by convincing them that their sacred fruit didn't confer the immortality they believed it to, but, quite the contrary, lured them with false, dangerous, and sinful knowledge? The strategy worked. Ever since Avitus's epic, it's been the apple that has tempted Eve and deprived both her and her unwitting spouse of eternal life in paradise. A seventh-century Old English translation of Genesis singles out the unfortunate fruit: God admonishes Adam, "Therefore shalt thou labour, . . . until that grim disease, which first thou tasted in the apple [*æple*], shall grip hard at thy heart."[17] And a thousand years later, it was still an apple that Eve longed for in John Milton's *Paradise Lost*: "To satisfy the sharp desire I had / Of tasting those fair Apples, I resolv'd / Not to defer."[18] To this day, it remains the apple that most of us believe to have grown on the tree of the knowledge of good and evil.

It turns out that the identification of the apple as the forbidden fruit has very little to do with the Bible and not much to do with the near Latin homonyms *mālum-malum* either, but instead everything to do with the conflicts that faced the Roman Church when it brought its Mediterranean religion to the lands of the Celts. Southern peoples had long been used to drinking and blessing their wine, whether according to the rules of the Bible or as the gift of Dionysus, the god of the vine. But what was to be done with a northern people whose foods were so very different, whose soil wouldn't produce olives and vines, and whose longed-for paradise wasn't Eden but a western isle of apple trees? What was to be done with a people who didn't transform nature—whether by agricultural or spiritual means—but who, quite simply, ate it right off the tree? Such barbaric heathens needed to be civilized and converted. They needed to be taught to subdue nature rather than just eat it. No Roman strolled out into his vineyard to pop grapes into his mouth; he pressed them into wine instead. And no one at all plucks olives off trees as a midday snack; we brine or cure them before indulging. It's no accident that one of the first stories in the Bible, Mediterranean book that it is, concerns the controlling of unruly physical appetites; nor is it an accident that the story took on special contours in northern Europe when the appetite in question turned out to be for an apple—wild, uncultivated, untransformed, and just as nature intended it to be.

Transporting a religion based on the grape and the olive to a hardy apple-loving people presented not only philosophical challenges but practical ones as well. How were the Christians even to procure the necessary foodstuffs so far from home? Olives flourished in the eastern Mediterranean, making the sacrament of extreme unction a convenient enough affair in Rome, but where was oil to be found for anointing the sick and dying in the north? If vines could scarcely be coaxed into growing in Britain, how was one to procure the wine necessary for communion, during which the faithful believed themselves to be drinking the blood of Christ? How were followers to perform the sacraments in such an inauspicious climate? From the moment of their arrival in Britain, the Romans had planted vineyards where they could, but even they had had to supplement their supply by importing amphorae from Gaul and the Iberian Peninsula. Wouldn't it have been a whole lot easier and less expensive for the Roman Christians to have used the fermented juice of an indigenous fruit? After all, Jesus had chosen the common drink of his time and place. Had he been born in northern Europe, he might very well have held up a horn or beaker at the last supper and bid his followers drink ale or cider in his memory. Why couldn't the common beverage of the northern climate do just as well as the wine of the Mediterranean? Why couldn't the sacrament of Holy Communion be celebrated with cider pressed from one of the only fruits hardy enough to grow in Britain? Perhaps it was.

It wasn't until as late as the sixteenth century that the Roman Church authoritatively decreed that the eucharistic element must be *vinum de vite,* wine of the grape, thereby forbidding the use of the fermented juice of any other fruit, including cider from apples and perry from pears—both northern fruits. The edict was issued at the Council of Trent. But Trent, or Trento, is in Italy where grapes are always at the ready. In fact, the council was convened to refute the claims and practices of the Protestant Reformation that had begun up north in Germany where neither olive oil nor *vinum de vite* was as easily procurable as in Italy. The same difficulty continued to bedevil English Christians until as late as the nineteenth century, when the Anglican Church was still resolutely insisting upon the precise nature of the liquid to be used during the Eucharist. In the 1888 *Cautels of the Mass,* the directions for the proper administration of the sacraments in the Episcopal Church, we read:

> In respect to the matter of the Blood, see that it be not home-made, or wine so weak, that by no means it hath the nature of wine. It must not be water red from being strained through a cloth which has been steeped in red wine. It must not be vinegar, or wine at all corrupted; nor must it be claret, or wine made of mulberries or pomegranates; because they retain not the nature of wine.

An important note is added to the passage: "or a wine made from apples—perhaps cider."[19]

Why forbid what's never been attempted? Why would both the Roman and Anglican churches have had to frame their specifications so narrowly unless they were responding to local churches that did in fact make use of indigenous products rather than those imported from the Mediterranean? It seems entirely likely that British churches celebrated their communions with apple cider, the fermented juice of the fruit that had featured so prominently in both Celtic and Germanic myth and religion, the fruit that had inspired Merlin and assuaged the spirits of the deceased on the pre-Christian festival of Samhain. No wonder the Church came down so hard on the homegrown apple. If its Celtic associations alone weren't enough to incriminate it, the fact that it had been identified as the very same fruit that had caused the expulsion from Eden would certainly have been more than enough to disqualify its juice from standing in for the *vinum de vite*, the wine of the grape that flourished in the warm southern Mediterranean sunshine.

THE ESTUARY OF APULDRE

At the coronation ceremony of the Anglo-Saxon king Æthelred II in 978, apples were specifically asked for as a blessing. Less than a century later, the Normans conquered England and brought with them the *pommes* for which Normandy is still famous to this day. According to the *Anglo-Saxon Chronicles* that narrate the history of the Germanic people from the fifth to the twelfth century, the fatal encounter between the two contenders for the kingship took place at Apuldre, the older spelling of Appledore, a town on the northern coast of Devon. But Apuldre, appropriately enough in this fruit-filled context, was also the Old English word for *apple tree*.

> Meantime Earl William came up from Normandy into Pevensey on the eve of St Michael's mass; and soon after his landing was effected, they constructed a castle at the port of Hastings. This was then told to King Harold; and he gathered a large force, and came to meet him at the estuary of *Apuldre*.[20]

The chronicle drily relates the momentous end of the battle: "King Harold was killed . . . and the French remained masters of the field." The victorious Normans went to work transforming the legal and ecclesiastical structures of the country over which they were now in control, which is why so many words heard in our English-speaking courts of law and churches come from French: *judge, plaintiff,* and *defendant; priest, parish,* and *prayer.* They also went to work transforming the language of food, but it seems that some words gave them a harder time than others, as we can see when we look to the written records of the period. Since the earliest English cookbooks appeared several centuries after the Norman Conquest, it's not to them that we turn for evidence of changing food words. Instead we can look to various translations of the Bible, for it was not only the most often translated book of the time, but it also—conveniently for us—happens to be filled with stories about food.

In a pre-Norman translation of Genesis, for instance, the Hebrew word for fruit had been rendered by the now extinct and archaic-looking Old English *wæstm.* After the conquest, however, *wæstm* was replaced by the French *fruyt*: "We schulden not eate of the fruyt of the tre," Eve tells the wily serpent. Obviously *wæstm* did not survive, perhaps because it was the Normans whom England had to thank for so many new fruits—and their names—including pears, peaches, quinces, cherries, and so many more. All were grown in France according to the grafting techniques and methods that the Romans had developed more than a thousand years earlier and all now made their way to the royal courts of England. Shortly after, with the return of the Crusaders from the Holy Land, the first citrus fruits appeared in England, and spice ships from southern Europe brought raisins, currants, prunes, figs, and dates from the eastern Mediterranean. Every one of these fruits today bears a French name. But not the apple, which had flourished in the north since time immemorial. Thus it is that the same version of the Bible in which Eve succumbed to the "fruyt of the tre," has the besotted maiden in the Song of Songs comparing her lover to "an apple tre among the trees of wodis" and moaning to her attendants to "Cumpasse ye me with applis; for Y am sijk for loue." *Fruyt* had by this time entirely eclipsed the older *wæstm,* but the Old English *apple* was never re-christened a Norman *pomme.* Duke William had a far easier time taking the throne from King Harold than he did taking the *æppel* from his new subjects.

Of course the apple might have survived because it was one of the only fruits known in Old English. There simply were no native words for pears, peaches, or cherries, so they couldn't be called by any but foreign names. And yet history could have taken another course, as it did several centuries earlier—and of all places, in Normandy itself. To this day the northwestern coastal region of France is famous for its apples but they haven't always been called *pommes.* Nor were the Normans themselves always French. The area owes its name to the "Northmen," or Norse-men, to whom Charles the Simple gave the northwest part of his country in 911 in his attempt to put an end to their incessant raping and pillaging. The word for apple that those Northmen, whom we tend to refer to today as Vikings, would have used was the north Germanic *epli,* yet if you order a *crêpe à la normande* today, it will be filled not with *eplis* but *pommes.* When the Vi-kings traded their spears for plows and became Normans, they traded the *epli* for the *pomme* as well. Within the space of less than a century, the Normans had become French. But when the Anglo-Saxons merged with the Normans to become the English-speaking people we know today, unlike the Vikings, they held onto their *apples.*

Thus, in the pages of the first cookbook printed in England, *The Forme of Cury,* assembled in the 1390s by the French-speaking chefs of King Richard II, we find many foods that would never have appeared on Anglo-Saxon tables sitting cheek by jowl with the Old English staples of yore. Figs, raisins, and dates flavor a fishy sort of mincemeat pie called *tart de brymlent*, but the dish calls for good old-fashioned apples as well.

Tart de brymlent

Take fyges & raysouns, & waisshe hem in wyne, and grinde hem smale with apples & peres clene ypiked. Take hem up and cast hem in a pot wiþ wyne and sugur. Take calwar samoun ysode, oþer codlyng oþer haddok, & bray hem small, & do þerto white powdours & hoole spices & salt, & seeþ it. And whanne it is sode ynowz, take it up and do it in a vessel and lat it kele. Make a coffyn an ynche depe & do þe fars þerein. Plaunt it above with prunes damysyns: take þe stones out, and wiþ dates quartered rede and piked clene. And couere the coffyn, and bake it wel, and serue it forth.

Tart for Midlent

Take figs and raisins and wash them in wine. Grind them small with apples and pears picked clean. Take them up and cast them in a pot with wine and sugar. Take boiled young salmon or codling or haddock and chop them small and add white pepper and whole spices and salt. And seethe it. When it is boiled enough, take it up and put it in a vessel and let it cool. Make a coffin an inch deep and put the filling inside. Lay on top damson plums, with the stones taken out, and quartered dates, picked clean. Cover the coffin, bake it well, and serve it forth.[21]

Note: The whole spices would probably have included cinnamon sticks, black peppercorns, and cloves. "Coffin" was the standard way to refer to what we know as a pie shell.

The distinction between the elegant French nomenclature in the recipe's title and the humble Germanic ingredients appears on virtually every page of the *Forme of Cury*. Another recipe makes the point even more clearly. A fairly standard feature in early English cookery books, *apulmose* (also spelled *appulmoy, apple moyle, appilmose*) was typically medieval in its blending of sweet and savory flavors: stewed apples were strained into a beef broth that was flavored with the common trinity of ginger, saffron, and pepper; the resulting soup was then thickened with bread. A meatless version for Lent and fast days replaced the broth with almond milk and olive oil.

For to make apulmose

*T*ak applys & seeþ hem and let hem kele, & after make hem þorwe a cloþ & do hem in a pot. & kast to þat mylk of almaundys, wyþ god broþ of buf in flesch dayes; do bred ymyed þereto. & þe fisch dayes, do þereto oyle of olyue, & do þereto sugur & coloure it with safroun, & strew þeron powder & serue it forþe.

To Make Soft Apples

Take apples, seethe them, let them cool, and after put them through a cloth and then into a pot. Add almond milk, with good beef broth on meat days, and minced bread. On fish days, add olive oil. Add sugar & color with saffron. Strew powder on and serve it forth.[22]

Note: The "powder" would probably have been a mixture of ginger, saffron, and pepper.

The unusual combination of flavors in this soup is rivaled by its equally unusual name. *Apul* is self-explanatory, and in its earliest written version, all the ingredients, with the sole exception of *Buf*, are called by their Old English names: *applys, mylk, flesch, bred, fisch. Mose* alone needs translating because, obviously, the word isn't English. It's the Old French for *soft* (*mou* or *molle* today). The king's master chefs were savvy enough to know that "soft apples" sounded dangerously close to the unwanted scraps thrown to hungry swine; graced with the Norman *mose,* however, the dish was fit to set before the king.

Occasionally, apple dishes went entirely French. To call a sweetened rice pudding flavored with almonds, saffron, and apples *pommys morles* certainly makes it sound far more refined than the plain old English "soft apples." But the two names mean exactly the same thing.

For to make pommys morles

Nym rys & bray hem wel, & temper hem up wyþ almaunde mylk & boyle yt. Nym applyn & pare hem & sher hem smal als dicis, & cast hem þereyn after þe boylyng, & cast sugur wyþal, & colowre yt wyþ safron & cast þereto pouder, & serue yt forthe.

To Make Soft Apples

Take rice, boil it well, add almond milk and boil it. Take apples, pare them, dice them and cast them therein after the boiling. Add sugar and color with saffron. Sprinkle with powder and serve it forth.[23]

What we see in these early cookery manuals is precisely the same inferiority complex, the same split personality that we English speakers still suffer from today. On the one hand, we assume that if it's French it's got to be better. *Pommys morles* sounded as superior to soft apples as *tarte des pommes à la normande* does today to an apple pie, even though in each case the ingredients are virtually identical. When it comes to the pear, the cherry, or the peach, neither Richard II's chefs nor we have a choice but to use the names imported by the Romans and the Normans. But in the case of the ingredient itself, the apple, whose provenance stretches back through the millennia, the less sophisticated part of our food personality asserts itself. Despite our love of French cuisine and our reverence for toque-wearing chefs and *pâtissiers*, when it comes to our native apples, we English speakers have historically chosen to snub the snobs.

"AS ENGLISH AS APPLE PIE"

From the time the Romans first landed in Britannia to the cookery books that appeared more than a thousand years later, it was all but invariably assumed that if a foodstuff bore a Latin or French name, it was more civilized, more elegant, and just plain better than the very same food called by its local name. To this day, a *tarte tatin* sounds more sophisticated than an apple cobbler— but why? Are the ingredients so very different: apples, butter, flour, and sugar? Even though the upside-down *tarte* was created entirely by accident when Stéphanie Tatin realized she had forgotten about a bottom crust and cleverly salvaged the dessert by flipping it over onto a serving plate, it nonetheless exudes an aura of refinement that eludes the homespun cobblers, not to mention the crisps, crumbles, grunts, slumps, brown betties, pandowdies, and buckles beloved by speakers of English on both sides of the Atlantic.

Food names have long served as barometers of national solidarity. During World War I, suspicion of all things German resulted in a name change for the hamburger: suddenly it was a Salisbury steak. Similarly, when France protested the U.S. invasion of Iraq in 2003, Republican representatives Robert W. Ney and Walter

B. Jones Jr. insisted that french fries and french toast be replaced by "freedom fries" and "freedom toast" on the menus of restaurants in the House of Representatives. What we call our food says a lot, not only about our preferences but about our allegiances as well, and apples are a prime example. Invading peoples have tried to impose their names, but one after another, they have gone down in defeat. The Celts refused to trade in their *aballo* for the Roman *malum*; the Anglo-Saxons shunned the Latin *pomum* and the Norman *pomme*, insisting on their *æppel*; and a few centuries later, English middle-class cooks fought back against the French chefs who were magisterially usurping their kitchens.

"I sing of food by British nurse design'd," penned the seventeenth-century poet William King in mock-Homeric fashion in his *Art of Making Puddings*. Dipping his "swilling plume in fragrant cream," he celebrated copious quantities of milk and butter in such English desserts as sackposset, oatmeal pudding, and the fanciful dessert of yesteryear known as hedgehog, on account of its characteristic almond spikes. But his noblest efforts of all went into the patriotic tribute called, appropriately, "Apple Pye." Here is the first stanza:

> *Of all the delicates which Britons try*
> *To please the palate or delight the eye,*
> *Of all the sev'ral kinds of sumptuous fare,*
> *There is none that can with applepie compare.*[24]

Some fifty years later, King's celebration of English food was echoed by a very unpoetic writer who stoutly mocked the francophile pretensions of her countrymen: "So much is the blind Folly of this Age, that they would rather be impos'd on by a French Booby, than give Encouragement to a good English Cook!" The words belong to Hannah Glasse, whose 1747 *Art of*

Cookery Made Plain & Easy disdained the "high, polite Stile" of haute cuisine and dared to call French *lardoons* by their plain-English name, "little Pieces of Bacon." By the same token, Glasse gave her recipes such no-nonsense names as "Apple fritters," "Pupton of Apple," "Apple Pudding," and "Apple Pye." Not a single *pommes molles* or *tarte aux pommes* is to be found in her collection.

Apple Fritters

Beat the Yolks of eight Eggs, the Whites of four well together, and strain them into a Pan; then take a Quart of Cream, make it as hot as you can bear your Finger in it, then put to it a quarter of a Pint of Sack, three quarters of a Pint of Ale, and make a Posset of it. When it is cool, put it to your Eggs, beating it well together, then put in Nutmeg, Ginger, Salt, and Flour to your liking. Your Batter should be pretty thick, then put in Pippins sliced or scraped, and fry them in a good deal of Butter, quick.[25]

Note: Sack was a fortified white wine from Spain or the Canary Islands; a sweet sherry is a modern substitute. A posset was a hot sweetened milk curdled with wine or ale.

On the other hand, a popular cookbook of the next century opens by advising its readers to imitate those with "greater culinary skill" so as to "remedy our own defects." The writer was Eliza Acton and in her 1845 *Modern Cookery for Private Families,* she wondered "why . . . the English, as a people [are] more ignorant than their continental neighbours of so simple a matter as that of preparing [nourishment] for themselves."[26] Gone, consequently, are Hannah Glasse's plain and easy names, replaced by the likes of *Pommes au beurre* (no more, no less than *buttered apples*) and *Charlotte de Pommes* (so much lovelier-sounding than a homegrown Apple Charlotte). The almond-spiked "trembling lump" that William King knew as hedgehog now makes its appearance as the elegantly foreign *Suédoise*.

Apple Hedge~Hog, or "Suédoise"

This dish is formed of apples, pared, cored without being divided and stewed tolerably tender in a light syrup. These are placed in a dish, after being well drained, and filled with apricot, or any other rich marmalade, and arranged in two or more layers, so as to give, when the whole is complete, the form shown in the engraving. The number required must depend on the size of the dish. From three to five pounds more must be stewed down into a smooth and dry marmalade, and with this all the spaces between them are to be filled up, and the whole area to be covered with it; an icing of two eggs, beaten to a very solid froth, and mixed with two heaped teaspoonsful of sugar, must then be spread evenly over the suédoise, fine sugar sifted on this, and spikes of blanched almonds, cut lengthwise, stuck over the entire surface: the dish is then to be placed in a moderate oven until the almonds are browned, but not too deeply, and the apples are hot through. It is not easy to give the required form with less than fifteen apples; eight of these may first be simmered in a syrup made with half a pint of water and six ounces of sugar, and the remainder may be thrown in after these are lifted out. Care must be taken to keep them firm. The marmalade should be sweet, and pleasantly flavoured with lemon.[27]

Like a fairy godmother waving her magic wand, Acton similarly transforms Apple Soup into *Soupe à la Bourguignon*. But what is a *soupe à la bourguignon*? An aromatic, winey, possibly vegetarian cousin to the well-loved *boeuf à la bourguignon* we've taught ourselves to cook from the pages of Julia Child's *Mastering the Art of French Cooking*? Hardly. Turns out that it's no more than Acton's invented French name for the old medieval dish known as *apulmos*. It was the late English food writer Jane Grigson who revealed the act of prestidigitation. Bothered by Acton's obvious love of all things French and skeptical of the dish's French provenance, Grigson set to work and sleuthed out the earliest printed source of the medieval dish. "Although Miss Acton attributed it to Burgundy," she concluded, "it does not appear in any French collections of Burgundian recipes. In the end I came across the original version, in a reprinted manuscript from the Bodleian Library at Oxford, of the beginning of the fifteenth century. It's called Apple moys, or apple mush (from the French mol, meaning soft)."[28]

Despite the long-standing love affair English speakers have had with all things French, when it comes down to basic home

Apple Soup
Soupe à la Bourguignon

Clear the fat from five pints of good mutton broth, bouillon, or shin of beef stock, and strain it through a fine sieve; add to it when it boils, a pound and a half of good cooking apples, and stew them down in it very softly to a smooth pulp; press the whole through a strainer, add a small teaspoonful of powdered ginger and plenty of pepper, simmer the soup for a couple of minutes, skim, and serve it very hot, accompanied by a dish of rice, boiled as for curries.[29]

cooking, Cinderella's magic coach becomes a pumpkin once more and the *pommes aux beurre, suédoises*, and *soupes à la bourguignon* are restored to their humbler status as buttered apples, hedgehogs, and apple soups. Thus in cookbooks with titles like *Good Things in England, Food in England,* and *English Food,* we read time and again sentiments that "French Cookery is, of course very good, but there has always been a great sameness about it," and "English cooking is old-fashioned, because we like it that way." Florence White, who decisively affirmed the first of these statements, recounted an amusing anecdote about the nineteenth-century foreign minister Lord Dudley, who refused to translate the name of his—and indeed England's—favorite dessert by any other name.

> The late Lord Dudley could not dine comfortably without an apple pie, as he insisted on calling it, contending that the term *tart* only applied to open pastry. Dining, when Foreign Secretary, at a grand dinner at Prince Esterhazy's, he was terribly put out on finding that his favourite delicacy was wanting, and kept on murmuring pretty audibly, in his absent way: "God bless my soul! No apple pie."[30]

Dorothy Hartley's patriotism led her to open her 1954 *Food in England* with a sketch of English history from the time of the earliest Devonian cave dwellers, through the invasions of the Celts, Romans, Saxons, and Danes, ending with the Norman Conquest, when "the Saxon slave, resentfully lugging in the firewood, learnt the new name 'mutton' for his slaughtered sheep."[31] Among her dessert offerings are "Chaucer's Roast Apples" (apples roasted with sugar candy and galingale syrup) and "Apple Tansy, medicinal" (a tansy was originally a purgative sort of porridge, useful in the days before modern laxatives), not to mention such standards as apple pasties and "Ancestral Apple Pie."

Chaucer's Roast Apples

Apples roasted with sugar candy and galingale syrup (a very delicate dish). Galingale is a lumpy spice, with the aroma of damask roses, usually to be got through a wine spicery. Peel the apples finely and set level on a platter. Stew the galingale root in enough water and honey to fill the platter. Drain over the apples, and bake gently; withdraw from the oven, and serve cold, scattered with crushed white sugar candy. They should look like frosted pink roses, in a syrup the colour of rose quartz.[32]

Such culinary patriotism reached its pinnacle in Jane Grigson's 1974 *English Food*. Grigson denied the blue ribbon to French cuisine and spoke instead about the borrowing and adapting that have taken place since the dawn of time, or, at least, since the dawn of cooking.

> No cookery book belongs exclusively to its country, or its region. Cooks borrow—and always have borrowed—and adapt through the centuries. Though the scale in either case isn't exactly the same, this is as true, for example, of French cooking as of English cooking. We have borrowed from France. France borrowed from Italy direct and by way of Provence. The Romans borrowed from the Greeks, and the Greeks borrowed from the Egyptians and Persians. What each individual country does do is to give all the elements, borrowed or otherwise, something of a national character.[33]

Not a single apple recipe in Grigson's history has a French name; instead we find a "Fretoure owt of lente" (fifteenth-century apple fritters) and an "English Apple and Raisin Pie," which, in a fairly unprecedented turning of the tables, the renowned French chef Carême himself wasn't too proud to include in his 1828 gastronomical classic, *Le Cuisinier Parisien*.

THE BIG APPLE

To this day we English speakers still rely on the ancient name that once referred to the wild crab apple even though we so obviously prefer the dizzying array of cultivated varieties, from the Aceymac to Zuccalmaglio's Reinette. Apples—not *malums*, not *pommes*, but apples—are still, after all the centuries since the Romans brought literacy and agriculture to Britain, the most English of fruit. As Mrs. Beeton noted in her *Book of Household Management* almost a hundred and fifty years ago, "The most useful of all the British fruits is the apple, which is a native of Britain." She added a surprisingly modern note: "apples grown in the vicinity of New York are universally admitted to be the finest of any."[34] Whether we agree with her appraisal or not, almost every schoolchild today knows that apples were the first fruit the English settlers brought with them to the shores of America. Long before Johnny Appleseed embarked on his legendary tree-planting mission throughout New England and the Midwest in the early nineteenth century, the earliest settlers were already planting orchards with seeds brought from the old country. Apple lore holds that the longest-lived apple tree in the United States was planted in 1647 by Peter Stuyvesant, the first governor of what was then called New Amsterdam, on the grounds of his Manhattan property near today's Third Avenue and Thirteenth Street. Even though historical records prove it to have been a pear tree, people nonetheless imagine it to have been an apple tree, going so far as to suggest that New York owes its nickname, "The Big Apple," to Stuyvesant's tree.

Today it's the apple that is the most American of fruits. We call the ones we love "the apple of our eye" and we croon to them, "Don't sit under the apple tree with anyone else but me." We speak of things that are "as American as apple pie." Chevrolet's catchy ad campaign could never have included a pear tart in its lyrical listing of American icons: "Baseball, hot dogs, apple pie, and Chevrolet." It's an apple that keeps the doctor away and apples that grateful students leave for their teachers. Even the computer on which I am writing these words is adorned with an apple and bears the name of "Mac." The pear, on the other hand, still strikes us as vaguely foreign, aristocratic, and Old World, with such varieties as Anjou (named after the French province) and Comice, whose full name is Doyenne du Comice. A pie (from the Middle English *pye*) can be filled with apples, but pears go into a tart (from the French *tarte*). A sliced apple demands a sharp Cheddar (whether English or Wisconsin), whereas a pear calls for a ripe Camembert or Roquefort. Fermented, the apple gives us cider, applejack, or Calvados, that specialty of Norse-settled Normandy; distilled with *eau de vie*, the pear becomes *poire William*.

"An apple a day," the saying goes. Whether McIntosh, Red or Golden Delicious, or Granny Smith, the apple is without question the most comforting of fruits, the one whose name we could no more do without than those of our other staples, bread and milk. Even though the apples we eat are the products of grafting that was written about so authoritatively by the ancient Romans, and even though the Church so convincingly and permanently transformed the sacred apple of northern legend into the fruit of the tree of the knowledge of good and evil, still our apple echoes the uncultivated Anglo-Saxon *æppel* and, even more remotely, the wild Celtic *aballo*.

But the conquerors did leave an imprint. Otherwise, why would the study of apples, and more generally of fruit, be known as *pomology*? Why would the *Oxford English Dictionary* call "a fruit of the apple kind or resembling an apple" a *pome*? Why would the apple-shaped balls filled with sweet-smelling aromatics once used to ward off infection be known as *pomanders* and the hair gel that once contained apple pectin be known as *pomade*? Because we English speakers, insecure in our rustic primitive northernness, prefer erudite-sounding Latin names for our scientific terminology and romantic French names for the products of our *toilettes*. No "appleology" for us, and certainly no "amber apple" or "apple ointment," even though that's all that pomanders (*pommes d'ambre*) and pomades amount to. When it comes to our refined vocabularies, we go French and Latin virtually every time. When it's a matter of the foods we eat day in and day out, however, we put our feet down and insist on the names we have known them by for countless centuries, the names on which we have built our myths and even our religious beliefs. Inextricably entwined with our very conception of what fruit is all about, the apple has become second nature to us.

But what apple? The towering and precariously balanced pyramids of McIntoshes and Granny Smiths that inevitably await us as we wend our way through the produce sections of our supermarkets? Is this what the fruit of legend has been reduced to? A uniformly shiny orb that looks and tastes the same every single time? In reaction, a grassroots movement has arisen that's been winning more and more adherents who seek to overthrow the pomological tyranny of our supermarkets and return to the way things used to be, when an almost inconceivable variety of apples were harvested by hand after long lazy days in the sun—rather than exposure to ethylene gas—had brought them to the perfect pitch of ripeness. Why limit ourselves to the same few predict-

able and engineered varieties when there's a world of red, orange, yellow, brown, and even dark purple apples out there with
names like Esopus Spitzenberg, Sheep's Nose (also known as the
Black Gilliflower), and Chenango Strawberry? Such locally grown
and quirkily named heirloom apples have become all the rage as
we try to throw off the yoke of agribusiness that has controlled
our culinary choices for so long.

And yet the irony is that no matter how heirloom they are,
such old-fashioned apples are nonetheless still the engineered
products that have resulted from the grafting that dates back to
the Romans, the Greeks, and, ultimately, the Chinese. If all human intervention were suddenly to come to an end and our carefully tended orchards left to fend for themselves, apples as we
have known them since the days of antiquity would gradually
revert to their truly natural state and become wild *Malus sieversii*
once more, the sour little things indigenous to the Eurasian
steppes where those ancient Proto-Indo-European peoples once
called them *abel*. Closer to hawthorns and rosehips (to which
they are botanically related) than to the fruit we have come to
rely on, those eminently natural wild apples would make us cringe
and pucker up. They'd make us long for the sweetness of cultivated fruit. However much we may claim today to prefer "all-
natural" foods, as no Roman ever would have, we still want the
sweetness that ancient horticultural expertise bequeathed to us.
In short, we want our apples but, contradictory creatures that we
are, we want to eat them too.

CHAPTER TWO

Leeks: Weeds or Vegetables?

"If You Can't Beat 'Em, Eat 'Em"

Eat leeks in March and ramsons in May
And all the year after the physicians may play.

—Traditional English proverb

If your Majesties is rememb'red of it, the Welshmen did good service in a garden where leeks did grow, wearing leeks in their
Monmouth caps, which, your Majesty know, to this hour is an
honorable badge of the service; and I do believe your Majesty
takes no scorn to wear the leek upon Saint Tavy's day.

—Shakespeare, *Henry V*

And, by the bye, the unsubtle English cultivate and cherish the
very subtle leek. A cross between asparagus and green peas, it is
one of the earth's most delicate and tender creatures, as well as the
national flower of Wales. Let the Gauls match that with onions
sublimated by art if they can!

—Robert P. Tristram Coffin, "British Breakfast" (1941)

Proto-Indo-European: *leug*

GERMANIC: **laukaz**   CELTIC: *c-n*   LATIN: **porrum**   GREEK: **prason**

Finnish: *laukka*   Irish: *cainnenn*   Italian: *perro*

Swedish: *lök*   Scottish: *cainneann*   French: *poireau*

Danish: *løg*   Welsh: *cenhinen*   Spanish: *puerro*

Dutch: *look*   Cornish: *kenin*   Romanian: *praz*

German: *Lauch*   Breton: **kinnen**

Old English: *leac*

English: *leek*

ynneleac: Old English *onion*

garleac: Old English *garlic*

According to Jane Grigson's *Vegetable Book,* an alphabetical look at edible plant life from artichokes to yams, the "one English contribution to the basic treasury of the best vegetables" is the nutritious herb of the mustard family known as sea kale.[1] Sea kale? With all due respect to the late and great British food writer Jane Grigson, I feel confident in stating that apart from a few traditional seaside towns on the fringes of England and Ireland, sea kale is nowhere eaten today on anything like a regular basis. Nor has the vegetable even been heard of here in the United States, even though Thomas Jefferson—not only our third president, but also an avid gardener—liked it enough to feature it in no fewer than nineteen separate entries in his 1809 *Garden Book.* He went so far as to special-order fifty earthenware pots from a pottery near Richmond, Virginia, to cover the young shoots as he had seen a friend do; like asparagus, a far more well known spring delicacy, sea kale is most highly valued when it is deprived of light during its growth and harvested when its stalks are a pale yellowish white.

Despite its current obscurity, its praises have been sung

throughout the centuries by many eminent gardeners and cooks. In 1699 John Evelyn, the man whose dream it was to transform England into an "Elysium britannicum," whose gardening and forestry plans are largely responsible for greening up the English landscape, and who introduced his countrymen to previously unfamiliar vegetables he had discovered while traveling on the continent, nonetheless deemed the "sea-keele . . . growing on our coast" as delicate as the "broccoli from Naples."[2] Three hundred years later, Darina and Myrtle Allen, whose Ballymaloe House near Shanagarry, County Cork, is a leading force in the revival of traditional Irish food, similarly pronounced sea kale to be "one of the most exquisite of all vegetables." Come the end of February or early March, they write in their *Complete Book of Irish Country Cooking*, "devotees keep an eye out for the first leaves" as eagerly as any mycologist does for the elusive trumpet-shaped chanterelle in the cool days of autumn. They provide detailed instructions for how to grow the vegetable at home and how to cook it. Wash it thoroughly, they recommend, because, like leeks, its stalks can hide an enormous amount of sand and grit; cut it into four-inch lengths, boil it in salted water for ten to fifteen minutes, and drain it well. Like asparagus, it is best served with melted butter.[3] Tempting as their descriptions are and much as I would like to taste this delicate vegetable so beloved by President Jefferson, I have never been able to find it. In fact, I'm sure that very few of us, whether English, Irish, or American, would even recognize sea kale if we were to see it in the produce section of our local supermarkets, and even fewer of us would know what to do with it if it somehow magically appeared in our kitchens.

All our more familiar vegetables—the ones that we buy at the store or grow in our backyard gardens, and then steam, braise, blanch, boil, sauté, roast, bake, or eat raw—came to England, and consequently to the English language, from somewhere else.

Sea kale growing on a beach.

Our artichokes, broccoli, and zucchini are virtually unchanged from the Italian *articiocco, broccoli,* and *zucchini*; in our carrot and onion we hear the French *carotte* and *oignon*; the very names of our brussels sprouts and savoy cabbage betray their provenance.[4] And then of course there are the vegetables that arrived on European shores from the New World and Africa: the potato, from the Spanish *patata,* itself derived from the Taino *batata*; the tomato, from the Central American *tomatl*; and the yam, from the West African *nyamba*.[5] You only have to run your eye through any cookbook index to realize that almost all our vegetables are little more than resident aliens. Sometimes we can date with remarkable accuracy when a previously unknown and hence exotic plant food made its appearance on English or European soil. We first read of endive, chicory, and burnet, for instance, in John

Evelyn's *Acetaria: A Discourse of Sallets,* published after his self-imposed exile in Italy, Holland, and France during the Cromwellian years of the seventeenth century. When the monarchy returned to England, so too did Evelyn, and he brought with him seeds that he encouraged his countrymen to plant. We also know that many of our most commonly eaten vegetables—our potatoes, tomatoes, and peppers—were imports from the New World, all arriving in Spain in the 1550s and wending their way to the British Isles sometime during the 1590s.

But even after several hundred years of naturalization—and in some cases much longer than that—vegetables still don't come readily to mind when we think of English food. Nor have they ever. In his *Travels in England in 1782,* the German writer Karl Philipp Moritz commented on a typical dinner; the vegetable side dish—cabbage in this case, although it might as well have been watery turnips or mushy peas—doesn't sound particularly appetizing:

> For an English dinner, to such lodgers as I am, generally consists of a piece of half-boiled, or half-roasted meat; and a few cabbage leaves boiled in plain water; on which they pour a sauce made of flour and butter. This, I assure you, is the usual method of dressing vegetables in England.[6]

Even a dyed-in-the-wool Anglophile like the Oxford-educated, Pulitzer Prize–winning poet Robert Peter Tristram Coffin once admitted that "the British lack variety in vegetables," immediately noting, however, their insignificance: "But, after all, what is a vegetable but grass? The British do run too much to bare potatoes and cabbage and Brussels sprouts. . . . People, apparently, eat such things."[7]

When most people think of English food—and there are plenty who would rather not think of it at all—they think of crumpets and scones, roast beef and sausages, even, perhaps, curry, the culinary legacy of British colonial rule in India and the unofficial national dish of England. But rarely do vegetables come to mind. As soon as we think fresh produce, our mind's eye heads south. It is both appropriate and ironic that the same imaginative migration happened to "the food writer to whom is given by common consent most credit for leading British tastes, from the 1950s onwards, in a new direction."[8] The writer so highly praised here for having revitalized British cooking is Elizabeth David, whose first published work bore the title *Mediterranean Food*. In it, she invited her vegetable-deprived readers to taste, if only in their imaginations, "what is so often lacking in English cooking."[9] Courgettes (better known to Americans as zucchini) had to be identified parenthetically as "(very young marrows)"; ratatouille had to be described as a "Provençale ragout of vegetables, usually pimentos, onions, tomatoes, and aubergines, stewed very slowly in oil"; and fennel, "Florentine, or sweet fennel," that is, "much cultivated in southern Europe for its thick and fleshy leaf stalks," had to be distinguished from "the common fennel, which will spread like a weed in any English garden." Clearly reacting to the stodgy English dinner of meat and two veg, she highlighted the starring role vegetables play in southern European cooking: "Many of these vegetable dishes," she noted, "constitute a course in themselves, and are intended to be served as such, after the meat or fish, when their full flavour will be appreciated."[10] To whet her readers' appetites still further, she prefaced her chapter on vegetables with a description of a Palermo market from D. H. Lawrence's *Sea and Sardinia* that no one could possibly confuse with the wooden shelves of cabbages, beets, and parsnips found in a typically drab English produce shop of the 1950s:

Abundance of vegetables—piles of white and green fennel, like celery, and great sheaves of young, purplish,
sea-dust-colored artichokes, nodding their buds, piles of
big radishes, scarlet and bluey purple, carrots, long
strings of dried figs, mountains of big oranges, scarlet
large peppers, a last slice of pumpkin, a great mass of
colours and vegetable freshnesses.[11]

Of course a lot has changed since then—in part thanks to
Elizabeth David herself—and one of the top tourist destinations
in London is the wildly extravagant Food Hall that Mohamed al
Fayed refurbished when he took over the ownership of Harrod's
Department Store, complete with gleaming glass display cases and
mouthwatering displays of fruits, meats, cheeses, pastries, breads,
teas, chocolates, and yes, even vegetables from all over the world.
Granted, none of this would have been possible back when
David's book first appeared in 1950; England was recovering
from the war and "almost every essential ingredient of good
cooking was either rationed or unobtainable."[12] Nonetheless, it
remains true that even today, when the only ration books around
are those being sold as collector's items, that when most of us
imagine a vegetarian feast, we do not tend to think of the traditional side dishes of British pubs: mushy peas, bashed neeps, and
potato mashes.

The importing of both edible plants and their names is no
more a modern phenomenon than is England's ambivalent gastronomic relationship with southern Europe—and with Italy
above all. Generally speaking, culinary historians attribute most
vegetables that are grown in the British Isles today to the first
four hundred years of the Common Era, the period of the Roman
occupation of Britain. Cultivated vegetables, that is. For there is
an enormous difference between wild plants, not all that different from weeds, and deliberately cultivated vegetables. In her

book on Mediterranean food, Elizabeth David not only introduced her compatriots to cultivated Florentine fennel, but she also took care to distinguish it from the wild northern variety. Similarly, after so highly touting her native sea kale, Jane Grigson observes that although it "was being grown in English gardens by the early decades of the 18th century," it had been "transferred from its natural habitat, which John Gerard in his *Herball*, of 1597, had evocatively described as 'the bayches and brimmes of the sea, where is no earth to be seen, but sande and rolling pebble stones.' "[13] England's one great contribution to the world's vegetable repertoire turns out to be a coastal weed. Again and again we find the same estimation. Darina and Myrtle Allen emphasize that sea kale "grows wild on sandy, pebbly strands around the coast" and "is rarely if ever seen for sale."[14]

We might begin to wonder what our word *vegetable* actually means. Most of us would unhesitatingly agree with the *Oxford English Dictionary*'s definition: "a plant cultivated for food; esp. an edible herb or root used for human consumption and commonly eaten, either cooked or raw, with meat or other articles of food." Vegetables are what we eat for dinner, usually as a side dish accompanying the more substantial part of the meal, most often some form of meat, poultry, or fish. This is the culinary definition of vegetable. The *OED* provides another meaning of the word, however: "a living organism belonging to the vegetable kingdom or the lower of the two series of organic beings; a growth devoid of animal life; a plant in the widest or scientific sense." According to this second, scientific definition, daisies, boxwood shrubs, and even pine trees qualify as vegetables, but we don't generally eat them. Many weeds are edible for that matter, but we don't eat them either. Today we use the word *vegetable* to mean not just vegetation or plant, and not even just edible plant, but palatable plant. We want to like eating what we eat, not just to stay alive. And so we prefer peas and carrots (or at the very least acknowledge them to be vegetables) to docks and mallow, both of which were regularly eaten in the past by those less able to buy or grow their own food than we are today and who would have been more willing to understand the word in its broader scientific sense (toxic vegetables aside) than in the restricted culinary sense we've come to assign to it.

The older meaning of the word, though, hasn't vanished entirely. In the guessing game Animal, Vegetable, or Mineral, the middle term has very little to do with edibility, but instead is opposed to cows, chickens, and lions, on the one hand, and copper, steel, and basalt on the other. According to the rules of the game, crabgrass and ragweed would count as vegetables.

Ultimately, our distinction between vegetables and weeds says more about us than it does about the natural state of things. We may distinguish between edible and inedible forms of plant life as between cultivated and wild, but our distinction is not absolute; rather, it's entirely determined by the time and place in which we live—not to mention how much money we have to spend on what we eat. Centuries ago people simmered nettles, plantains, and the other "potherbs" they found during their long hours of foraging in the wild, whereas today we'd no more eat nettles than we'd use the word *potherb* in the first place. When we make soup, it's carrots, celery, potatoes, and onions that we use to flavor the broth—each and every one unquestionably a vegetable in the culinary sense of the word, rather than a weed.

And yet even though the world of vegetation has today been categorized and classified according to genus and species, still there are rebels that don't seem to toe the line. In the animal kingdom, no one seems able to decide whether the red panda is a bear (genus: *Ursus*) or a raccoon (genus: *Procyon*), but no one doubts that it's an animal. When we turn to vegetables, we're even less sure of what's what. We know the common dandelion belongs to the genus *Taraxacum* within the family Asteraceae, but we can't seem to figure out whether it's a weed or a vegetable. Gardeners view dandelions as the banes of their otherwise green lawns and doggedly try to uproot them, but gourmets and foodies buy the locally grown organic variety at upscale greengrocers. Whole Foods sells them for $3.29 a pound—something to keep in mind the next time you're struggling to pull those long taproots out of your backyard. In her wonderful book *In Nonna's Kitchen: Recipes and Traditions from Italy's Grandmothers*, Carol Field comments on what we might call the gentrification of weeds traditionally foraged by those who could afford no better: "*Andar per erbe*, to go hunting for wild greens, was once considered the province of the poor. . . . Ironically, what the poor once picked for free now arrives on Italian tables at great expense."[15]

Closer to home, we might consider the ramp, the odiferous weed that grows as far south as the Carolinas and as far north as Canada. Although it's an entirely distinct species of allium—technically classified as *A. tricoccum*—it's known colloquially as a "wild leek" because it's so much easier for us to think of weeds as a kind of leek than as a kind of onion. Residents of West Virginia hold festivals in honor of the ramp every spring—often called, to add to the confusion, "Feasts of the Ramson"—even though its odor—"off-puttingly smelly when raw," is how the *New York Times* recently described it—frequently sends visitors running in the opposite direction with their noses tightly clamped between thumb and forefinger. After two eight-hour shifts cooking ramps at one such recent spring celebration, retired coal miner Don McClung literally stank. His daughter Patricia, who assisted him throughout the festival, wore an apron bearing the dubious title the "King of Stink." Her explanation of why she's never tasted so much as a single ramp, even after serving as sous-chef to her father: "I don't want to smell bad."[16] Their malodorousness notwithstanding, celebrity chefs Emeril Lagasse, Bobby Flay, and Mario Batali have all devoted segments of their television shows to cooking with ramps, driving prices in the New York area up to between $10 and $15 a pound. Yoshi Yamada, a chef from Batali's West Village restaurant Babbo, "dreams of ramps. To me nothing announces the end of winter like the arrival of ramps"; when they finally appear at farmer's markets, he sautés them in olive oil, sears them until the whites soften, adds garlic, linguine (cooked al dente, of course), and bread crumbs, before sprinkling pecorino romano over the top. "It may be my favorite pasta ever."[17]

So, in the end what are the wild leeks we call ramps? Stinky smelling weeds or eagerly anticipated spring delicacies?

While we're on the subject, what about the whole category of what's come to be called "edible weeds"? Burdock, chickweed, lamb's-quarters, plantain, and purslane are all technically considered weeds, defined as "wild plants growing where they are not wanted," and yet more and more often, they're appearing in soups and salads in fine restaurants. A recent article in the *Boston Globe Magazine,* titled "In the Weeds," claims that purslane is "a flavorful green to those in the know (but a pesky plant invading the yard to others)" and quotes chef Champe Speidel whose restaurant was almost named after the perennial weed: "It can come from the backyard, from the sidewalk, or better yet, for culinary purposes, our favorite herb grower."[18] My local farmstand has just begun to sell purslane, at over $3 a pound, sandwiching it in between the watercress and arugula. Quite a fuss over a weed that sprouts out of the sidewalk. What would dinner guests think if they knew that their salad greens had been pulled out of the cracks in the driveway's asphalt?

At what point does a pesky dandelion become a delectable green waiting to be tossed with a balsamic vinaigrette or sautéed in garlic and oil? At what point does a pest become a delicacy? When does a weed become a vegetable? When does wild become cultivated? And when did cultivated vegetables eclipse wild plants in the first place?

Myrtle and Darina Allen include a chapter in their book of traditional Irish cooking called "Food from the Wild," in which they feature recipes for wild garlic, nettles, crab apples, and seaweeds with names like sloke, samphire, dulse, and carrigeen moss. "Nowadays," they write,

> in times of relative plenty, many of these wild foods are neglected and often left to rot in the hedgerows. . . . For years Ballymaloe House has encouraged local children to forage in the countryside and to bring their finds to the kitchen door for use in the restaurant.[19]

The Allens no doubt have the legacy of the Irish Potato Famine in mind as they teach their children to forage for berries, nuts, nettles, and wild mushrooms. But poverty and famine are certainly not why trendy chefs today have begun to hire professional foragers to supply them with the best of local produce, whether wild mushrooms found in the forests near Santa Barbara or lacinato kale purchased direct from the grower at New York's Union Square Greenmarket. Alice Waters's legendary Chez Panisse might have been the first American restaurant to add a professional forager to its payroll back in the 1980s, but the Berkeley landmark is no longer a lone voice in the wilderness. From Wolfgang Puck's Spago in Beverly Hills to April Bloomfield's New York gastropub The Spotted Pig, restaurants across the country are increasingly relying on foragers to track down seasonal delicacies and—in the words of the popular San Francisco blog Local-Forage—"to look, even beyond the organic realm, to the culinary traditions of our ancestors." "What hunter-gatherers did for ancient societies," writes Maria Hunt in the *Christian Science Monitor*, professional foragers "do for modern haute cuisine."[20]

And it's not just our *chefs de cuisine* who stalk the wild mushroom. Steve "Wildman" Brill has made a name for himself leading foraging tours through the woods and meadows of New York's parks. For $15 (more or less), Brill will teach you to identify such edible wild plants as carnelian cherries, elderberries, lamb's-quarters, sheep sorrel, and sassafras. So successful have his tours been that, on the order of Parks and Recreation Commissioner Henry J. Stern, Brill was once arrested for eating the dandelion greens that grew wild in Central Park's meadows: "It's a violation of park regulations. You don't want people eating up your park."[21]

That fashionable restaurants and edible herb specialists should promote foraging—in many cases of plants that we would dismiss as weeds—is an enormous reversal of culinary attitudes that date back almost two millennia to the Romans' disparagement of the hunter-gatherers they encountered when their empire moved north and west. The first-century Roman historian Tacitus commented on the Germanic tribes he encountered in the north: "The fact is that although their land is fertile and extensive, they fail to take full advantage of it because they do not work sufficiently hard. They do not plant orchards, fence off meadows, or irrigate gardens."[22] In other words, they foraged. Unlike the Allens, who collect nettles and sloke and have made it their mission to educate the public about such wild vegetables, the Romans were happiest dining on vegetables that had emerged from carefully fenced, irrigated, and cultivated gardens. And by and large, it's still the Roman definition that we so uncritically accept today when we oppose broccoli and celery to burdock and purslane. Our modern word *horticulture*, the science of cultivating plants, derives from the Latin word for garden, *hortus*. Classical writers such as Cato the Elder, Varro, and Columella devoted volume upon volume to farming techniques and all things agricultural, painstakingly detailing how to improve soil, graft desirable cuttings onto hardier but wild fruit trees, and tend vegetable beds. Leaves, seedlings, roots, and other wild plants, all collectively known as *herbae,* were regarded as no better than fodder for animals—or for people who were so poor as to be reduced to the level of animals. According to Roman logic, if the people living in the north foraged for their food in the wild, they couldn't be all that different from animals.

Certainly the pre-Roman inhabitants of Britain ate the roots and green leaves of wild plants that today are considered weeds more than vegetables—nettles, for instance, and plantains, mallows, and docks. In the winter, they dug up carrots, parsnips, and turnips, all of which still grow wild in the fields and hedgerows of the English countryside. The native plants of the onion family—including wild garlic, onion, and leeks—were used as potherbs, or flavorings, for the otherwise bland stews that sustained much of the country. It was the Romans who transformed vegetable growing and eating in Britain. Most of the plant foods we eat today—even here in the United States—are the engineered products of Roman horticultural expertise. According to Jane Renfrew, culinary historian of the English Heritage Society, the Romans "introduced a number of vegetable crops such as cabbage, the onion, leek, shallots, carrots, endive, globe artichokes, cucumber, marrow, asparagus, parsnip, turnip, radish and celery.[23] Wild forms of many of these vegetables might already have been growing for untold centuries before the Romans arrived, but, as Elizabeth David has noted, there's a world of difference between Florentine fennel, "much *cultivated* in southern Europe" (emphasis added) and "common fennel, which will spread like a weed." It can come as no surprise that each of the imported cultivated vegetables on

Renfrew's list—with the exception of leeks—bears an imported name as well, most of them from the Latin. Radish comes from *radix,* as cucumber does from *cucumer,* asparagus from *asparagus,* and carrot from *carota.* Even the word *vegetable* itself, as I noted earlier, comes to us from the Romans.[24] As in the case of the word *fruit,* both our general term for edible plant foods and the specific varieties the Romans brought with them are known by their classical names.

Weed, on the other hand, has no such distinguished Latin provenance. Like so many of the less desirable things we eat, the word *weed* comes to us from the language spoken by the Germanic people who took over the island after the Romans departed, leaving their villas, fish ponds, orchards, vineyards, and gardens to go to ruin. The Germanic peoples were not known for their consumption of vegetables, if vegetable is understood to mean carefully tended horticultural produce. Uncultivated, wild, and foraged herbs and grasses collectively referred to as *weodes* grew just fine without any human toil whatsoever. To this day only a very few edible plants indigenous to Britain are still known by their non-Roman names, whether Celtic or Germanic, and they are not, generally speaking, the stuff of which vegetarian dreams are made.

ON LEEKS AND ONIONS

The *bean,* the *beet,* and the *leek*: these are our only European vegetable names that don't derive from Latin, Italian, or French. Not nearly as glamorous—or as polysyllabic—as asparagus or radicchio, the bean, the beet, and the leek were about the only plant foods available on a daily basis in northern Europe before Roman times. And we're not talking about kidney, lima, or green beans, all native to the New World and unknown in Europe before Columbus's voyages across the Atlantic. We're talking about the broad bean, described as early as the first century by the Greek physician, pharmacologist, and botanist Dioscorides as "windy, flatulent, hard of digestion, causing troublesome dreams." Hardly as lyrical a name as *scorzonera,* our modern English word for bean is identical to its Anglo-Saxon forebear; French and Italian, on the other hand, derive their bean words from the Latin *faba*—hence *fève* and *fava.* The beet, generally identified with the borschts and herring salads of the Germans, Russians, and Poles, is one of the only vegetable names that was borrowed by the Romans, who had not encountered the bloodred root until they ventured north. They transformed the Celtic name into *beta,* from which the French derive their *betterave* and the Italians their *biete.*

And then there is the leek. Whether considered as word or thing, no other vegetable is quite as confusing as the leek. And the more we try to resolve that confusion, the more we find our-selves embroiled in the divide between north and south, between Germanic peoples and the Roman Empire, the hunter-gatherers and the agriculturalists, the wild and the cultivated—between weeds and vegetables. When you think about it, the fact that we consider the leek to be part of the onion family (as opposed to the onion being considered part of the leek family) has every-thing to do with the triumph of the south, the Romans, and the Romance languages. *Onion*—the name, that is—only came to England centuries after the native leek had lent its name to the entire family of pungent edible plants. Its earliest written refer-ence dates to about 1130—after the French-speaking Normans arrived in England, bringing with them all their many new foods and words. Before then, the onion had been considered a type of leek—an *ynneleac,* an "onion-leek," or, to translate even more precisely, a "unified leek," an accurate enough description when you compare its single globe-shaped bulb to the many segments that comprise a shallot or the many cloves that form a head of garlic. The leek is the perfect vegetable for northern countries, far easier to grow than other alliums, accommodating itself to poor soil conditions and hardy enough to withstand the long cold winters of Germany (where it's called a *Lauch*), the Netherlands (*look*), Denmark (*løg*), Sweden (*lök*), Russia (*luk*), Lithuania (*lukai*), Latvia (*kiploki*), Estonia (*kuuslauk*), and Finland (*laukka*).[25]

The leek isn't the only allium that has kept its northern name over the centuries, but its primacy is undeniable when we realize that the other, garlic, derives its second syllable—*lic*—from the leek. Its first syllable was the Old English word for spear; either the long bladelike leaves of the garlic plant were thought to resemble spears or perhaps the individual cloves were thought to look like spearheads, but in any event, the point remains the same. Garlic was regarded as a kind of leek, as it was similarly in Germany and the Netherlands, where *Knoblauch* and *knoflook* mean "knotted leek."

In countries where Romance languages are spoken, on the other hand, the leek was never any kind of a *pater familias*. The Latin leek was a *porrum*, which gave the French their *poireau*, the Spanish *puerro*, and the Italians *perro*—but it was a Roman word for onion, *allium*, that lies behind the names for garlic: *ail, ajo*, and *aglio*.

An obvious conclusion can be drawn: what the leek was to northern Europe, the onion was to the Roman Empire.

In the end, though, it's no easy business distinguishing between the different members of the allium family. Are scallions the same as green onions or spring onions? Some say yes, some say no. Is elephant garlic just a bigger form of the more compact heads we use more often? Actually, it's more closely related to the leek than to garlic. The blurry boundaries are reflected in the stories that lie behind the names we've given to our alliums. Despite the best efforts of Linnaean taxonomy, the names of the various members of the genus *Allium* are as tightly interwoven as the plants themselves. Today the botanical classification system incorporates hundreds of species, including *cepa* (onions), *ampeloprasum* (leek), *schoenoprasum* (chives), *ascalonicum* (scallions and shallots), and *sativum* (garlic). What we call the onion bears the scientific name *Allium cepa*, and what we know as the leek is the *A. ampeloprasum*; but *cepa* was simply another Latin word for onion (still heard in the Spanish *cebolla* and Italian *cipolla*), and *ampelo* and *prasum* were the Greek words for vine and leek. Translated into its various components, the scientific nomenclature thus winds up meaning "onion-onion" and "onion-vine-leek."

The names of all the other members of the *Allium* genus turn out to be variations on either the onion or the leek. The shallot, for instance, is referred to as *A. eschaninii*, which simply means "onion from Ascalon," a port in present-day Israel. In classical times it was known as a *cepa ascalonia*; as the years went by, the name gradually became the Old French *eschalotte*. The same story holds for the scallion, or *A. ascalonicum*, in which it's easy to see another variation on the theme of the Ascalon onion. Chives, on the other hand, weigh in on the leek side. Their botanical name, *A. schoenoprasum*, is formed from two Greek words: *schoinos,* a kind of rush or grass, and *prason,* leek. "Grass-leek," when you think about it, is an appropriate name for the slender-leaved dark green chive. The modern Greek words for leek and chive are almost identical—*prasum* and *praso*—suggesting that to the Greeks, anyway, the two amount to more or less the same thing.

Whether their names are traced back to the leek or the onion, however, the genus to which they all belong is *Allium*—onion. By the same token, despite the fact that it was once the foremost member of the genus eaten in northern Europe and remains to this day a staple in the northern European diet, the leek nonetheless plays second fiddle to the onion. In the United States, it's all but unknown other than as a component in *vichysoisse* or *potage parmentier,* whereas it's almost impossible to imagine most of our everyday dinners without the onion. Cookbooks regularly describe onions as the workhorses of our kitchens. *The Joy of Cooking* calls them "one of the most versatile seasonings in a cook's repertory" and yet has to explain to its presumably ignorant readers what leeks are by comparing them to something else, that something else being the more familiar and well known onion: "Milder and more subtle than onions," "Looking like enormous scallions with flat rather than hollow leaves." Helpful notes are appended, suggesting that if they're too hard to find in the store or too expensive, leeks may be replaced by onions. It can be no coincidence that it was the onion the French Chef— not the northern but the French Chef—famously lauded. "It's hard to imagine civilization without onions," Julia Child once noted. The humble and virtually eclipsed leek, on the other hand, has been the butt of jokes since Shakespeare's time at least when "to eat one's leek" meant to be humiliated.

What became of the native leek? Why was it uprooted by the imported and cultivated onion?

"THE COCKIE-LEEKIE IS A-COOLING"

Time was—granted, a long long time ago—when the leek reigned supreme on the island of Britannia. Even before the Angles and Saxons arrived in the sixth century, the leek was the favorite allium of the Celtic peoples, and it remains so in Ireland, Scotland, and generally throughout the Celtic fringe of Britain to this day. Known in Welsh as a *cenhinen*, in Irish as *cainnenn*, in Cornish as *kenin*, and in Breton as *kinnen*, the leek is the foundation of many of the most traditional dishes. Cockie-leekie or cock-a-leekie, for instance: no Scottish cookbook could fail to include a recipe for the most famous of Caledonian soups, the soup that King James VI of Scotland (later James I of England) is said to have been inordinately fond of and that inspired Sir Walter Scott, author of the Waverley novels, to close his *Fortunes of Nigel* with, "And, my lords and lieges, let us all to dinner, for the cockie-leekie is a-cooling." Its name, legend has it, derives from the cockerel, or rooster, that was defeated in the days of cockfighting and so ended up simmering away in the stew pot with leeks and prunes (the rice being a modern addition). In Ireland, *brotchán roy,* literally "a broth fit for a king," is an oatmeal-thickened broth made of either milk or meat, but always flavored with leeks. Also known as *brotchán foltchep,* it is reputed to have been a favorite of Saint Columba, the greatest Irish religious figure after Patrick.[26] Not to be undone in the matter of legendary soups, Wales claims that its traditional leek broth, *cawn cennin,* dates back to King Cadwallader's defeat of the Saxons in the fifth century. It is said "to strengthen the heart cords of anyone with Welsh blood."

Cock-a-Leekie *(serves 4–6)*

4 lb oven-ready chicken, with giblets, if possible
salt and black pepper
5 cups water
1 chicken stock cube, if needed
1 large onion, peeled and chopped
1 bay leaf
a few stalks of fresh thyme, or 1 teaspoon dried
1 lb leeks, trimmed and washed, and cut into thin diagonal slices
18 ready-to-eat unpitted prunes
2 tbsp long grain rice
2 tbsp chopped parsley

1. Wash the chicken and season it very well inside and out. Put it, breast down, in a deep saucepan or flameproof casserole with the water. Add the giblets, if you have them, or the stock cube, crumbled. Bring slowly to the boil, skimming off any scum that rises to the surface.

2. Add the onion, bay leaf and thyme, cover tightly and simmer very gently for 1 hour, turning the chicken over halfway through.

3. Remove the giblets from the pan. Add the leeks, prunes, and rice and continue to simmer gently for 15–20 minutes, or until the chicken is cooked (the juices will run clear when the chicken is pierced with a skewer).

4. Lift out the chicken onto a warmed dish. Season the broth to taste and add the parsley. Either serve the chicken and the broth separately, or cut the chicken into serving pieces or shreds and serve in the broth.[27]

Brotchán Roy (serves 2)

8 oz leeks, washed
2 tablespoons butter
2 cups stock or milk or water
½ cup oatmeal
Salt and freshly ground pepper
Pinch of powdered mace
1 tablespoon parsley

Slice the white and pale green parts of the leeks finely. Melt the butter in a saucepan, toss in the leeks, cook for a minute or two, add the liquid, bring to a boil then sprinkle in the oatmeal. Bring back to a boil, stirring all the time, season with salt, freshly ground pepper, and a pinch of mace. Cover and simmer for about 45 minutes or until both vegetables and oatmeal are cooked. Add the parsley, boil for a minute or two, then serve.[28]

Cawn Cennin (serves 6–8)

4 slices bacon
6 thick leeks, trimmed of the roots and dark green, then chopped
10 cups (2½ quarts) chicken stock

Salt and pepper to taste
A few circles of sliced leek, for garnish

To prepare:
1. Sauté the bacon in a large soup pot over medium heat until crisp, then remove it from the pan, drain on paper towels, and reserve for the garnish.
2. Prepare the remaining ingredients as directed in the recipe list.

To cook:
1. In the soup pot, reheat the bacon grease over medium heat and stir in the leeks, turning to coat them and sautéing them for several minutes, until they take on a little golden color.
2. Pour in the stock, bring to a boil over high heat, then reduce the heat to low and cook, uncovered, for 15 minutes. Remove from the heat. Puree the soup, solids first, then pour back into the pot. Season with salt and pepper.

To serve:
Reheat the soup over medium-high heat, then ladle it into bowls and top with crumbled bacon and circles of leek.[29]

The leek remains the national emblem of Wales and in 1985 was depicted on the one-pound coins celebrating the four parts of the United Kingdom—right up there with the English oak, the Scottish thistle, and Irish flax. It's proudly worn on Welsh caps every March 1, the day honoring Saint David, the country's patron—or Saint Tavy, as he's known in Wales. Whether historically accurate or merely legendary, the story holds that the sixth-century saint ordered his soldiers to wear leeks on their helmets to distinguish themselves from the Saxon enemy on the battlefield. The battle itself is believed to have been fought in a field full of leeks. Today many Welshmen substitute daffodils for leeks, perhaps because the name for the flower in Welsh is *cenhinen Bedr*, "Peter's leek" (leeks and daffodils are both members of the lily family). Or perhaps daffodils simply smell better.

Shakespeare had his fun with the Welsh in *Henry V,* when he caricatured not only the appalling pronunciation of his Welsh officer Ffuellen whose *b*'s are consistently aspirated as *p*'s, but also his predilection for leeks. "The Welshmen did good service in a garden where leeks did grow," Ffuellen boasts to the king, before taking his revenge on the English knave who humiliated him by making him "eat his leek."

> FFUELLEN: I say, I will make him eat some part of my
> leek, or I will peat his pate four days. Bite, I pray you, it
> is good for your green wound and your ploody coxcomb.
> PISTOL: Must I bite?
> FFUELLEN: Yes, certainly, and out of doubt and out of
> question too, and ambiguities.
> PISTOL: By this leek, I will most horribly revenge—I eat
> and eat—I swear—
> FFUELLEN: Eat, I pray you. Will you have some more
> sauce to your leek? There is not enough leek to swear
> by. (V.i.40–51)

Apparently, the tradition of humiliating the Welsh by maligning their leeks is still alive and well, as is the stereotypical belligerent response. When the July 1, 2004, edition of the *London Evening Standard* hit the newsstands, it bore the headline, "Welshman Beat Up Englishman over Leek." The story itself was even better: "A Welshman who attacked an Englishman outside a Chinese takeaway in Scotland over a jibe he made about a leek was jailed today for five years."

So intimately entwined are the leek with the Celts, most especially the Welsh, that it's hard to find references to the vegetable that do not in some way involve the inhabitants of Cymru. John Evelyn's discussion in his *Acetaria* is no exception:

> Leeks, and cibbols, *Porrum*; hot, and of vertue prolifick;
> since Latona, the mother of Apollo long'd after them: the

> Welch [sic], who eat them much, are observ'd to be very
> fruitful: they are also friendly to the lungs and stomach,
> being sod in milk; a few therefore of the slender and green
> summities, a little shred, do not amiss in composition.[30]

Some Welsh historians go so far as to speculate that the leek might have played a special role in the land's religion and culture centuries before the time of Saint David. Before Christianity ever arrived in Britain, the priestly Druids, who worshipped trees and plants, had a special veneration for the leek, which was considered to have both medicinal and magical properties. It was believed, for instance, that if maidens put a leek under their pillows, they would be granted dreams in which they could see the faces of their future husbands.

Even when shrouded in fanciful pseudohistory and endowed with dubious magical properties, the point remains that the leek is nonetheless and consistently associated with the Celts. To this day, Wales often attributes its tradition of fine singing and its internationally known *eisteddfodau,* or musical festivals, to regular consumption of its national vegetable, which suggests that maybe there is something to the belief in the leek's health-giving qualities. After all, how different were medicine and magic in a prescientific age?

Its illustrious role in myth, religion, and the arts notwithstanding, the native Celtic leek has all but vanished from our kitchens. If we want to find it today, we need to comb through British seed catalogues that specialize in native fruits, vegetables, and bulbs. Shipton Bulbs, for instance, describes the native leek as "the ancestor of allium porrum, the leek. In the wild in the British Isles it occurs on some rocky coasts of Cornwall, the Scillies and of course here in South Wales." Chiltern Seeds writes similarly of the variety known as the Babington leek—"a very showy and rare plant endemic to the British Isles. Found in clefts of rocks and sandy places near the coast of Cornwall and Dorset and western Ireland." The catalogue concedes, however, that "it is thought to be a relic of former cultivation."

In fact, recent food writers have gone so far as to call the indigenous status of the beloved Celtic allium into question. It might be, writes Alan Davidson in his authoritative *Penguin Companion to Food,* that it was none other than "the Romans [who] introduced the leek to Britain and therefore to the Welsh, who subsequently made it their own special vegetable."[31] Heresy, say those from the Celtic camp who, whether accurately or wishfully, refer to "pre-Roman times," "an age before Christianity," and Druids, Mother Nature, and ancient Celtia. Perhaps there's a grain of truth behind their belief that if the leek was imported at all, it wasn't by Romans, but by Phoenician traders centuries earlier. The Greek merchant-geographer Pytheas had circumnavigated most of Britain in the fourth century BC; he was also the first to use the name Britannia and to mention the Germanic tribes, as well as the midnight sun, the aurora, and polar ice. In the first century BC, the Roman official Publius Crassus visited the Cassiterides, the Tin Isles, or what we today know as Cornwall and the Scilly Islands, in an effort to organize an already existing tin trade. It's not impossible that a visitor centuries before the Romans brought the leek with him. Nonetheless, most culinary historians agree that it was the Romans who brought their prized cultivated leeks with them in the first century of the Common Era when they passed through Gaul and arrived on the island of Britannia. Bringing with them both agricultural expertise and literacy, the historians tell us, they planted their own leeks. According to Celtic sources, what they did was cultivate and rename the indigenous variety.

If leeks did grow on the island before the arrival of the Romans, they would probably have been what we today call the

Allium ampeloprasum, possibly the Babington leek. But the variety that the Romans prized so highly and upon which they had expended so much of their agricultural knowledge was what we know as *A. porrum*, the forerunner of the leek that we find today in farmers' markets and the produce aisles of today's supermarkets. The Roman broad-leafed leek looks like what comes to mind when we think leek; what the Celts ate looks like a weed.

We are right back where we started, with the fuzzy distinction between weeds and vegetables. At what point does the dandelion become a salad green? At what point did the wild leek become the

Wild leeks, *Allium ampeloprasum*.

Cultivated leeks, *Allium porrum.*

cultivated one? When it was deliberately planted and tended, rather than simply foraged in nature? When it was cross-pollinated to become the broad-leafed variety we recognize today? When its taste grew milder and sweeter? When it was bred to mature from seed to full-grown plant in only four months? When its Celtic name and druidical associations disappeared from the pages of history, replaced by the Latin *porrum,* which had already earned quite a reputation for itself back home in the Mediterranean?

THE IMPERIAL PORROPHAGUS AND THE PYRAMID BUILDERS

According to Pliny's first-century *Natural History,* the Emperor Nero ate such enormous quantities of leeks that his subjects nicknamed him Porrophagus, "Leek-Eater."

> It may also be suitable to mention the leek in this family
> of plants, especially as importance has recently been
> given to the leek by the emperor Nero, who on certain
> fixed days of every month always ate leeks preserved in
> oil, and nothing else, not even bread, for the sake of his
> voice.[32]

The emperor might not have been completely wrong and he
was far from alone in his faith in the medicinal power of the
leek. One theory, no doubt fanciful, even holds that the word
leek is a corruption of *loch*, the Latin word for a medicinal substance that could be licked to cure a sore throat (perhaps the
Welsh are onto something after all when they attribute their
renowned singing ability to their regular consumption of leeks).
In his *De materia medica,* Dioscorides touted the health benefits
of the entire allium family, leeks not excepted, and none other
than Hippocrates, the founder of Western medicine and author
of the oath still sworn by newly minted physicians today, pre-
scribed the leek as a cure for nosebleeds. Centuries later, the
medieval medical treatises known as leechdoms (no relation to
leeks) recommended the vegetable for many ailments, most especially those involving the throat. The leek was used as an an-
tidote to poison and was called into service in the diagnosis of
the severity of abdominal injuries. A wounded man would be
fed leeks and his wound sniffed an hour later. If an oniony odor
were detected, it was clear that the digestive tract had been rup-
tured and death was deemed imminent—a logical conclusion in
a time before antibiotics, when intestinal ruptures would inevitably have spelled systemic infection and death. Our belief that
it's an apple a day that keeps the doctor away dates only to the
early twentieth century; in the medieval period, it was the
healthfulness of the leek that was touted: "Eat leeks in oile and

ramsines in May, / And all the year after physicians may play"
(a *ramsine*—today spelled *ramson*—is wild garlic).

Their medicinal value aside, leeks were also esteemed in the
ancient world for their flavor. Probably owing to their milder
taste, leeks—cultivated ones, that is—were treated as the aristo-
crats of the allium family. Poor people could eat their humble
and bitter-tasting onions—or *cepae,* as they would have called
them—but only the *porrum* was fit for an emperor. The Roman
epicure Apicius provided four recipes featuring leeks in his *De re
coquinaria*—boiled in oil, wrapped in cabbage leaves, cooked with
laurel berries, and served with green beans cooked in the leek-
infused water—but not a single recipe for either the onion or
garlic. Only the leek was worthy of standing on its own.

Centuries before the Romans, the Egyptians had similarly
distinguished between onions and leeks. Their variety, the Middle Eastern species *A. kurrat,* had been cultivated as early as the
fourth millennium BC, and the broader-leafed vegetable they
produced was so beloved that they depicted it in their tomb paintings. Only the wealthy would have had ornately decorated tombs;
the rest of the population would have been laid to rest in unmarked
graves and, while still alive, would have subsisted on bread and
onions. In the fifth century BC, the Greek historian Herodotus
claimed that the pyramids had been built by those who survived
on "radishes, onions and leeks." It's hard to believe, though, that
the laborers would have had access to the new and improved cultivated leek. It's a tricky business knowing what words that look
familiar once referred to. Were the golden apples of the Hesperides really apples? It all depends on how we understand the
Greek *melon,* which in a contemporary dictionary is translated as
apple, but back then might have referred to, for instance, a
quince. So too with the leek. We might not even really know

what the ancient words for the vegetable referred to. I'll give an example.

According to the Bible, after the Israelites escaped from their Egyptian taskmasters, they wandered in the desert for forty years. So much is well known. During those forty years, the people had to eat, but deserts being deserts, not a lot of food was to be had. Before God took matters into his own hands and rained down manna on his chosen but hungry people, they complained to Moses, nostalgically recalling the "cucumbers, the melons, the leeks, the onions, and the garlic" that they used to feast on back in the good old days in Egypt (Numbers 11:5). But there's a problem here, apart from the obvious one of the Israelites' faulty memory: how often do slaves feast on anything, much less cucumbers and melons? According to John Cooper, a historian of Jewish food, the word translated as *cucumber* could not have meant what we imagine it to be because cucumbers were unknown in ancient Egypt.[33] It must have been a different gourd that the Israelites had in mind, perhaps the muskmelon. By the same token, the word rendered *melon* should more precisely be translated as *watermelon*. With *onion* and *garlic* we stand on surer ground; the Hebrew words used in the Bible have maintained their meanings over the centuries. But the word for leek—*hatzir*—is a problem. In Israel today, a leek is *karti*; look up *hatzir* in a dictionary and you'll find it translated as *grass* or *hay,* which is what it means in all other biblical passages where it appears. When the Lord punished Ahab for his apostasy with a drought, for instance, the rebellious northern king commanded his prophet Obadiah to " 'Go through the land to all the springs of water and to all the wadis; perhaps we may find grass [*hatzir*] to keep the horses and mules alive, and not lose some of the animals' " (1 Kings 18:5). It seems highly unlikely that Ahab would have fed leeks to his horses while his people were dying. When the prophet Isaiah described the desolation devastating a neighboring kingdom, he noted that "the grass [*hatzir*] is withered, the new growth fails, the verdure is no more" (15:6). Are we to believe that Isaiah was concerned with the withering of leeks?

Translators have long had a hard time knowing what to make of the confusion and have rendered *hatzir* according to context. Thus, in the Greek Bible the Israelites remember the *prasa*, or leeks, they used to eat in Egypt, even though in all other instances *hatzir* is understood to mean plants or grass. In the Latin Bible, the story is much the same: it's *porri* (plural of *porrum*) the Israelites dream of, but *herba,* grass, that Ahab commands his prophet to feed his livestock and *herba* that has withered in Isaiah's prophecy.

When we try to distinguish between *A. ampeloprasum*, the leek indigenous to northern Europe, and *A. porrum,* the cultivated vegetable of the Romans, we're in much the same position that the biblical translators found themselves in when they had to decide between the weedy variety and the cultivated Mediterranean one. In both cases, it comes down to a matter of class. The pharaohs would have feasted on tended leeks; the Israelite slaves (and the Egyptian commoners) would have had to make do with wild grass. No doubt what the ancients Celts ate was similarly wild and weedy.

My local nursery, by the way, sells two varieties of leek. On a recent trip I bought a four-inch potted *A. porrum* and planted it in the garden. Everyone instantly recognized it to be a leek. The four-inch potted *A. ampeloprasum* that I planted, however, looked an awful lot like a weed and I had to keep reminding myself not to pull it out of my herb garden. Heirs to Roman agriculture (and perhaps to Egyptian as well), we want our vegetables to look like vegetables and our leeks to look like the ones the Romans so masterfully reengineered, not the weedy ones. Nonetheless, we still call them both leeks.

ON *PORLEACS* AND *YNNELEACS*

Our word for the broad-leafed allium has never had any relationship with any of the names derived from the Latin *porrum*. In fact, our leek is barely changed from the *leac* central to the diet and imaginations of the Anglo-Saxon invaders of Britain. Their alphabet—if we can call their runic system of writing an alphabet—had symbols for ice, elk, cattle, and leeks. They seem to have believed it to possess magical and life-sustaining properties. Perhaps the entire onion family did. In his seventh-century life of Saint Cuthbert, the Venerable Bede relates a story about the unusual diet that kept the holy man alive for five days when a violent storm stranded him on an uninhabited island off Lindisfarne where his monks waited and worried about their bishop. When the storm abated and they sailed to his rescue at last, they found him surprisingly fit. It was onions that had sustained him during the storm—or so said the Venerable Bede:

> "Now, from the moment of my coming until the present time, during a space of five days and five nights, I have sat here without moving." "And how have you supported life, my lord bishop?" asked I; "have you remained so long without taking food?" Upon which, turning up the couch on which he was sitting, he showed me five onions concealed therein, saying, "This has been my food for five days; for, whenever my mouth became dry and parched with thirst, I cooled and refreshed myself by tasting these."[34]

But was it onions that Cuthbert survived on, or was it leeks? Bede's Latin had two distinct words—*cepae* and *porri*—but

Cuthbert's Old English had only *leac*. In the garden plans of an early seventh-century monastery, we can see that the monks planted *cepas* (onions), *alias* (garlic), *ascolonias* (shallots), and *porros* (leeks), but of course the plans are in Latin. In the Old English leechdoms, on the other hand, we read about *ynneleac, cropleac, garleac, secgleac, bradeleac,* and *holleac*—all members of the allium family, and all, judging from the common suffix, considered types of leeks, with the Latin prefix specifying the variety. Thus an *ynneleac* was an onion-leek and a *porleac* a leek-leek. Garlic is easy to see in *garleac,* and chives were probably what was meant by *cropleac. Secgleac, bradeleac,* and *holleac* are anyone's guess.

In fact, *leac* might have cast as large a net in the world of vegetables as the apple did in the world of fruit, referring not just to oniony vegetables but to edible plant foods other than roots, which were known as *wyrt.* As medieval food historian Ann Hagen has noted, a common Anglo-Saxon word for garden was *leactun,* literally, "place of the leek," and a common term for gardener was *leactunweard,* literally, "ward of the leek-place." Many English towns and cities have names that mean something like "settlement or town of the leek": Leighton, Leyton, Laughton, Leckhampstead, and Leckhampton. Loughrigg, in the Lake District, means "leek ridge" and Lawkland, in North Yorkshire, is "leek land."

By the time the Angles and Saxons were naming parts of the country, though, the Romans had occupied the land for some four hundred years. They had already introduced many of the herbs and vegetables they needed for the elaborate dishes they must have so desperately longed for—onions, shallots, chives, not to mention chervil, coriander, dill, fennel, garden mint, hyssop, parsley, rosemary, rue, sage, savory and sweet marjoram, and thyme, all were imported by the Romans. They had also brought their southern variety of leek and, in addition, had cultivated the native wild one, calling both, confusingly, by the same name: *porrum.*

In order to get to Britannia, the Romans had made their way through Gaul, the region of today's France. Leeks have long been a favorite ingredient in French cuisine—just think of such potato-leek soups as *potage à la bonne femme* and *potage parmentier,* not to mention the famous leek pies, or *flamiche aux poireaux,* of Picardy. Before Caesar conquered Gaul, the leek would have been called by a version of the Celtic *c-n* name used throughout Britannia at the time. Today, however, the French word is *poireau,* obviously derived from the Latin. In England, on the other hand, similarly occupied by the Romans, the vegetable has kept its northern name.

For a while it seemed the pendulum could have swung either way. As we saw in the garden plans for the seventh-century monastery, northern and southern names coexisted happily for a time, resulting in the now-obsolete *ynneleac* (onion-leek) and *porleac* (leek-leek), with Latin providing the first syllable and Anglo-Saxon the second. Sooner or later, though, the onion lost the northern part of its name while the leek lost the Latin part.

Fast forward a few centuries and we find onions, scallions, shallots, and chives being called by names that look far more familiar to us than the old *cropleac, secgleac, holleac,* or *bradeleac.* Some of the earliest references appear in books that were printed within a few years of each other. The 1390 *Forme of Cury* calls for *oynouns, lekis,* and *chybolles* galore. A simple recipe called *Salat,* for instance, includes all three, plus a few extra.

A recipe found in virtually every early cookery book in one form or another was for a dish known as *porray,* a sort of stewy concoction in which vegetables were simmered in almond milk (on fast days) or meat broth with bits of bacon (on meat days). Spelled many different ways, *porray* is obviously derived from *porrum,* leeks being a principal ingredient, but the Latinate title notwithstanding, the instructions invariably call for leeks by

Salat

*T*ake persel, sawge, grene garlic, chibolles, oynouns, leek, borage, myntes, porrettes, fenel, and toun cressis, rew, rosemarge, purslarye; laue and waische hem clene. Pike hem. Pluk hem small wiþ þyn honed, and myng hem wel with rawe oile; lay on vyneger and salt, and serue it forth.

Salad

Take parsley, sage, green garlic, scallions, onions, leeks, borage, mint, green onions, fennel, garden cress, rue, rosemary, purslane; rinse and wash them clean. Peel them. Tear them into small pieces with your hands, and mix them well with raw oil; lay on vinegar and salt, and serve it forth.[35]

their Old English name, as in the recipe for a *Blawnche Perrye* from a manuscript dated to about 1420: In this linguistic melting pot of the most literal kind, Northern *lekys, mylke, hony,* and *elys* simmer together with the newly imported *almaundes, rys, sugre,* and *venysoun,* yet never is the dish called a leek stew, whether white, black, green, or chaplain's (a popular version was known as a *porrey chapeleyn*).

That French names were used in the cookbook is hardly surprising; it was written by the master chefs of the French-speaking king Richard II and freely borrowed from earlier continental cookbooks. Nor are we terribly surprised, things being what they were, that the first English Bible should have called for onions rather than for *ynneleacs,* as it did in the passage I referred to earlier from John Wycliffe's 1388 translation: "We thenken on the fischis whiche we eten in Egipt freli; gourdis, and melouns,

For to make Blawnche Perrye

Take þe Whyte of the lekys, an seþe hem in a potte, an presse hem up, & hacke hem small on a bord. An nym gode Almaunde Mylke, an a lytil of Rys, an do alle þes to-gederys, an seþe an stere it wyl, an do þer-to Sugre or hony, an dresse it yn; þanne take powdered Elys, an seþe hem in fayre Water, and broyle hem, an kytte hem in long pecys. And ley .ij. or .iij. in a dysse, and putte þin perrey in a-noþer dysshe, an serue þe to dysshys to-gederys as Venysoun with Furmenty.

To Make White Porray

Take the whites of leeks and seethe them in a pot. Press the water out of them and cut them into small pieces on a board. Take good almond milk and a little rice, and put all this to-gether; seethe and stir it well. Add sugar or honey and stir it in. Then take dried eels, seethe them in fresh water, broil them, and cut them in long pieces. And lay them in a dish, put the porray in another dish, and serve the two dishes together as venison with furmenty.[36]

and lekis, and oyniouns, and garlekis comen in to mynde to vs." By the time Wycliffe translated the Bible, the onion had con-quered the northern word as effectively as King William had the Angles and Saxons and had thoroughly naturalized itself on En-glish soil once and for all. Only the leek—humble, wild, more weed than vegetable—kept its Old English name in both cook-book and Bible.

As time went by, the vegetable once beloved by saints and kings, proudly worn onto the battlefield, believed to possess magical properties, and after which dozens of towns are named, lost much of its former stature. Most people will be surprised to learn that porridge, hardly the food of the wealthy, is neither originally Scottish nor originally made of oats; it was made of leeks, from which it derives its name. "By reason of their mild nature," the 1717 *Dictionarium rusticum, urbanicum & botanicum* succinctly states, "they [leeks] are much used in porridge, which had its name from the Latin *porrum,* a leek."[37] From soup fit for a king to humble porridge: oh, how the mighty have fallen.

THE ECLIPSE OF THE LEEK—AND ITS COMEBACK

Despite their prestigious, often legendary history and their thoroughly English name, leeks are nonetheless cooked and eaten less often than onions, both in Britain and certainly here in the United States. They scarcely appear in the most popular cookery books of the eighteenth and nineteenth centuries. Hannah Glasse's best-selling book *The Art of Cookery Made Plain and Easy* (1747) has not a single recipe featuring leeks. Eliza Acton's 1845 *Modern Cookery for Private Families* includes only "Boiled Leeks," with the terse instruction to "send melted butter to table with them." In the entirety of her encyclopedic *Book of Household Management* (1861), Isabella Beeton provided only two brief recipes for the leek, the first for the accurately if unpoetically named "Leek Soup," and the other for the famous Scottish cock-a-leekie, which Mrs. Beeton noted "was largely consumed at the Burns Centenary Festival at the Crystal Palace, Sydenham, in 1859."[38] Victorian through and through, Mrs. Beeton appended a cautionary note that must have made matrons throughout the land nervous: although the leek "is very wholesome," she wrote, "to prevent its tainting the breath, [it] should be well boiled."

Twentieth-century English cookbooks hardly fare better and by the close of the century Jane Grigson, the untiring champion of English food, referred to the "social collapse of this ancient vegetable."[39] She attributed its disappearance to plain old bad English cooking. As with so many other vegetables, from peas to cabbage, leeks were often boiled into a greenish gray oblivion, most likely by cooks overzealous in heeding Mrs. Beeton's well-meant advice for preventing bad breath. Or perhaps it was all the sand and grit lurking inside its leaves that relegated the leek to the dustbin of culinary history: "a servant girl in a dark kitchen without running water," Grigson wrote, "would not have had much success in cleaning leeks properly."

But we might wonder whether overcooking and poor lighting were the sole culprits in the disappearance of the leek. Or did it have something to do instead with a prejudice against that most "ancient vegetable," and a belief that cultivated vegetables, rather than dirty weeds, are what civilized people are meant to eat. By the time Isabella Beeton published her *Book of Household Management,* the English were on top of the world and the Celts— viewed collectively—were regarded as a less evolved people. The satirical *Punch* magazine went so far as to caricature the Celts as having apelike or Neanderthal features; they were even described in the pseudoscientific treatise *Races of Britain: A Contribution to the Anthropology of Western Europe* (1862) as similar to Cro-Magnon man who hunted and gathered his food in the wild. John Beddoe, founder of the Ethnological Society, president of the Anthropological Institute, and member of the Royal Society, distinguished between advanced races that tended to be "orthognathous" (that is, have receding jaws) and the Irish and the Welsh, who were "prognathous" (have large jaws).[40]

Who says that history doesn't repeat itself? Those in power have always looked down on those without it. The cast of characters may change, but the story remains the same. Hundreds of years ago it was the Romans looking down on the hunter-gatherers of the north; now the English, descendants of the

IRISH IBERMIAN.   ANGLO-TEUTONIC.   NEGRO.

A caricature of Irish-Iberian, Anglo-Teutonic, and Negro physiognomy by
H. Strickland Constable, first published in *Harper's Weekly* in 1899.

Anglo-Saxon hunter-gatherers, were looking down on the Celts.
And those in power do not like to share their food with those
they've conquered. In seventeenth-century China, a new strain of
dark purple rice was hybridized exclusively for the Kangxi emperor of the Qing dynasty; it was not to be eaten by commoners,
hence its name "forbidden rice." Nor do those in power like to
eat the food of those below them on the social hierarchy. If the
apelike Celts ate leeks, then, not surprisingly, the English wanted
as little to do with the weedy allium as possible.

It was thus largely in the culinary traditions of those wild
Celtic peoples—and the more rugged peoples of the northern
counties of England—that the leek remained a vital ingredient.
North Country leek pudding, a leek-, bacon-, and sage-stuffed
pastry roll; Cornish leek pie; Anglesey eggs (*Wyau Ynyn Mon* in
Welsh), a leek-and-potato mash into which quartered hard-
boiled eggs are nested, the whole covered with a cheese sauce;
Welsh leek-and-mutton broth; the mashed potato and leek dish
known as leek champ: such are a few of the dishes in which the
leek is cast in a starring, rather than supporting, role. In Ireland,
Myrtle and Darina Allen seek "to recapture some forgotten

flavours, or to preserve some that may soon die," and so provide their renditions of such old favorites as leek and cheese pie and Saint Columba's beloved *brotchán roy*. On the other side of the Irish Sea, Claire Macdonald, wife of the laird of the clan Donald and author of numerous books of Scottish cookery, has a seemingly endless repertoire of leek dishes, including leek and bacon potato cakes; leek and mushroom salad; chicken, leek, and parsley pie; and leek and potato soup.

Now, none of this is to suggest that leeks are cooked, eaten,

Cornish Leek Pie (serves 4)

½–¾ lbs leeks, cleaned & sliced
4 tbsp butter
¼ lb bacon rashers
1 cup heavy cream
1 egg and 1 egg yolk
salt & pepper
short pastry made with ½ cup flour
For glazing: 1 egg yolk or cream

Cook leeks gently in the butter for 10 minutes, in a covered pan, without browning them. Remove from the heat. Add bacon cut into ¼-inch-wide strips, and turn into a pie dish or plate. A good size is 8–9 inches in diameter, and 1½ inches deep. Mix cream and eggs well together, season—allowing for the bacon's saltiness—and pour over the leek mixture. Cover with a pastry lid. Brush with beaten egg or cream and bake for 20–30 minutes in a moderate oven (375 degrees). Like all custard mixtures, this pie tastes best warm, rather than hot.

Note: For a Welsh leek pie, put a layer of pastry below as well as above the filling.[41]

Chicken, Leek & Parsley Pie *(serves 8)*

1 large chicken, about 4½ lb
2 onions, peeled
1 carrot, peeled and cut in chunks
bouquet garni
salt
a few black peppercorns
3 oz butter
4 good-sized leeks, washed, trimmed, and cut into ½ inch pieces
1 rounded tsp curry powder
2 oz flour (⅓ cup)
20 oz milk
10 oz chicken stock
freshly ground black pepper
2 rounded tbsp finely chopped parsley
12 oz puff pastry
Milk for glazing

Put the chicken in a large saucepan and cover with water. Add 1 onion, cut in quarters, the carrot chunks, bouquet garni, salt and peppercorns. Bring to the boil, cover with a lid and simmer gently for 1 hour or until the juices run clear when the point of a knife is stuck into the chicken thigh. Cool the chicken in the stock in which it cooked. When cool, strip all the meat from the bones, and put in a deep 3½ pint (2 liter) pie dish. Finely chop the remaining onion.

Melt the butter in a saucepan. Add the sliced leeks and the chopped onion and cook gently for about 10 minutes, when the onions should be soft and transparent. Stir in the curry powder and the flour. Cook for 1–2 minutes longer, then gradually stir in the milk and the chicken stock, stirring until the sauce boils. Season with salt and pepper. Stir in the finely chopped parsley. Pour over the chicken meat in the pie dish, and mix well.

Roll out the puff pastry, and use it to cover the pie. Decorate the pie with pastry leaves and brush the surface all over with milk. Bake in a hot oven, 425 degrees, for 20 minutes, then lower the heat to 350 degrees for a further 20 minutes, or until the pie is golden brown.[42]

and celebrated *only* in the Celtic parts of Britain. But it is certainly true that the Celtic fringe—the westernmost shores of the island to which the early inhabitants were pushed when other more powerful peoples conquered their land—has never had to rediscover the leek because it never lost it in the first place.

The curious part of the story is that although the English turned their backs on the native vegetable that once sustained them, preferring imported onions, shallots, scallions, and chives, they nonetheless never traded in the name for the allium they had so heartlessly abandoned. The old *ynneleacs, holleacs, cropleacs,* and *bradeleacs* are all gone for good, but as far as the linguistically extant member of the family is concerned, the conquests of the Romans, the Christians, and the Normans, with their cultivated *porri* and *poireaux,* left virtually no trace on the English language.

"IF YOU CAN'T BEAT 'EM, EAT 'EM"

Despite both its long-standing popularity in the Celtic parts of Britain, and its recent revival in England, here in the United States the leek remains almost as unknown as sea kale, even though—or perhaps *because*—it grows in the wild from Canada to Mexico, from the Atlantic to the Pacific. As the famed outdoorsman Euell Gibbons wrote in his 1962 classic guide to foraging, *Stalking the Wild Asparagus,* "America is blessed with many kinds of Wild Onions . . . many Indian tribes considered them hearty staples, and ate them in great quantities."[43] Heirs to the English language and culinary traditions rather than to Native American customs, we have traditionally preferred cultivated to wild, vegetables to weeds, and most of us nod in agreement when we read the question that opens Gibbons's book: "Why bother with wild food plants in a country which produces a surplus of many domestic food products?" When we can so easily buy anything we might have a yen for at the supermarket—whether Chinese, Japanese, Thai, or Sicilian eggplant or jicama, chayote, or nopal trucked in from Mexico—why would we want to forage for weeds in alleys and parking lots? "I have collected fifteen species that could be used for food on a vacant lot right in Chicago," Gibbons boasted; maybe so, but who wants to eat them? We read incredulously of the "wild parties" he and his wife, Freda Fryer, used to host—wild not in the sense of hanging from the chandeliers, but in the sense of *foraged*. In the Gibbons household, guests were regularly treated to meals in which all the main ingredients had been foraged in the wild: daylilies were tossed in a salad, cattail roots ground into flour and baked into biscuits, frog's legs were chicken-fried, and muskrats dressed, soaked, cut up, and baked with potatoes, bacon drippings, and seasonings in a dish called "Maryland Potted Marsh Rabbit" (presumably even Gibbons knew his guests were likely to balk at the idea of eating a muskrat).

Another recipe sounds more appetizing. Despite its elegant name, "Forager's French Onion Soup" turns out to be a soup of weedy wild leeks—*A. tricoccum*, or ramps, "the sweetest and best of the wild onions . . . with a mild onion flavor with a hint of garlic, which I find delicious."

Last I looked, my local supermarket had not a single daylily, cattail, or frog's leg, and certainly no muskrat has ever been advertised in the weekly circular. Of all the foraged foods that Gib-

Forager's French Onion Soup

Clean the bulbs by removing the outer fibrous skin, then slice them thinly crosswise. Saute 1 cup of these sliced leeks in 2 tablespoons of butter. Add 1 can of consommé and 1 can of water. Simmer for 20 minutes over low heat, and you'll have a good onion soup without doing any more. But if you want to make it a real occasion, add 2 tablespoons of cooking sherry to the soup and pour it into individual ramekins. Cut a round of toast for each bowl and float the toast carefully on top of the soup. Sprinkle the toast with grated Parmesan cheese and set the bowls in a hot oven for ten minutes to let the cheese melt slightly.[44]

bons set before his guests, it's only the plant that goes by the name of *leek,* not *onion* but *leek,* that regularly appears in one form or another in both supermarket and nature. At once cultivated vegetable (*A. porrum*) and wild weed (*A. tricoccum*), the leek defies categorization.

Yet it still has to be identified, described, and explained. Most home cooks have never grown, bought, or prepared it and it suffers from an inferiority complex in relation to the onion: we use a hundred onions for every one leek. Why? The pragmatist might answer that leeks cost more, $2.99 a pound, as compared to yellow onions at $1.59 a pound (the store that advertised these prices, by the way, Whole Foods, hangs an obviously-intended-to-be-helpful sign above its leek display: MILD WITH A RESEMBLANCE TO LARGE SCALLIONS). But the comparative prices merely beg the real question at hand. Leeks cost more because fewer of them are grown and fewer of them are grown because there's less demand for them. And why is there less demand? Because despite their high price today, they have long been associated with and dismissed as the food of the poor and the powerless. In the seventeenth century, the gardener John Parkinson noted that leeks were the food of the impoverished in England and that leek pottage was "a great and generall feeding in Wales for the vulgar [i.e., average] gentleman."[45] A common way to refer to the leek was "poor man's asparagus," none too flattering an epithet but one that suggests leeks weren't historically as expensive as they are today, whether because they were wild or simply undervalued.

Associated as they were with the downtrodden Celts and the lower classes, pawned off as poor man's asparagus, and considered unworthy of the language of haute cuisine, leeks have nonetheless kept their Old English name. Gone are the *ynneleacs, cropleacs,* and *holleacs* of yore, replaced by French onions, shallots, scallions, and chives. But the familiar, native, and humble leek has not only survived, it has grown more popular in recent years. The forager is now a professional, the salad greens you're served are likely to be wild, and the leek, whether cultivated or not, is in demand once more—not *despite* its weediness but *because* of it. In recent years the so-called wild leek, or *A. tricoccum,* has even won for itself quite a band of enthusiastic foodies.

Consider the following response, recently posted on a gardener's online chat group under the title "Rampant Wild Leeks." A desperate woman appealed to her readers, asking if anyone knew of a way to get rid of the wild leeks that were taking over her property. "Is there anything that will eradicate them?" she asked in frustration. The response her query elicited must have taken the poor woman aback:

> You really have a huge stand of ramps (aka wild leeks)??
> Did you know they are an increasingly popular and

much sought after gourmet treat? If that's really what you've got growing there, I'm sure you can get someone to come and harvest them for you in the spring. Definately [sic] the stuff of tres trendy haute cuisine.[46]

In his article "Ravenous for Ramps," the chef from Babbo who dreams of ramps all winter wrote similarly of a farmer whose land was being overrun by the odiferous weed:

> One farmer I know, who used to sell us ramps by the garbage bag, claimed to have been desperate to kill the weed that suddenly appeared, took over a fifth of his usable land, and radically shrunk the yield of his salable crops. He tried everything he could think of that wouldn't poison the soil, but the ramps would not die. I think his despair lifted when crackpots calling themselves chefs began showing up at his farm and offering to buy the weed at outrageous prices not unlike those, of, well, weed.[47]

Perhaps there's hope for our good old Germanic *leacs* and *weodes* after all. Even when not hallucinogenic, they can be every bit as tasty as the cultivated vegetables that the Romans brought with them when they set out to conquer the world.

CHAPTER THREE

Milk and Dairy
"Stone Age Brits Got Milk"

It is a remarkable circumstance, that the barbarous nations which subsist on milk have been for so many ages either ignorant of the merits of cheese, or else have totally disregarded it; and yet they understand how to thicken milk and form there from an acrid kind of liquid with a pleasant flavour, as well as a rich butter: this last is the foam of milk, and is of a thicker consistency than the part which is known as the serum. We ought not to omit that butter has certain of the properties of oil, and that it is used for an ointment among all barbarous nations, and among ourselves as well, for infants.

—Pliny the Elder, *Natural History of the World* (first century AD)

And so, brothers and sisters, I could not speak to you as spiritual people, but rather as people of the flesh, as infants in Christ. I fed you with milk, not solid food, for you were not ready for solid food. Even now you are still not ready, for you are still of the flesh.

—1 Corinthians 3:1–3

Why, sir, alasse my Cow is a commonwealth to mee, for first sir, she allowes me, my wife and sonne, for to banket our selues with-all, butter, cheese, whay, curds, creame, sod [boiled] milke, raw-milke, sower-milke, sweete-milke, and butter-milke . . . And now to loose my cow! Alas, Maister Usurer, take pittie upon me.

—Thomas Lodge & Robert Greene, *A Looking Glass, for London and Englande* (1590)

Proto-Indo-European: *melg, galag*

GERMANIC: *meolc*	CELTIC:[1]	LATIN: *lac*	GREEK: *gala*
Norwegian: *melk*	Irish: *bainne*	Italian: *latte*	
Swedish: *mjølk*	Scottish: *bainne*	French: *lait*	
Danish: *mælk*	Welsh: *llaeth*	Spanish: *leche*	
Dutch: *melk*	Cornish: *leath*	Romanian: *lapte*	
German: *Milch*	Breton: *laezh*		
Old English: *meolc*			
English: *milk*			

---

[1] The Celtic languages of the British Isles are divided into two broad groups, known as *Brythonic* and *Goidelic* (from *Brittonic* and Gaelic). To the former belong Welsh, Cornish, and Breton; to the latter, Scottish, Irish, and Manx. Because it was the *Brythonic* languages that were spoken in the southern parts of Britain during the Roman period, there are more traces of Latin in Welsh, Cornish, and Breton than in the Gaelic languages of Ireland and Scotland, both of which lay beyond the heavily fortified borders built by the Romans. It is for this reason that we can see the Latin *lac* in the Welsh *llaeth*, Cornish *leath*, and Breton *laezh*, but not in the Irish and Scottish *bainne* or the Manx *bainney*.

ON MOTHER'S MILK

Although apples are almost always the first fruit eaten by infants (who can imagine the baby food industry without applesauce and apple juice?) and although onions are the building blocks of virtually all of the world's many and diverse cuisines, it's unquestionably milk that's the most basic food of all. Mother's milk, that is, about which absolutely nothing need be said as far as discovery or travel routes are concerned. We are mammals, after all, from the Latin word for breast, *mamma*. But we are weaned from the breast at such an early age that we barely remember ever having suckled and so if we want to have any dairy in our grown-up diets at all, we must take the milk that other animals produce for the benefit of their own offspring—whether calf, lamb, kid, or almost any domesticated baby herbivore other than the piglet.[2]

Therein lies the dilemma of milk. Or, to put the matter more precisely, therein lies the dilemma of our attitude toward milk. We drank it when we were babies, but we're not babies anymore. And we're certainly not the ones for whom that other milk was intended. Which means that to drink milk as a grown-up is to steal food from a baby. And that it's not just our morals that haven't matured: neither have we. Nature didn't mean for grown-ups to drink milk, which is why babies are generally weaned sometime after they cut the first teeth that allow them to enter the wonderful world of solid food. And just as we would look askance at an adult who freely chose to dine on strained peas, puréed squash, and rice cereal, so too many of us would look down our noses at a full grown man who poured himself a tall drink of milk—or worse still, was brash enough to order it in a restaurant. Yet there clearly are plenty of people who not only continue to drink milk into adulthood but who actually enjoy doing so—much to the stomach-turning horror of others who regard it as no more than a raw material waiting to be transformed into butter, cream, buttermilk, cottage cheese, yogurt, kefir, koumiss, sour cream, quark, topfen, cheeses of all sorts from the Dutch Aalsdammer to the Spanish Zamorano, and—last but certainly not least—ice cream.

And so the battle lines are drawn. On one side stand the confirmed and recalcitrant milk drinkers who see nothing at all wrong with the calcium-rich liquid in the exact state that nature created it. On the other side are the equally staunch milk transformers who are delighted to be served a platter of well-selected artisanal cheeses and who happily dollop mounds of *crème fraîche* on top of their *gateaux* and *tartes*, but who blanch at the thought of a glass of the ice-cold stuff and positively gag at the idea of a mug of warm milk before bedtime.

Such a food prejudice can only be the tip of a vast and submerged iceberg. Seldom do we loathe simply on the basis of taste. If we did, why would some cultures treasure a fruit that others describe as smelling like rotting flesh, old gym socks, and even raw sewage? Why would a sticky salty brown spread that looks more like dirty engine grease than it does a savory sandwich filling be so popular in some countries and so despised in others that its own marketing slogan is "Love It or Hate It"? In the first instance, I refer to the durian, the fearsome-looking thorn-covered fruit native to Southeast Asia, and in the second, to the yeast extract sold mainly in England and Australia under the brand names Marmite and Vegemite. In cases such as these, it's easy enough to make the claim that if you weren't exposed to it in childhood, it's not likely that you're going to acquire the taste later in life. The same cannot be said of milk, however, since we were all exposed to the taste from the earliest possible age. We have to wonder, then, what lies behind the aversion so many of us feel to the liquid that's really pretty mild-tasting when all is said and done. Why do so many of us react to it as strongly as we do?

It's often thought that our prejudice against the food that nature designed to sustain us in our infancy goes hand in hand with the repulsion we feel when we see an innocent baby happily playing, blithely indifferent to the dirty (and smelly) diaper he's sitting in. Our own toilet training was so effective, this argument holds, that as adults, we've completely forgotten that once upon a time we were just as unbothered by the sight, smell, and even feel of excrement. Today we pinch our noses as we gaze at the none-too-sweet-smelling little angel, but the point is, we weren't born with that olfactory revulsion; we acquired it. By extension, the aversion non–milk drinkers feel to the idea of drinking milk might have more to do with their hard-won maturity and sense of superiority toward those who imbibe than it does with exposure or taste preference. Who drinks milk? Babies.

But this explanation goes only so far, because plenty of fully toilet-trained and mature adults actually like to drink the stuff. In a recent blog, Joanne Goddard made this confession: "I have something really weird to tell you . . . I drink milk. When I order it in coffee shops, people think I'm nuts and never know what to charge me. But milk is so delicious."[3] As though seeking solace in numbers, she ended her admission with a question: "Do you drink glasses of milk, dear readers? I'm so curious!" The answers to her query—dozens of them—ran the gamut from unequivocal hatred to impassioned love:

> Nope. I never liked it, not even as a child. Cheese, though, that's an entirely different story.
>
> NOOOOOOOOOOOOOOOO!!!!!!!!!!!!!!!!!!! Hate it!
>
> I LOVE MILK. And yes, whenever I order it at restaurants everyone I'm with is always like what are you, 6 years old?
>
> Yes! I love milk! I order it at restaurants even and people think I am either childish or weird. I say what's so wrong with milk, it is so delicious and nutritious!

It's hard to think of another food that elicits such extreme avowals. Raw fish and meat, perhaps, although it seems pretty clear once again that the horror many people feel at the idea of eating sushi or steak tartare is more cultural than individual. Do the Japanese balk at the thought of *nigiri sushi*? Similarly, although it might be hard for us to imagine tucking into a dinner of raw meat that's been tenderized under the saddle during a long day's ride, no self-respecting nomadic Tatar of the Central Asian steppes would have turned up his nose at such a dinner. As I noted a moment ago, however, unlike sushi and steak tartare, we're all brought up on milk. So the question remains: why do some cultures continue to drink it into adulthood while others don't?

Perhaps we get closer to the mark when we look more closely at which cultures are doing the quaffing.

> I'm swedish—we all drink milk! My father is the biggest milkdrinker i know.

Of course I drink milk! Living in Sweden this is a totally normal thing, everyone here drinks milk.

Hih, maybe a part of you is Northern European by spirit, as it is really common to drink milk here, people of all ages do it, as . . . mentioned above. I'm Finnish, and I've drank [sic] milk all my life, and will continue to do so.

No surprise here. The blue ribbon for milk-drinking goes to the Swedes—and to the Scandinavians in general, who continue to drink milk long after they've been successfully toilet trained. In other words, there seems to be no *necessary* reason that the drink has to be associated exclusively with childhood. The pairing of the two is not so much inevitable as it is cultural. Further, it goes hand in hand with taste preference. Southern Europeans generally associate milk with childhood and don't like drinking it; northern Europeans don't make the connection and keep quaffing.

And we Americans? Well, according to one final response I'll cite in full and that I suspect will strike a chord with many of us, it's not all that unusual for us to drink it at home, but not too many of us are bold enough to order it in a restaurant, unless we happen to be in one of the popular new milk bars that have begun to spring up in sophisticated urban centers. But it's one thing to order a Lavender Infused Milk or Choco-latte Milk Cocktail at Chelsea Market's Ronnybrook Milk Bar or to stand in line for a Cereal Milk at one of David Chang's Momofuku Milk Bars; it's quite another to order a glass of the plain old stuff at a three-star Michelin restaurant.★ Much as we like it, we just don't want to be

---

★ "Milk bars" originated in Australia in the 1930s and soon after became popular in Britain where they were considered healthy and morally pure alternatives to pubs. In the 1940s, milk bars became a short-lived feature in the United States where they sold groceries and nonalcoholic beverages until they were eclipsed by the fast-food restaurants of the 1950s and 1960s that similarly did not sell alcohol.

caught drinking in public what deep down we suspect to be a childish beverage. As one reader, Dawn, replied:

> I do drink milk—usually with richer meals. I grew up in the Midwest and my family had milk for dinner often— none of us are lactose intolerant. But I can't think of a time when I ordered it when I was eating out. I guess I subconsciously repressed the urge to drink it when out with others.

To my mind, this reply speaks volumes. Dawn grew up in the Midwest, the part of the country settled by northern Europeans whose descendants still eat hearty meat-and-potato meals that aren't found as often on the more ethnically diverse coasts. Did Dawn leave the land of her birth? Is she living in a more culinarily sophisticated world, dining regularly on *moules marinières* and Thai curries? Is she ashamed of being thought childish by the Merlot- and Pinot-swilling adults around her? Is she embarrassed at being considered too Midwestern by all those fast-paced, fast-talking Angelinos and New Yorkers? Can she even distinguish between the two possible sources of her embarrassment? Can we?

Dawn's inferiority complex—or what we might even call her split lactic personality—is our collective American inferiority complex as well, and like so many of our food preferences and prejudices, it's as old as the hills.

ON BABIES AND BARBARIANS

With milk as with no other food, there's a connection between what goes into our mouths and the sounds that come out of them. What that connection is, though, has been debated for centuries. According to the psychoanalysts, it was when we pulled away from the breast and stopped slurping milk that we first made the remarkable discovery that our own bodies were not physically attached to our mothers'. We were not just extensions of her but people in our own right, people who got hungry yet were so incapable of feeding ourselves that we would die if it weren't for the sounds that announced our hunger to the world. And so it was just about the time we were weaned that we began to babble the incoherent noises that over time formed themselves into words—words like *mama*, which sounds an awful lot like the ancient Latin word for breast, *mamma*. Such is the connection that the psychoanalysts make between weaning and language. But there's another version of the story that focuses not on mother and child but on more and less developed peoples.

More than two millennia before Freud ever put pen to paper, the ancient Greeks had already associated milk drinking with incoherent babbling, but they weren't referring to children. They had in mind entire groups of people whom they regarded as no better than children: the barbarians. In Greek, *barbarian* didn't mean an uncivilized aggressive person, as it does today, but instead one whose speech sounded like the nonsensical "bar bar"—the ancient equivalent of our "blah blah"—that the word sought to onomatopoetically echo. A common synonym for *barbaros* was *galaktopotes*, literally, "milk drinker." Who were those horse-riding, nomadic, and fiercely aggressive Scythians whom Homer called "the proud mare-milkers, drinkers of milk" and whose fermenting of raw milk into the beverage known as *koumiss* was described in the fifth century BC in Herodotus's *Histories*? Barbarians and milk drinkers alike. What else would such a primitive and strange-speaking people drink?

As far back as Homer's *Odyssey,* the barbaric, one-eyed, milk-drinking Cyclops was outsmarted by the ever-resourceful, highly civilized, thoroughly Greek, cheese-eating Odysseus.

> Next he sat down and milked his sheep and his bleating goats, / each of them in order, and put lamb or kid under each one / to suck, and then drew off half of the white milk and put it / by in baskets made of wickerwork, stored for cheeses, / but let the other half stand in the milk pails so as to have it / to help himself to and drink from, and it would serve for his supper.[4]

Even though the Cyclops has somehow acquired the know-how to make cheese, it's the milk that furnishes his supper. Odysseus and his men, indifferent to the raw substance, are completely unable to resist their appetites for the "baskets . . . heavy with cheeses." They wait for the Cyclops to leave the cave, and then "built a fire and made sacrifice, and helping ourselves to the cheese, we ate." That the Cyclops exacts his revenge on Odysseus by eating a few of his men—"entrails, flesh and the marrowy bones alike"—only adds fuel to the fire. What more could be expected of a milk drinker?

As they did with so many other aspects of Greek culture, the Romans adopted their predecessors' views of non-Mediterranean peoples whose language sounded like infantile babbling and whose milk-drinking habits amazed, disgusted, and repelled. Civilized people, according to the ancient classical world, spoke Greek and Latin and drank mead (fermented honey) or wine (the fermented juice of grapes)—but they did not drink milk and they certainly didn't drink strange things like koumiss. The Roman statesman Cassiodorus went so far as to make up an etymology that many people still believe today. Barbarian, he claimed, comprised *barba* (beard) and *rus* (flat land) because the hirsute subhumans lived out in the open fields like wild animals, hunting and gathering their food and drink.

I've already noted that Caesar's first observation about the people he encountered in Britain concerned their strange dietary customs. Obviously he was struck by a people he perceived as decidedly not Roman. They were barbarians and they drank what Caesar himself would never have let pass his lips: raw milk. Good for softening the skin, perhaps, but certainly not for human consumption. In his first-century *Natural History*, Pliny the Elder reported that the wife of the emperor Nero made it part of her beauty regimen to regularly bathe in ass's milk—going so far as to bring five hundred female donkeys (technically called jennies) with her when she traveled—but he nowhere notes that she drank it.

Caesar's comment was to be echoed throughout the centuries. Fourteen hundred years later, *The Forme of Cury* similarly informs us that "the Aborigines of Britain . . . lived on milk and flesh."[5] Seen as bookends of a historical period that opens with the Roman invasion and ends with the Norman Conquest, the two comments share more than a casual observation. In my next chapter, I'll turn to the horror and amazement the carnivorous northern Europeans aroused in the vegetable-loving people of the Mediterranean; for now I focus on the lactic half of the equation. Dismissed as the food of babies and barbarians, milk has long been a litmus test of one's degree of maturity or civilization, so it could almost have been predicted that when the sophisticated peoples of the Mediterranean ventured north to conquer the strange blue-skinned savages, one of their first comments should have concerned the repulsive (to them) habit of drinking milk.

ON MILKY MYTHOLOGIES AND LACTOSE INTOLERANCE

Even the most civic-minded Greeks and Romans were once babes at the breast, so it's not surprising that they too should have something positive to say about milk—even if only about its role in the beginning of things. Whether it's called *gala* (as it was in Greek) or *lac* (as it was in Latin), milk was the basis of an enormous number of myths in the ancient world. The Roman poet Ovid opened his *Metamorphoses* with a description of a pristine and primordial earth, where, in addition to the usual agricultural bounty, the rivers flowed with milk and honey:

> *And Earth, unplowed, brought forth rich grain; the field,*
> *Unfallowed, whitened with wheat, and there were rivers*
> *Of milk, and rivers of honey, and golden nectar*
> *Dripped from the dark-green oak-trees.*[6]

It wasn't only the earth that flowed with milk, but the entire galaxy as well. The Milky Way came into being, or so holds the myth, because of Hera's anger at her philandering husband, Zeus. When Hera suddenly realized she had been tricked into suckling another's child, the infant son of Zeus's dalliance with a mortal woman, she tore the baby from her breast, causing her milk to spew across the sky. Consequently, the Greek word *galax* derives from *gala*—thus making the Milky Way Galaxy something of a redundancy.

Similar milky cosmogonies are to be found the world over. Hindus believe that the universe came into being when a primordial milky ocean was churned into the solid world, just as cream is churned into butter. Norse legend holds that among the first creatures was the primeval cow Audhumbla from whose unimaginably massive udders flowed four great rivers of milk. The Celtic holiday that celebrates the return of spring, when dairy animals once again begin to produce milk, was called Imbolc or Oimelc, which, translated literally, means "in-milk" (or perhaps "ewe's milk"). To this day in Nepal, an annual butter dance is performed, in which dancers encircle statues of the gods molded out of ice-cold, brightly colored butter; as the dancers' body heat melts the statues, the butter flows into the earth to ensure the next season's fertility.

People the world over are sustained by milk during our earliest days, so it's no surprise that cultures as distinct as Hindu, Norse, Greek, and Roman should consider milk to be a primal element and associate it with innocence, purity, and new life. It's the food we don't have to work for, the food that comes naturally to us, the food that nature designed for our earliest years, whether those years belong to our own infancy or to a mythical golden age. So identified with childhood is milk that today's dairy industry currently pumps millions of dollars into one of the most famous advertising slogans in America in its attempt to dispel the single-minded association. Created for the California Milk Processor Board, the "Got milk?" campaign has been running continuously since 1993 and is given credit for ending a twenty-year decline in milk sales nationwide. Its milk-mustachioed celebrities (from Britney Spears to Tony Bennett), supermodels (Christie Brinkley, for example), sports stars (Tom Brady, Tiger Woods, Venus and Serena Williams), and even such cartoon characters as Batman and Superman, and the puppet Kermit the Frog all try to convince teenagers and adults that not only children can drink the calcium and vitamin D–rich substance.

Why so much effort? Because in reality few people continue to drink milk after about the age of two, largely due to the inherited inability to metabolize the sugars in raw dairy products. This is known as lactose intolerance, and it occurs in so much of the world's population that it's the ability to drink the stuff that's more likely to be the abnormality—the result, apparently, of certain people's practice—notably, northern Europeans—of drinking milk in adulthood since time immemorial. According to the biologists, milk drinking in adulthood has resulted in a genetic adaptation that allows northern European peoples to benefit from a convenient and full-fat source of protein. Because of lactose intolerance, many adults will drink almost anything—tea, coffee, wine, beer, soda, water, juice—other than milk. According to a recent study of lactose intolerance, 66 percent of Greek Cypriots and 71 percent of Sicilians stop producing lactase, the enzyme necessary to break down lactose, by about age four and so are unable to digest milk; only 5 percent of the British and Danish populations and a mere 2 percent of Swedes stop producing the enzyme ("I'm swedish—we all drink milk!").

But I'm not a biologist and I'm not as concerned here with the physical phenomenon as I am with attitudes toward the lactose-rich substance that certain people are able to digest and others not—attitudes that are captured in the words we use. When we narrow our perspective to the European canvas, we see a fairly tidy correlation between milk drinking and milk naming. Those people who drink milk call it by a word that sounds much like our English *milk* (German *Milch,* Dutch and Danish *melk,* Swedish *mjolk,* Norwegian *melk*), and those who don't call it *lait, latte, leche, lapte,* or some other *l* word, all of which derive from the Latin *lac.*

In this linguistic (not to mention enzymatic) divide, as in so many others, we can see the march of historical forces, the rise and fall of empires, and the collision of cultures. We can also see the foundation of our blogger's insecurity complex—and, more largely, our own—when it comes to the matter of milk.

ON BUTTER, CHEESE, AND CURDLED MILK

Even though we share our word for milk with our northern European cousins, we don't do so for other dairy processes and products. Lactation, for instance. We English speakers tend to prefer Greek and Latin derivatives for our scientific and medical terminology—hence it's cardiologists, dermatologists, and podiatrists who treat our hearts, skin, and feet—so on one level it makes sense that the physiological production of the mammary glands should be called *lactation* whereas the product itself has kept its native name. Both French and German are more consistent in their terminologies: *la lactation* provides *le lait*; *die Milchabsonderung* produces *die Milch*. It's only English that merges the two, deriving lactation from the Latin *lac*, and *milk* from the Germanic *meolc*.

On another level, though, our dairy terminology reveals quite a lot about the inferiority complex that so bedevils us English speakers. We wouldn't feel as confident in a heart doctor as in a cardiologist, would we? Nor do we feel confident ordering a glass of milk in public, and we wouldn't be as willing to pay exorbitant sums at our local Starbucks for a "large milky coffee" as we do for a "grande caffè latte" or a "venti latte macchiato." There's something about milk—both word and substance—that unsettles us and makes us profoundly uncomfortable. Butter and cheese, on the other hand, we've got no problems with; not coincidentally, their names come from Greek and Latin even though they were already being produced in Britain before the Romans made their way there.

Pliny the Elder wrote that "they [the Britons] understand how to thicken milk and form therefrom an acrid kind of liquid with a pleasant flavour, as well as a rich butter." He noted that it was most often made from cow's milk—hence the name *butter,* from the Greek *boutyron,* "cow cheese." Cheese was also being made long before the arrival of the southern Europeans: archaeologists have found perforated colanders in pre-Roman British sites, suggesting that whey was being drained from milk solids to produce cheese, which derives its name from the Latin *caseus*. In fact, according to a recent *Boston Globe* article, "Stone Age Brits Got Milk," the dairy industry may have preceded the Romans by some four thousand years. With the new ability to chemically distinguish between milk and meat fat residues, the article explains, scientists can positively identify the traces of protein found on ancient pottery vessels as the remains of some sort of dairy product.

> Six thousand years ago, neolithic Brits might have enjoyed sips of milk with their steaming haunches of meat. Researchers from England's University of Bristol report in the Proceedings of the National Academy of Sciences that they have discovered milk-fat residue on 6000-year-old pottery fragments. It is the earliest direct evidence of dairy farming ever found.

"Considering milk's short shelf life, it's probable the ancient Britons were making and eating butter, cheese, or yogurt," the article concludes.[7]

Northerners were not only drinking milk, but also making butter and cheese long before the Romans ever appeared with their *butyrum* and *caseus,* yet the names that were used in England throughout the Middle Ages were easy adaptations of these Latin words: *cubutere* (literally, "cow butter") and *cyse.* But milk—the raw material with which the barbarians were so regularly identified—kept its native name. That the products of human labor are known by Latin names whereas the natural excretion of the mammary glands is known by its Germanic one is evidence of our attitudes, and those attitudes were—and still are—the legacy of the Romans.

Tacitus summed up the matter neatly when he wrote that the northerners just "do not work sufficiently hard." Rather than actively and energetically cultivating the land as the Romans did, the barbarians were lazy and content enough to subsist on the most primitive of diets. "Their food is plain," Tacitus concluded, "wild fruit, fresh game, and curdled milk." Curdled milk? What is curdled milk? Milk gone bad? The Latin phrase that Tacitus used, *lac concretum*, might be more accurately translated "solid milk," but what's that? Cheese? If so, why didn't he just say *caseus*? Word choice reveals a lot about attitude. Just think of the difference between vinegar and sour wine. Even though *vin aigre* means "sour wine," no more, no less, it looks a lot better on a label than "aged balsamic sour wine." Sour wine is simply wine gone bad, whereas vinegar is the result of a careful process of fermentation and aging. We might say that vinegar is to sour wine as cheese is to *lac concretum*—milk that has naturally soured or fermented by the action of acid-producing bacteria until it hardens into a semisolid state. As the food historian C. Anne Wilson has noted, "No art was needed to achieve this result."[8] Hard cheese, on the other hand—cheese that's stored and aged, rather than eaten fresh—requires work to produce, as well as understanding of the fermenting qualities of rennet, the digestive juice secreted in the stomach bags of certain mammals.

The Romans didn't invent cheese—references to it abound in ancient literature—but they certainly mastered the process of manufacturing it. Along with bread and wine, those other produced foodstuffs that owe their being to fermentation, cheese represents a perfect example of what the food scientist Harold McGee has called "a process of limited, controlled spoilage."[9] It's neither as appetizing nor as poetic to think of cheese as an attempt to stave off inevitable putrefaction as it is to celebrate it as, in the words of Clifton Fadiman, "milk's leap toward immortality." The fact remains, however, that left to its own devices, milk has a woefully short shelf life. But then almost all raw ingredients would have soured, gone rancid, rotted, or fermented in a matter of days, if not hours, in a time before refrigeration or canning. Smoking, fermenting, salting, and cooking were all ways to beat the clock and wrest control from nature's hands. To acknowledge that raw ingredients putrify is to state the obvious. It does not explain why certain people—the Romans, for instance—were so fond of controlling the process, while others—the northerners—were content with the natural process of spoilage. At least that's how the Romans so frequently depicted the matter. Milk was meant to be transformed.

ON SPIRITUAL MILK

The Roman Empire may have fallen, but its preference for *produced,* as opposed to *natural,* foodstuffs lived on in the food symbolism of Christianity, which is in so many ways its heir. Bread, wine, and oil—the foods central to both the empire and the new religion—are all produced substances. From its very inception, Christianity set out to transform milk as well, and it's no accident that during the long centuries of the Middle Ages, it was the monastic houses of Europe that kept alive not only the knowledge of how to make the wine needed for communion, but also how to make cheese. The so-called Trappist cheeses that we still eat today—Epoisses, Limburger, Munster, Pont-l'Evêque, and Port-Salut—were all made by the religious orders of France, Belgium, Switzerland, and Germany.

In the monasteries of Europe, milk might have been solidified into cheese, but in the New Testament itself, it was spiritualized into the means of salvation. "Like newborn infants, long for the pure, spiritual milk so that by it you may grow into salvation—if indeed you have tasted that the Lord is good" (1 Peter 2:2). The raw stuff was for infants and nonbelievers who "need milk, not solid food, for everyone who lives on milk, being still an infant, is unskilled in the word of righteousness" (Hebrews 5:12–14). It was the spiritual beverage that nourished those who were reborn in Christ—or, as we would call them today, the born-agains. By this logic, the Jews and the barbarians had quite a lot in common: neither was skilled in words of righteousness (in fact, the barbarians weren't skilled in words at all), and they both preferred milk of the unspiritual variety.

Seen in this context, Saint Paul's vision of a blinding light from heaven on the road to Damascus resulted not so much in his conversion as in his weaning. "When I was a child, I spoke like a child, I thought like a child, I reasoned like a child; when I became an adult, I put an end to childish ways," he later wrote; and he might just as well have added that he also put an end to his childish suckling. From that moment on, he made it his life's purpose to similarly wean the world. "I fed you with milk, not solid food," he told the people of Corinth, "for you were not ready for solid food."

Paul would have found it relatively easy to wean the Mediterranean because its people had long been wary of milk anyway; oil, rather than butter, was their traditional cooking fat, and wine, rather than milk, was the beverage of choice. Degree of latitude alone might be all the explanation needed to justify the southern European dislike of raw milk: if it isn't refrigerated (obviously an impossibility in the first century), fermented into yogurt, or preserved as cheese, it quickly turns rancid. But what then can account for the high esteem in which another Mediterranean culture—one that Paul had more difficulty weaning—held the fresh raw liquid?

The Jews must have had just as hard a time keeping their milk fresh as any Greek or Roman, and they too either drank most of their milk in the soured form known as *laban* or ate it in the semisoft state called *chemah,* curds. But whereas the Greeks and Romans looked down on raw milk, the Jews did not. In the Old Testament, milk is offered as a sign of gracious hospitality. It was both curds and milk that Abraham served his angelic visitors in the book of Genesis, and later, in the book of Judges, we read that when the enemy general Sisera of the nine hundred chariots of iron asked for the biblical equivalent of a glass of water to refresh himself, the prophetess Jael went above and beyond the call of duty and poured him milk instead. Of course she went on to drive a tent peg through his skull, but the point remains that the milk she offered him was a sign of hospitality, however devious that hospitality might have been.

> He asked water and she gave him milk,
> She brought him curds in a lordly bowl.
> She put her hand to the tent peg
> And her right hand to the workmen's mallet;
> She struck Sisera a blow. (Judges 5:25–26)

Not all people of the ancient Mediterranean viewed fresh milk with revulsion—only those who, like the Greeks and the Romans, believed that transforming nature into culture was what they had been put on this earth to do. Even though raw milk could rarely have been drunk in ancient Israel, it was nevertheless associated with purity and innocence in the Old Testament. In fact, it was precisely because it was so pure and innocent, so unchanged from its natural condition, that it was believed to be superior to any cultured dairy product. If what God created at the beginning of time was good, then any change could only be for the worse. Same climate, but entirely different attitudes toward the natural world and, consequently, toward milk.

Neither taste nor climate alone, then, can answer the question of why certain people valued the raw stuff while others insisted on cultured derivatives. We get a lot closer to the mark when we think about what's involved in the words I keep returning to: *natural*, *unspoiled*, and *unchanged*. Earlier I quoted Tacitus's patronizing observation about the northern tribes' laziness and lack of agricultural know-how. Tacitus was a Roman and to a Roman, land was there to be worked. None of the three indispensable ingredients of the Mediterranean diet—bread, wine, and oil—is found in nature. Each results from a carefully controlled process in which a natural ingredient is transformed into a civilized product. Such tireless industry not only won the Romans their empire; it also resulted in the agricultural legacy that we still benefit from. It bequeathed to us as well the attitudes that lie behind so many of the food choices we make today. So deeply ingrained are our culinary attitudes that we often forget—if we were ever aware—that they're not so much individual or natural as they are cultural. Our food prejudices, too, are the products of history—like the prejudice so many of us have against milk.

The irony of fate, though, was that when the Bible was read to newly baptized Christians in Britain, the same people whom Caesar had described as living on milk and meat were now exhorted to wean themselves from a beverage that they in no way associated with immaturity, childhood, or incoherent babbling. Northern Europe was converted to Christianity, to be sure, but in today's English-speaking countries, people are still famous for drinking the milk that is so maligned in the New Testament.

SAINT BRIGID

In his *Ecclesiastical History of the English People,* the Venerable Bede tells an amusing story. On a day in the late sixth century, the future pope Gregory the Great was wandering about a Roman marketplace when he saw some light-skinned, blond-haired boys for sale. Asking where they had come from, he was told that they were pagans from the island of Britain. And what is the name of their race? Gregory asked. Angles, his companion informed him. " 'That is appropriate,' he punned, 'for they have angelic faces.' "[10] When he became pope several years later, Gregory remembered those fair young boys and sent missionaries to the far-off island to save their souls from damnation. The hitch was that the gospel the missionaries brought informed those milk-drinking angelic pagans that the time had come for them to wean themselves of a drink to which they were very partial.

We've already seen that milk drinking had an illustrious history in the British Isles. Long before the Angles and Saxons had settled there, milk was not only drunk but even honored by the Celtic peoples at one of the four great seasonal festivals. Celebrated on February 1, *Imbolc* marked the return of spring and new life, when cows and ewes gave birth and milk flowed plentifully once again. The Celts believed that both the holiday and the season as a whole belonged to the nurturing mother-goddess known as Brigid. It's no coincidence that one of the most well known Irish saints has the same name as that earlier Celtic goddess: when Christianity ousted indigenous religions, it often accommodated local gods and rituals into its own practices. Thus, throughout the Middle Ages, February 1 was now dedicated to the beloved Saint Brigid, who was invariably depicted with a bovine companion and a pair of milk buckets.

Certainly no one would expect the life of a saint to make for realistic reading, but the seventh-century *Life of Bridget* is a whopper. Written by one of the monks of the Kildare monastery she is believed to have founded, it dates her to the late fifth or early sixth century but

A hand-carved statue of Saint Brigid with her cow.

anachronistically identifies her as both Mary's midwife and Jesus' wet-nurse. We expect miracles to feature prominently in accounts of saints' lives, but somehow the miracles in Brigid's life seem more like the tall tales told of such folk heroes as John Henry and Paul Bunyan than the life story of a revered religious figure. They all involve milk, usually in vast quantities. As an infant she was bathed in it. As a child, she was unable to eat ordinary food and could digest only the output of a special red-eared white cow. As an adult, she was accompanied by a cow that supplied her with all the milk she needed. After becoming the abbess of Kildare, she increased the milk and butter yield of the abbey cows exponentially. One account affirms that her cows produced a lake of milk three times a day and that her churning alone filled hundreds of baskets with butter. Accurate? Of course not, but such lactic excess couldn't have come from nowhere. "It seems reasonably certain that behind this alleged holy woman, of whom no contemporary or near-contemporary records survive, stands a pagan goddess of the same name," notes historian Ronald Hutton.[11] Turns out that Saint Brigid might be a Christian avatar, so to speak, of the pagan goddess Brigid.

When the Angles and Saxons arrived in the fifth century, they were convinced to abandon their pagan beliefs in favor of Christian ones, but they too were unwilling to wean themselves of milk. It was their mythology that featured the primeval cow Audhumla, and dairy products loomed large in their everyday lives, judging from their wills, leechdoms, and estate records in which repeated mention is made of *Þinre meolc, meolc wœtre gemenede, flete, ream, clut, clœne niwe buteran,* and *sealte buteran* (skimmed milk, milk mixed with water, curds, cream, clotted cream, pure new butter, and salted butter), not to mention syllabubs, junkets, and frumenty. Butter provides the subject of one of the riddles from the late medieval Anglo-Saxon Exeter Book; obviously the vigorous churning required to transform cream into butter brought another equally vigorous activity to mind:

> There came a young man to where he knew her to be, standing in a corner. The lusty bachelor approached her, lifted up his clothes and thrust something stiff under her girdle where she stood, had his way, so both of them were shaking. The thane worked hard; his good servant was sometimes useful, but, though strong, he always became tired and weary of the work before she did. Beneath her girdle there began to grow what good men love in their hearts and buy with money.[12]

The answer to the riddle? The dasher that's inserted into the top of a butter churn and plunged quickly up and down.

It was in order to convert these milk drinkers that Pope Gregory sent his missionaries to the shores of Britain, preaching the words that had made perfect sense to listeners in the south: "Everyone who lives on milk, being still an infant, is unskilled in the word of righteousness." The message worked just fine when Paul sought to convert the Greek- and Latin-speaking gentiles, but it used exactly the wrong image to convince the northern pagans to abandon their native ways—had they been able to understand what was being preached to them in the first place.

In his *Ecclesiastical History*, Bede writes that among the first converts to Christianity was Egbert, the king of Kent, who, in the final years of the sixth century, not unreasonably asked for the gospels to be read in his native language. When his subjects heard the Bible in words they could understand, they realized they were being implored to wean themselves of good old Anglo-Saxon *meolc*. But they had no reason to share the Mediterranean disdain for milk. What was to be done? It was just about this time that the fruit sacred to the northern peoples, the apple, was singled out as the forbidden fruit that had caused the expulsion from Eden. Milk couldn't suffer the same fate, but it did pose a similar dilemma to the early Christians who were doing all they could to convert the hardy milk-drinking pagans into northern versions of themselves.

As the saying goes, if you can't beat 'em, join 'em. Such seems to have been the logic of the missionaries. Somewhere between the fifth and seventh centuries, a new holiday appeared in the Christian calendar—exactly at the same time as the springtime festival that had once been dedicated to the Celtic goddess Brigid. In the Mediterranean countries, February 2 was a solemn holy day on which one fasted and prayed in memory of the purification of the Virgin Mary after the birth of the baby Jesus. In northern Europe, though, February 1 had already been given over to Imbolc and, later, to Saint Brigid's Day, both of which were festivals involving music, revelry, and celebratory meals featuring lots of cheeses and freshly churned butter. Either Imbolc or Saint Brigid's Day would have been a lot more fun than a solemn Christian day of worship. It was clear to all concerned that the Mediterranean holy day would need some tweaking to appeal to northerners, whose long cold winters left them needing light, food, regeneration, and festivity more than they did abstinence and purifying rituals. Such tweaking was duly made.

Instead of commemorating Mary's purification, the northern holiday celebrated the presentation of the baby Jesus. It was called Candlemas and throughout the Middle Ages parishioners celebrated by carrying candles representing the divine light of both the Christian son and the celestial sun. Celebrated on February 2, Candlemas occurred only one day after Imbolc and Saint Brigid's Day. Conceding that people used to carousing on that date were none too willing to swap their feasting for fasting, the

Church decided to give the people what they wanted. It was at the same time that Brigid was identified as the midwife to Mary and wet nurse to the baby Jesus. She was even affectionately nicknamed "Mary of the Gaels." Completely anachronistic and logically impossible, the association of Brigid with Mary interwove the pagan and Christian festivals even more tightly. The Celtic goddess who had already become the Christian saint now became wet nurse to the baby Jesus.

ON "WHITE MEAT"

As Christianity gradually spread throughout the British Isles, questions continued to crop up about how to adapt Roman customs to the colder northern locale. Exporting religions is never an easy business, especially when their most important rituals involve food. If you're going to insist that communion with God can be achieved only by drinking wine, then you'd better be sure wine is readily available or you run the risk of losing your clientele.

Even rituals that involved the *lack* of food can pose problems. Fasting, for instance. It's one thing to reduce your calorie intake if you're living in the sunny Mediterranean; it's quite another when you live in the bleak and chilly north, where you need a lot more fuel just to maintain body heat, not to mention doing any physical labor, which is what most people spent their time doing. Animal proteins are the most calorie-dense foods around, but they were precisely what was forbidden on Christian fasting days, which included all Wednesdays, Fridays, Saturdays, major saint's days, three days at each of the quarter days, and the whole of Lent. The Church couldn't possibly have expected to stay in business if it required believers to abstain from all food for more than half the year, but it did insist that followers abstain from animal products—the idea being that by refraining from meat, one could recreate the bloodless innocence of Adam and Eve's vegetarian life before the Fall. When you think about it, though, the fact that the couple was restricted to eating fruits and vegetables reveals as much about Eden's climate as it does about divine intention. It's a dead giveaway that the garden was in a warm and sunny land where vegetables flourished and fruit trees prospered. How many "plants yielding seed" and "trees with seed in their fruit" grow in cold climates?

All these food issues were to pose a challenge for the early Church when it ventured out of the world of its birth. In the Mediterranean, the rules for fast days wouldn't have seemed all that stringent, since they only denied what people didn't eat that much of in the first place. Early Eastern monasticism encouraged its followers to restrict themselves to diets of little more than bread, water, wild herbs, nettles, and even occasionally grass. Stories were told of saints and hermits who ate so sparingly that they became too weak to stand upright and of noble women who subsisted on barley bread and broth made of nothing but herbs steeped in water. Yet such diets, although certainly an exaggeration of the normal, were not qualitatively different from what would have been eaten on nonfast days. Even now, a Tuscan specialty is the soup known as *acqua cotta,* which literally means no more than "cooked water." In other words, your average Italian could have sat down to a meal of bread, oil, and vegetables, whether the day was a fast day or not.

Conditions were different in the cold and drafty monasteries of England where it became clear early on that no one could survive on such a Spartan diet. So what was a devout and well-intentioned northerner to do when, in the mid-sixth century, the founder of Western monasticism enumerated no fewer than two hundred fast days during the course of the year, for all of which he decreed a complete abstinence from meat, fish, and eggs, and from cheese and butter as well? Although born in France, Saint Benedict was educated in Rome, wrote in Latin, and, at the time of his death, had established twelve monasteries, the first of which was Monte Cassino in southern Italy. He would certainly never have been a big milk drinker and his food would have been cooked in olive oil, not butter. But how could his rule be followed by a hungry population who relied on dairy products that, to make matters worse, they regularly referred to as "white meat"? How were penitent northerners to survive the almost two hundred fast days every year?

Well, according to Saint Chrodegang, an eighth-century bishop, they could indeed eat their white meat, if they did so sparingly and with a good conscience. "He who is genuinely able to abstain from eggs and cheese and butter and fish and wine is of great strength and virtue," he wrote, before concluding on a more lenient note: "He who cannot really abstain from them because of weakness or any other reason may eat them." Unlike Benedict whose career was spent mostly in Italy, Chrodegang was the bishop of Metz, in the Lorraine region of today's France, and accommodations such as his were made throughout the dairy-producing lands of northern Europe. Fast days were necessarily less strict than those in the south, and it's not unusual to read of English fasts that included milk, even if watered down. According to Bede's *Ecclesiastical History,* the eighth-century Bishop Egbert was a model of "humility, gentleness, purity, simplicity, and uprightness" and he allowed himself milk. "He used to keep the previous day's fresh milk in a flask, and having skimmed off the cream next day, he drank what was left with a little bread." A story is told of Saint Columba, founder of the monastery on the island of Iona off the west coast of Scotland, who believed himself to be fasting on a diet of no more than nettles simmered in water. When he was complimented on his surprisingly hardy appearance, his cook confessed that he had been adding milk to the broth, thus allowing the pious but nutritionally naïve saint to maintain his strength. Rather than chastising the well-meaning man, Columba blessed him.

But skimmed or watered-down milk was one thing, richer dairy products quite another. Butter, for example. No one was sure whether butter was allowed as a cooking fat, because the monastic rules had been written in Italy where cooks used olive oil. It wasn't until the fourteenth century that the Church issued its first explicit prohibition against butter on fast days, with the clear implication being that it had been used for centuries. Shortly after the Church's prohibition, however, dispensations allowing for the use of butter became so common that another northerner, this time a German by the name of Martin Luther, complained that the Roman Catholics had turned the innocent act of eating butter into a sin right up there with lying, blasphemy, and adultery.

> In Rome, they make a mockery fasting, while forcing us to eat an oil they themselves would not use to grease their slippers. Then they sell us the right to eat foods forbidden on fast days . . . but they have stolen that same liberty from us with their ecclesiastical laws. . . . Eating butter, they say, is a greater sin than to lie, blaspheme, or indulge in impurity.[13]

Martin Luther, of course, is far better known for the ninety-five theses he nailed to the door of the church in Wittenberg on that fateful morning of October 31, 1517. Many of those theses concerned corruption in the Church, such as the selling of what were called indulgences, or releases from undesirably strict prohibitions. One commonly purchased indulgence allowed the well-off buyer to eat butter on fast days.

Historical events as tremendous as the Protestant Reformation turn out to be not all that removed from the everyday life of the kitchen. As Maguelonne Toussaint-Samat observed in her *History of Food,* the butter-oil divide that's so often identified as the primary distinction between northern and southern European cooking played an enormous role outside of the kitchen as well. "Those countries which use butter for cooking," she wrote, "are almost identical with those which broke away from the Catholic Church in the sixteenth century. . . . We should bear in mind that those countries of northern Europe which became Protestant are countries with a tradition of dairy farming."[14]

It would be far-fetched to claim that the northerners' love of dairy products caused the Protestant Reformation. But that it was the Germanic countries that broke away from the Roman Catholic Church testifies to the difficulties that beset the Mediterranean religion when it moved north. If a religion uses food for its symbols and sacraments, it had better make sure those foods are easy to come by when it moves outside its native region or it will have to contend with indigenous substitutes. Milk had never been a feature of Mediterranean cuisine nor was it esteemed in the pages of the New Testament. Yet despite being looked down on by wine-drinking Roman legionnaires and Christian missionaries alike, northern Christians continued to drink their *meolc.*

ON NORTHERN MILK

The last major invasion of Britain occurred in October 1066 when the Normans landed at Hastings and defeated King Harold's army of Angles and Saxons. Before William had earned for himself the title of Conqueror, though, he had been the Duke of Normandy, which means that had he been born only a few generations earlier, he would have been one of the Northmen. If medieval genealogies are correct, he might even have been a descendant of the Viking leader Hrolf to whom the French king Charles gave the land today called Normandy. Charles's plan to put an end to the Vikings' raids worked perfectly. The Northmen settled down to work their newly acquired land, which proved to be so much more fertile than the frozen tundra they had left back home. So fertile that the northern cattle they brought with them could graze all day long, producing the endless gallons of milk that would eventually be turned into some of the world's greatest cheeses: Camembert, Livarot, Pont l'Evêque, Neufchatel, Brillat-Savarin, Petit-Suisse, Boursin.

Long before they arrived in France, the Vikings had been famous for their butter and cheese, as Scandinavians still are to this day. They spoke a North Germanic dialect in which their favorite beverage was *mjolk,* butter was *smør,* and cheese was *osti.* Yet within the space of a mere hundred years or so, the Northmen were no more and the Old Norse they spoke was silenced. They had become Normans and their *mjolk* had been replaced by *lait, smør* by *beurre,* and *osti* by *fromage.* Today Normandy is officially one of France's twenty-two provincial regions, yet the descendants of the Normans who settled there more than a thousand years ago still look different and eat differently from other Frenchmen. They "are apt to be heavier and solider than the French average," wrote Waverley Root in *The Food of France,* "often taller as well and more often blue-eyed and light-haired than in other sections of the country, as one might expect from their Scandinavian origin."[15] In fact, they hardly seem French at all, he continued.

> Normans are notoriously big eaters. Perhaps they require
> more food because they are larger and heavier than the

average Frenchman; or perhaps they are larger and heavier because they take on more food. . . . The richness of Norman food is attributable in the first place to the importance of Normandy as dairy country and to the habit of absorbing its milk in its richest forms, not only in butter, but even oftener in cream—heavy cream.[16]

No French Paradox there: their steady diet of high saturated fat and cholesterol-rich butter and cheese resulted in the big-boned, blue-eyed, light-haired people of Normandy who look more like their Scandinavian forebears than they do stylishly slim Parisians. Nonetheless, they call the food for which they're still well known by the same names the rest of the country does: *lait, beurre, crème, fromage.*

When those Northmen-turned-Normans conquered England, however, only some of their food names stuck: thus, as we'll see in the next chapter, the words *beef* and *pork* were adapted from *boeuf* and *porc,* while the living breathing beasts kept their native names of *cow* and *pig.* A similar gentrification happened to our dairy vocabulary: the watery remnants and less desirable products given to the humble cowherds and milkmaids kept the names by which they had been known for the previous millennium—*whey, buttermilk, curds,* and *milk*—whereas the substance that was reserved for the rich and powerful was newly baptized with a French name as *cream* and incorporated into the elaborate preparations that graced aristocratic tables.

It was even believed that the upper echelons of society were constitutionally unable to digest milk. "The well-to-do rarely consumed milk in its raw state," noted food historian C. Anne Wilson, "for it was known to curdle in the stomach, and was thought to engender wind there."[17] According to this logic, the lowly born, who comprised the vast majority of the population, were born with hardy northern European peasant constitutions immune from gastric disturbance and so were physiologically suited to receiving their animal protein in the form of the so-called white meat, leaving the costlier red meat to those blessed (or cursed) with refined digestive systems. Today we know that the *crème de la crème* was suffering from gas, bloating, stomach rumbling, and diarrhea—the classic symptoms of lactose intolerance. We also know that however uncomfortable the cramps and flatulence made the lactically intolerant wealthy, their gassiness was no more an indication of social rank than is any other genetic condition. Just because Queen Victoria bequeathed the hemophilia gene to her daughters, who in turn passed the mutation to the royal houses of Spain, Germany, and Russia, doesn't mean that hemophilia is exclusively a royal disease; plenty of commoners suffer from it as well. So too with lactose intolerance: what we recognize to be a straightforward physiological condition was understood to be a class distinction and, even further, a national one. Milk—both word and lactose-rich liquid—was appropriate for the English peasant as cream was for the French aristocrat.

Even today there's a world of difference today between "burnt milk"—whole Web sites are devoted to suggestions for how to clean it out of pots and pans (a popular recommendation seems to be simmering lemon juice and water in the pan and then scraping with a wooden spoon or scouring with an abrasive pad)—and *crème brûlée,* a perennial favorite of the upscale restaurant dessert menu. But is "burnt cream" so very different from "burnt milk"?

Apparently yes—and it has been for centuries. In an early-fifteenth-century recipe collection, we find a dish that allowed for milk if no cream is available, but even so, the name of the dish says it all: Creme Boylede.

Apparently the split lactic personality that we English speakers suffer from has been ailing us ever since we were first exposed to Italian and, centuries later, French food. Then as now things just sound better in other languages. In the case of milk, our personality disorder takes on an added dimension. We want to drink it, but we're embarrassed to do so in public. And so, to satisfy the urges we find so hard to repress (remember Dawn from the on-line poll?), we disguise the childish drink by mixing it with an

Creme Boylede

Take creme or mylke, & brede of paynemayn, or ellys of tendyr brede, an breke it on þe creme, or ellys in þe mylke, an set it on þe fyre tyl it be warme hot; and þorw a straynour þrowe it, and put in in-to a fayre potte, an sette it on þe fyre, an stere euermore: an whan it is almost y-boylyd, take fayre yolkys of eyren, an draw hem þorw a straynowr, and caste hem þer-to, and let hem stoned ouer the fyre tyl it boyle almost, an till it be skylfully þikke; þan caste a ladel-ful, or more or lasse of boter þer-to, an a good quantite of white sugre, and a litel salt, an þan dresse it on a dysshe in maner of mortrewys.

Boiled Cream

Take cream or milk and wheaten white bread, or else soft bread, and break it in the cream or else in the milk, and set it on the fire until it is warm-hot; and pour it through a strainer and put it into a clean pot, and set it on the fire, and stir constantly. When it is almost boiled, take good egg yolks, put them through a strainer, and add them. Let it stand over the fire until it boils and until it is quite thick. Then add a ladleful, more or less, of butter and a good quantity of white sugar and a little salt. Dress it in a dish in the manner of a mortrewys.[18]

Note: A *mortrewys* was a dish of finely ground food that had been boiled in broth, named after the mortar used in its preparation.

adult beverage and calling it by another name—*café au lait* or *caffe latte* or even *café con leche*. In eastern Massachusetts where I live, a milk shake goes by the name of "frappe"—from the French *frappé*. If dessert menus can be taken as a gauge of popularity, milk puddings aren't doing too well these days, but there's no end in sight to the flavor possibilities of *crème caramel, crème brûlée, flans,* and *panna cottas*. The English boarding school dessert (or pudding to the Brits) known as milk jelly—or still worse, "shape"—sounds a whole lot better when it's called *blancmange*. By the same token, we all enjoy french toast on a Sunday morning, but when was the last time any of us sat down to the old-fashioned supper known as "milk toast"? Without knowing quite what it is, we know we don't want it for dinner, even with the assurances of no less than Marion Cunningham, author of both the *Fannie Farmer Baking Book* and the revised *Fannie Farmer Cookbook*. "Why in the world did we ever abandon milk toast?" she asked, we can hope, disingenuously. "Although it sounds deceptively bland and dull, it isn't; and as the Victorians discovered, it can revive the peaked or sad. Nourishing and soul-satisfying, milk toast will banish the blues."

FOOD FOR THE SICK

As the centuries kept rolling along, the English language gradually took on contours recognizable to us today, neither Anglo-Saxon nor French but simply the mutt that we know and love, which is why lactating mothers produce milk. The words we use so automatically—and, just as importantly, the attitudes conveyed by those words—reflect the split lactic personality that has been our lot since the Romans first came to Britannia. On the one hand, we still drink milk and call it *milk;* on the other, we have absorbed the attitudes of the lactose-intolerant Mediterraneans. That's why Midwestern Dawn of the online blog is embarrassed

Milk Toast

For each serving of the simplest of milk toasts, first lightly toast 2 slices of bread. Place the slices in a bowl. Pour 1½ cups milk into a saucepan, bring just to a boil, remove from the heat, and stir in 1½ tablespoon butter. If you like, add a tablespoon of sugar and a pinch of ground nutmeg. Pour the milk into the bowl over the bread. Cover, and let stand for 5 minutes—don't stir or you will spoil the texture. Serve hot.[19]

to admit to her savvier East Coast friends that she actually enjoys drinking the stuff. That's why so many of us happily pour a glass for ourselves late at night while we stand in front of dimly lit refrigerators in our bathrobes, but we would never dream of ordering it in public. Even in modern English, milk has kept the associations the Romans imposed on it when they dismissed it as the drink of babies and barbarians. Why else would the timid and self-effacing comic strip character of the 1920s have been named Caspar Milquetoast?

A Caspar Milquetoast
Christmas card.

Above all, milk has come to be identified with children, the poor, the sick, and, in Britain, where heathen barbarians no longer shave their bodies and paint their skin blue, with the downtrodden Celtic peoples who have never been considered fully English and who have always loved and been famous for their dairies. Kerrygold Pure Irish Butter wins awards to this day and in its purest form, Irish soda bread contains only three ingredients: flour, baking soda, and buttermilk. The Scots pour buttermilk on porridge at breakfast, simmer smoked fish in milk to make the soup called *cullen skink,* and for dessert, often serve a milky pudding called *cranachan,* a whisky-laced whipped double cream sprinkled with toasted pinhead oats (to us Americans, that would be steel-cut oats).

When recipes involving milk appeared in English cookbooks, on the other hand, they were almost always intended for the young, the old, and the sick. A bestseller of its day, Gervase Markham's 1615 *The English Housewife* opens with a long medicinal chapter that instructed the lady of the house to ease the pains of gout by boiling up a concoction of roots and herbs and then adding the "new milk of a cow," a measure of chimney soot, and—believe it or not—"the urine of a man that is fasting."[20] So too in her popular *Art of Cookery Made Plain and Easy* (1747), Hannah Glasse included a chapter called "Directions for the Sick" in

Artificial Asses Milk

Take two Ounces of Pearl-Barley, two large Spoonfuls of Hartshorn Shavings, one Ounce of Eringo Root, one Ounce of China Root, one Ounce of Preserved Ginger, eighteen Snails bruised with the Shells, to be boiled in three Quarts of Water, till it comes to three Pints, then boil a Pint of new Milk, and mix it with the rest, and put in two Ounces of Balsam of Tolu. Take half a Pint in the Morning, and half a Pint at Night.

which she provided a recipe for artificial ass's milk—ass's milk was believed to be closest in chemical composition to human milk and thus good for whatever it was that ailed you.

For those who had trouble laying their hands on hartshorn shavings and eringo root, Glasse offered an alternative that she claimed was almost as effective:

Cows Milk next to Asses Milk done thus.

Take a Quart of Milk, set it in a Pan over Night, the next Morning take off all the Cream, then boil it, and set it in the Pan again till Night; then skim it again, and boil it, set it in the Pan again, and the next Morning skim it, and warm it Blood-warm, and drink it as you do Asses Milk. It is very near as good, and with some consumptive People it is better.[21]

As usual it was Mrs. Beeton who summed up the matter concisely in her bible of Victorian domesticity: "Milk," she wrote, "is an important article of food for the sick."[22] As it was, of course, for children as well. Despite the fact that "many persons entertain a belief that cow's milk is hurtful to infants, and, consequently, refrain from giving it," Beeton nonetheless insisted that "sugar and milk should form a large portion of every meal an infant takes" and when the time came to graduate from nursery foods, she pronounced "milk soup" to be "a nice dish for children."

A less expensive version of milk soup—unsweetened and thickened with flour, which was cheaper than eggs—appeared in the 1852 *Plain Cookery Book for the Working Classes*. The book was written by Charles Elmé Francatelli, chief cook to Queen Victoria and

Milk Soup

Ingredients.—2 quarts of milk, 1 saltspoonful of salt, 1 tea-spoonful of powdered cinnamon, 3 teaspoonfuls of pounded sugar, or more if liked, 4 thin slices of bread, the yolks of 6 eggs.

Mode.—Boil the milk with the salt, cinnamon, and sugar; lay the bread in a deep dish, pour over it a little of the milk, and keep it hot over a stove, without burning. Beat up the yolks of the eggs, add them to the milk, and stir it over the fire till it thickens. Do not let it curdle. Pour it upon the bread, and serve.

Time.—¾ of an hour.
Average cost, 8d. per quart.
Seasonable all the year.
Sufficient for 10 children.[23]

Prince Albert before he turned his considerable talents to feeding the nation's poor. "I could feed every day a thousand families on the food that is wasted in London," he was often heard to boast, and he thus dedicated his book to those "who, from sickness or other hindrance, have not money in store."[24] To spend one's few pennies on an imported luxury item like tea, which was entirely lacking in any nutritional value, made no sense to Francatelli. Instead, he recommended good old English milk.

"REAL MILK"

The Celts, children, the poor, and the sickly. From the time the ancient Greeks first drew the connection between babbling barbarians and *galaktopotes* to the golden age of eighteenth- and nineteenth-century cookbooks to the contemporary "Got

Thick Milk for Breakfast

Milk, buttermilk, or even skim-milk, will serve for this purpose. To every pint of milk, mix a piled-up tablespoonful of flour, and stir the mixture while boiling on the fire for ten minutes; season with a little salt, and eat it with bread or a boiled potato. This kind of food is well adapted for the breakfast of women and children, and is far preferable to a sloppy mess of tea, which comes to more money.[25]

milk?" ad campaign that has tried so hard to reverse the traditional association, milk has been consistently linked with those *not* holding the reins of power. Who can be surprised that the world of art and literature is filled with tantalizingly pretty but poor dairymaids, completely at the mercy of their powerful seducers? Maybe the association of milk and powerlessness is inevitable, given the fact that it's the food nature intended for babies, whether human, bovine, porcine, or any other mammalian variety. Maybe the inability to digest milk that we call "lactose intolerance" is not a deficiency at all, but a normal part of the natural process of maturation. But if so, why have so many other people continued to drink milk long and happily well after they've left their childhood behind?

The belief that only those people drink milk who don't know any better turns out to be an attitude that can be traced straight back to the world of the ancient Mediterranean—to Julius Caesar's observation about those milk-drinking blue-skinned barbarians he encountered when he forged his way through Gaul, across the Channel, and onto the island of Britannia, to Tacitus's description of the "wild fruit, fresh game, curdled milk" that comprised the sum total of the diet of those hardy northerners. By and large, it was the Roman attitude toward milk that went down on record throughout most of history. Certainly it gave rise to the Christian image of milk drinking as a sign of spiritual immaturity that we see in the New Testament. But as I suggested at the outset, such an association is more cultural than it is inevitable. Winston Churchill is generally credited with the observation that "History is written by the victors." In the case of milk, this is undeniably true. We know only what was written, and because it was the Greeks, the Romans, and the Christians who were doing the writing, it was their attitude toward milk that won the day.

And so, all these centuries later, even we English speakers are embarrassed to admit that we like the drink, not of champions but of babes. We drink it at home but refuse to order it in restaurants. We look down on those who do. We think that the things we make out of it are better than the raw material. And yet at the same time we still call it *milk*. The Mediterranean *l* word used by Caesar, Tacitus, and the Latin Bible was never able to vanquish the northern *m* word that lacked those southern associations with the powerless, whether baby or barbarian.

Which brings us back full circle to the dilemma I began with, to the matter of our collective split personality. We look down on milk but we can't do without it either. We not only pour it for our children and bemoan its having been replaced by nutritionally empty sodas and overly caffeinated energy drinks, but we even occasionally drink it ourselves. We don't believe that milk is there only to be improved, processed, or transformed. Maybe, we think, it might be just fine exactly the way nature gave it to us: untransformed and unprocessed.

Unpasteurized and unhomogenized too. So believe thousands of Americans today who, whether they realize it or not, are fighting to reverse those age-old attitudes and beliefs about the most primary and natural of beverages. How can it be called natural, they ask, when it's been heated so as to kill off the salmonella and *E. coli* bacteria but when that heating also destroys healthy enzymes, diminishes vitamin content, denatures milk proteins, and kills off beneficial bacteria as well? Is it natural, they ask, to artificially break down butterfat molecules so that cream no longer rises to the surface? Is it natural for milk to emerge from the udders of cows that are kept on special diets of grain and antibiotics and that are treated with recombinant bovine growth hormones designed to triple their output? Absolutely not, they argue. Preferring to use the phrase "real milk," instead of "raw milk," which carries with it the implication that, like raw meat, the drink must be cooked or pasteurized, the Campaign for Real Milk is currently lobbying Congress to legalize the sale of untreated milk throughout the United States. CORPORATE COWS MOOOVE OVER! read a placard carried at a recent raw milk drink-in organized in downtown Boston to protest the Massachusetts Department of Agricultural Resources' attempts to limit the raw-milk buying clubs that have been cropping up across the state. Campaign members claim that the most natural of beverages has been so altered from its original state that in no way can it be seen as natural, or even healthy for that matter. They insist that pasteurization is an unnatural procedure that destroys the "good" bacteria and "denatures" milk proteins into forms that humans were never meant to digest. Further, they claim, it's pasteurization that's actually responsible for lactose intolerance. Once made necessary by the notoriously unsanitary conditions of nineteenth-century dairies, pasteurization is no more than a relic of the past, they maintain, "a defunct process" rendered obsolete by today's stricter hygiene regulations and stainless-steel equipment. One of the campaign's members, a self-confessed "germophobe," announced to the world that ever since she started buying real milk for her family, her husband, who never used to drink the stuff at all, began to consume "gallons and gallons" of it. Not only did her family decide that real milk tasted better, she claimed, but that it *was* better. Why? Because it hadn't been transformed or improved. Because unprocessed milk is just that: unprocessed, in "the original state that God gave it to us in."

"The original state that God gave it to us in." Neither fermented into yogurt nor immortalized into cheese. Neither pasteurized to remove the possibility of bacterial infection nor homogenized to prevent the cream from rising to the surface. Neither skim, 1 percent, 2 percent, nor even the industrial standard of 3.25 percent (the percentage of fat in what's sold as "whole milk"), but full-fat, whatever the percentage might be when it emerges from the udders of a single grass-fed Guernsey or Holstein.

Despite the risk of parasite- and bacteria-borne food poisoning and disease, we eat sushi and carpaccio, don't we? We believe raw oysters to have aphrodisiac qualities, and it's impossible to make a real mayonnaise or a real caesar salad without raw egg yolks. Yet we dig in our heels at the thought of fresh raw milk. Clearly it's not entirely a concern for our health that makes us balk as it is our attitude, and the more than two-thousand-year-long smear campaign that milk has been subjected to.

Yet, condemned though it's been for millennia as the drink of barbarians and babbling babies, milk is making a complete turnaround and is now being celebrated in all its unprocessed, raw, and real glory as not only permissible to drink, but actually *better* than its reengineered and "improved" versions. Can it be possible that after so many centuries, we English speakers are finally curing ourselves of our inferiority complex and our split lactic personality? Can we at last be shedding the attitude toward milk that was imposed on us by the Latin-speaking and lactose-intolerant people of the Mediterranean and instead be returning to that of the dairy-loving northern Europeans whose name for the drink they so loved we still use to this day?

It certainly seems that at long last the milk-drinking Joanne Goddards and Dawns of the world can order their favorite drink in public with neither shame nor fear of humiliation.

CHAPTER FOUR

Meat

"Forty Pounds of Meat— or No Less Than Sixty"

Whole nations, flesh-devourers (such as farthest northern) becoming heavy, dull, unactive, and much more stupid than the southern; and such as feed much on plants, are more acute, subtil, and of deeper penetration.

—John Evelyn, *Acetaria: A Discourse of Sallets* (1699)

I do not believe that any Englishman who is his own master has ever eaten a dinner without meat.

—Pehr Kalm, *Visit to England* (1748)

M. Curmer . . . tells us that . . . French beef is far superior to that of England. This is mere vaunting on the part of our neighbours, who seem to want *la gloire* in everything . . . No, M. Curmer, we are ready to acknowledge the superiority of your cookery, but we have long since made up our minds as to the inferiority of your raw material.

—Mrs. Beeton's *Book of Household Management* (1861)

Proto-Indo-European: *met, ple(i)k, (s)ker*

GERMANIC: *flaiskjan*   LATIN: *carnis*   GREEK: *kreas*

Norwegian: *kött*   Italian: *carne*

Swedish: *kjøtt*   French: *viande*

Danish: *kød*   Spanish: *carne*

Dutch: *vlees*   Romanian: *carne*

German: *Fleisch*

Old English: *flæsc*

English: *meat*

mete: **Old English** *food*

In the early fourth-century *Historia Augusta,* a collection of the lives of the Roman emperors from Hadrian to Carinus, we read of Maximinus I, also known as Maximinus Thrax or Maximinus the Thracian. The first barbarian to have worn the imperial purple, he was also the first Roman emperor never to have set foot in Rome. Born to a Goth father and an Alani mother, Maximinus was "strikingly big of body . . . handsome in a manly way, fierce in his manners, rough, haughty, and scornful." He was a behemoth of a man—"six inches over eight feet in height; and his thumb was so huge that he used his wife's bracelet for a ring"—and was ruthlessly ferocious in battle—"he hung men on the cross, shut them in the bodies of animals newly slain, cast them to wild beasts, [and] dashed out their brains with clubs." Comparisons to wild beasts pepper his life, as is only to be expected when we remember that the biography was written by a Roman, for a Roman, but about one of "low barbarian birth." Neither is the story surprising that, when he first came to the attention of Emperor Septimius Severus, Maximinus was "scarcely yet master of the Latin tongue, speaking almost pure Thracian." As we've seen, *barbarian* didn't refer to a boorish savage but to one unlucky enough to have been born outside of Greece or Rome. More specifically still, it referred to one who didn't speak Greek or Latin, but instead a language that to classical ears sounded like nothing more than the infantile "bar bar" that the word *barbarian* derisively tried to mimic. We've already seen how the Romans identified the northern barbarians with milk drinking; now we arrive at the carnivorous half of Caesar's observation: "*lacte et carne vivunt,*" "they live on milk and meat.

What is most memorable—and certainly most nauseating—about the life of the barbarian Maximinus is the description of his diet:

> It is agreed, moreover, that often in a single day he drank a Capitoline amphora of wine, and ate forty pounds of meat, or according to Cordus, no less than sixty. It seems sufficiently agreed, too, that he abstained wholly from vegetables, and almost always from anything cold, save when he had to drink. Often, he would catch his sweat and put it in a cup or a small jar, and he could exhibit by this means two or three pints of it.[1]

A "Capitoline amphora," for those unfamiliar with the ancient unit of liquid measurement, held a little over twenty-six liters, or almost seven gallons. No less than such a prodigious amount of wine would have been needed to wash down the forty to sixty pounds of meat that the barbarian emperor reportedly ate every day in order to maintain his legendary strength. As to the two to three pints of sweat he collected in a jar, no comment.

Some fifteen hundred years later and in a very different context, another observer marveled at the similarly colossal appetites daily satisfied at the Tavistock Hotel in London's Covent Garden.

There we could eat everything we fancied, and as much
of it as we liked, for two shillings. They offered us an
infinite number of steaks or placed in front of us a forty-
pound piece of roast beef along with a very sharp knife.
Then came the tea for all this meat to stew in.[2]

The writer of this passage was the French novelist who published
under the pseudonym of Stendhal. While visiting London in the
1830s, he was as struck by the carnivorous penchant of Englishmen
as our Roman chronicler was by that of the barbarian emperor
Maximinus, as well as by the sheer quantity of meat consumed.

Granted, prodigious feats of meat eating have never failed to
exert a certain nauseating attraction. We're still amazed by the
mammoth amount of meat that competitive eaters can cram down
their throats, not to mention the speed at which they do so. Gentleman Joe Menchetti, a frequent contender at eating competitions,
has been known to swallow nearly twelve 4½-ounce beef patties
in five minutes (that's 3.3 pounds of meat) in one contest and a
thirty-inch-long hot dog in 1 minute 53 seconds in another. Or
consider Joseph Christian "Jaws" Chestnut, the Californian who
recently set a new world record at the Southwest regional quali-
fier for Nathan's Famous Hot Dog eating competition. He consumed 59½ hot dogs with their buns in a mere twelve minutes,
easily beating the previous world record of 53¾ hot dogs held by
Takeru "Tsunami" Kobayashi.

Even when eating isn't competitive, we marvel at the amounts
people can pack away. The Yeoman Warders of Her Majesty's
Royal Palace and Fortress of the Tower of London, founded by
Henry VII in 1485, received the nickname the world knows
them by—Beefeaters—on account of the portions of meat they
were allotted during years when most of the populace had to
make do with only an occasional rasher of bacon. In 1813, their

daily rations consisted of eighteen pounds of mutton, sixteen pounds of veal, and twenty-four pounds of beef to be shared among the thirty men. That amounts to just shy of two pounds of meat per Beefeater per day. For the sake of comparison, consider that the current recommended protein allowance is .8 grams per kilogram of body weight, which for a 180-pound adult male could be satisfied by eating 9 ounces of meat a day. By today's standards, Maximinus' forty to sixty pounds of meat and the Tavistock Hotel diners' roast beef exceed the RDA by approximately 10,000 percent, and the Beefeaters' more moderate intake by almost 400 percent.

Needless to say, we're dealing with exaggerations here, at least in the case of Maximinus, but it's no accident that such wild exaggerations were made in the first case by a Roman about a barbarian and in the second by a Frenchman about the English.

James Gillray's caricature "John Bull taking a Luncheon."

Could the son of a Goth really have stood over eight feet tall in his stockinged feet and worn his wife's bracelet as a thumb ring? Could roast beef–eating Englishmen really have looked like the three-hundred-pound John Bull consuming platefuls of French battleships we see depicted in a popular eighteenth-century caricature? Of course not. But such tall tales and caricatures are more than simply exaggerated accounts of men who probably were above the average in height, strength, and appetite. They seem instead to have emerged ready-made from the stereotypical images of the non-Roman that the Romans had already held for centuries by the time Maximinus donned the purple, and, centuries later, from the equally stereotypical contrast between the stolid roast beef–eating English and the precious "kickshaw-eating" French ("kickshaw" was the English parodic pronunciation of *quelque chose,* the term used to refer to the light and fancy dishes dear to the French). Why else would the writer of the *Historia,* traditionally attributed to Julius Capitolinus, have dwelt at such length on the gargantuan carnivorous appetite of the non-Roman emperor? Why else would the French still refer to the English as *les rosbifs,* as they did in their graffiti opposing Tony Blair's involvement in Iraq, ROSBEEFS GO HOME? Why would former French president Jacques Chirac have found it so easy to joke in a 2005 summit meeting that the only thing the British have ever done for European agriculture was spread mad cow disease? "You can't trust people who cook as badly as that," he announced. "After Finland, it's the country with the worst food." Since the best defense is an offense, by the way, the response of the insulted British chefs was to be expected: "Bollocks . . . Chirac doesn't get out enough. Our beef is the best in the world. . . . All the langoustines they eat are Scottish. So I'd serve him langoustines followed by good Aberdeen Angus beef and then give him a heart attack with some sticky toffee pudding."[3]

A second stereotype almost inevitably accompanies such images of meat eaters. At the same time that it exaggerated his carnivory, the Roman biography went out of its way to note that the flesh-eating Goliath would have nothing whatsoever to do with vegetables—"he always abstained from vegetables"—and no one can doubt that other than boiled cabbage and mushy peas, vegetables have never played much of a role in English cooking either. The French, on the other hand, have long been famous for their *haricots verts* and *petits pois,* and the Romans, as we've seen, delighted in transforming wild plants into the cultivated vegetables we know and love today. Predictably, it wasn't vegetable beds that the barbaric Maximinus spent his youth tending, but livestock: "In his early youth," the *Historia* tells us, "he was a herdsman."

What is it about those non-Roman and non-French vegetable-deprived carnivores that so intrigues, fascinates, and repels? Why are the English and Americans still associated the world over with roast beef and hamburgers—not to mention Angus steaks, Omaha steaks, sirloins, chops, meat pies, and barbecue? And why is it that it's only in English that *meat* refers to the edible tissue of animals? Could it be only in countries where meat means what it does that the animal protein–rich Atkins Diet could be as popular as it is? Hard to imagine an Italian, or any Mediterranean for that matter, not only ready, willing, and able, but positively eager to give up pasta, gnocchi, risotto, polenta, foccacia, pizza, and bread, in addition to most fruits and vegetables. It turns out that the more we look at the matter, the more we see that the opposition between what today we call the grain- and vegetable-based Mediterranean diet and the animal protein–rich Atkins Diet is—like so many of our other culinary oppositions—by no means a modern phenomenon.

ON MEAT AND FLESH

Carnis. Translated as both "flesh" and "meat," the Latin *carnis* is at the heart of many of our English words—*carnage, carnal, carnation* (named after its pinkish flesh color), *carnival* (a portmanteau word combining *carne* and *vale*; literally, "good-bye to meat"), carnivore, incarnation, to name only a few. When it comes to the substance itself, however, English insists on *meat*. The Italians and the Spanish to this day eat *carne*, and the French refer to their *boeuf, mouton,* and *porc* as *les viandes,* which also comes from a Latin word, *vivere,* "to live," and hence means something along the lines of "living matter." But only in modern English does a carnivore eat meat. What's more, it's only in English that the word *meat* exists at all—in the specific sense that we use it. The Scandinavian languages have similar-sounding terms—the Danish *mad* and the Swedish and Norwegian *mat*—but in those countries, the word means "food" rather than "meat," which is there called *kød, kjøtt,* and *kött.* Why is it that only English-speaking people call their meat *meat*? And why is it that we respond so differently to *meat* and the word it was used interchangeably with for so many centuries: *flesh*?

Today, flesh is defined as "the soft substance, *esp.* the muscular parts of an animal body," and meat as "the flesh of animals used for food." The former is not necessarily eaten; the latter is. Which is why Shakespeare's Shylock might be a usurer but not a cannibal when he demands a pound of flesh as collateral for his loan of three thousand ducats to Antonio, the merchant of Venice: "A pound of man's flesh taken from a man / Is not so estimable, profitable neither, as flesh of muttons, beefs, or goats," and which is also why the infamous "Meat Grinder" issue of *Hustler Magazine* caused such an outrage. The cover of the June 1978 issue featured a woman's naked body descending into a meat grinder, with only her lower torso and legs still unmangled; emerging from the other end of the grinder was a mass of bloody meat. Her living, breathing flesh had turned into dead meat.

Yet these are contemporary understandings of the words; they have not always meant what they do today. In fact, a possible ancestor of our *meat* is the Proto-Indo-European root *met*, which originally meant no more than "a portion of food measured, or meted, out"—as simple as that. Another theory holds that *meat* traces back to *mad*, which had something to do with flowing, wetness, and moisture—all the unctuous qualities of fat, much more keenly appreciated back then than it is now in our calorie- and cholesterol-obsessed age. The Greek *madaros*, wet, and *mastos*, breast, derive from this root, as do the Latin words for moisture, *mador*, and drunkard, *madulsa*. The root also had something to do with a quality of food, and it is this sense that was developed in the Germanic languages. Words as apparently unrelated as *mast* ("a collective name for the fruit of beech, oak, chestnut, and other forest trees, *esp.* as food for swine"), *must* ("new wine; the juice of the grape either unfermented or before the fermentation is completed"), *muesli* (a breakfast cereal of un- cooked oats and fruit), and, according to this theory, *meat* all trace back to the essential wetness, juiciness, or moistness of what we eat. As John Ayto has suggested in *The Diner's Dictionary,* such related words "build up a picture of *meat*—'food, nourishment'—as something that flows from the mother's breast."[4] In this context, meat is a food provided by nature to sustain us almost as effortlessly—and as bloodlessly—as milk. It's easy to understand how in Old English, *mete* could have re- ferred to all forms of solid food, not just to beef, lamb, and pork. It continued to do so well into the seventeenth century: in the 1611 King James Bible, God tells Adam and Eve that he has "given [them] every green herb for meat." When today we refer to nutmeat and mincemeat, we're using the word in this older sense.

Flesh, on the other hand, which today refers primarily to living animal tissue, evolved from the Proto-Indo-European *ple(i)k,* which meant "to tear," and thus most literally means "a piece of animal tissue torn from the whole." It's related to *flay,* "to tear the skin from," and *fleck,* originally "a piece of skin or flesh." As violent and brutal as *meat* was originally bloodless, *flesh* emphasized the living whole from which a part had been ruthlessly torn. Thus the Old English *flæsc* referred specifically to animal tissue, much as *Fleisch* still does in today's Germany, where meat looms large in the nation's diet. In the words of the former *New York Times* restaurant critic and cookbook author Mimi Sheraton, "No people in the world like meat more than the Germans do, whether it is pork, beef, veal or lamb; the important thing is that it be served in enormous portions."[5] *Flesh*—like the related German *Fleisch*—seems to be the term favored by those with pronounced carnivorous propensities—the northern barbarians, for instance. In England, though, *meat* gradually came to refer to edible muscular tissue, while *flesh* was limited to tissue that was still alive.

Linguists speak of a process they call a semantic shift in which words move from one set of circumstances to another, resulting in either a broadening or a narrowing of the original meaning. Such a shift occurred in our meaty food words after the Norman Conquest, when Old English merged with French to become the recognizable forerunner of the language we use today. In today's English, thus, to eat meat is to eat what is meant to be eaten, whereas to eat flesh is to eat what was once, and perhaps still should be, alive. "Meat eater" might be the way the Romans described the barbarian who hunted his game in the wild, but "flesh eater" invariably brings cannibalism to mind—and not just to the

Roman mind, but to ours as well. "Oh, the bloody cannibals, what a meal they'd make of us if we were to take it into our heads to land!" the ship's captain told a young Herman Melville who, heedless of the warning, jumped ship and escaped into the interior of a Polynesian island, "But they say they don't like sailor's flesh, it's too salt."[6] Other than the sort of stereotypical cannibals in the pages of books set in the South Seas, few of us can eat flesh, human or otherwise, with impunity, which is why we are so titillated by stories ranging from the ancient Greek myth of Atreus, who served his brother's sons to him for dinner in revenge for having been cuckolded, to the Broadway musical *Sweeney Todd,* in which the demon barber of Fleet Street slits his clients' throats and delivers their bodies to Mrs. Lovett's Meat Pie Shop, to Fannie Flagg's *Fried Green Tomatoes at the Whistle Stop Cafe,* the book (later made into a movie) in which the body of the wife-beating Ku Klux Klan member is butchered, barbecued, and served up to none other than the investigating detective himself. When flesh is served up as meat, we shudder.

Yet there are some who are neither titillated nor appalled, even in our own culture, but who transgress boundaries and eat the unthinkable. Hannibal Lecter may be the first cannibal who comes to mind today, but he's an easy case because we write off his flesh eating as a symptom of insanity. What do we do with an ostensibly sane person who, for reasons of his own, decides to sample another human being? In the 1920s, the *New York Times* reporter William Buehler Seabrook, in the interests of research, obtained a chunk of human flesh from the body of a healthy man who had just been killed in an accident. He roasted it, ate it, and described the taste as follows:

> It was like good, fully developed veal, not young, but not yet beef. It was very definitely like that, and it was not like

any other meat I had ever tasted. It was so nearly like good, fully developed veal that I think no person with a palate of ordinary, normal sensitiveness could distinguish it from veal. It was mild, good meat with no other sharply defined or highly characteristic taste such as for instance, goat, high game, and pork have. The steak was slightly tougher than prime veal, a little stringy, but not too tough or stringy to be agreeably edible. The roast, from which I cut and ate a central slice, was tender, and in color, texture, smell as well as taste, strengthened my certainty that of all the meats we habitually know, veal is the one meat to which this meat is accurately comparable.[7]

Does Seabrook's calling the human flesh he ate "meat" and comparing it to veal, only "slightly tougher," make his cannibalism more or less nauseating? Does his calling it "meat" gloss over the atrocity of what he was doing?

Often the associations we have to words act on us even more powerfully than the things being named—especially in the case of the things we put in our mouths, and most especially of all when we'd rather not think too much about what we're putting into our mouths. Who wouldn't rather eat a *sweetbread* than a thymus gland or a pancreas? *Lights* rather than lungs? *Variety meat* rather than entrails, internal organs, or offal? We certainly don't like to think of our own flesh as meat, or even worse, as food, as Jonathan Swift knew when he modestly proposed an easy and eminently logical way to profit from the surplus of babies born to impoverished Irish families. "A young healthy child well nursed," he wrote in his eighteenth-century satire, "is at a year old a most delicious, nourishing and wholesome food, whether stewed, roasted, baked, or boiled; and I make no doubt that it will equally serve in a fricassee or a ragout." Who of us would order a blue-plate special of "flesh loaf and mashed potatoes"?

Yet *flæsc* was what meat was called for almost a thousand years—the years during which the Angles and Saxons either spit-roasted or boiled the flesh of sheep, swine, boar, cows, deer, and even horses—or, as they would have been called then, *scæp, swin, bar, cu, deor,* and *hors.* In times past people don't seem to have suffered overly much from the sort of finickiness that lies behind terms such as *sweetbread* and that requires us to separate flesh from meat. Of course they might not have minded the idea of eating flesh—or what we might call human meat—in the first place. On the walls of caves by the river Hönne in northern Germany there are almost two thousand representations of cannibalistic feasts, and it was Saint Jerome himself— the translator of the Latin Bible—who left an account of having met members of the Celtic tribe of the Atticoti who, he claimed, boasted to him that they regularly enjoyed eating "the buttocks of the shepherds and the breasts of their women" as a delicacy.[8]

Today, few of us eat human buttocks and breasts, and most of our languages happily make distinctions that ancient ones did not. *Flesh* and *meat* no longer mean what they did before the Norman Conquest, after which culinary tastes were refined and many native words replaced with French equivalents that to this day sound more sophisticated—not to mention mouthwatering. *Fatty liver* simply doesn't sound as appetizing as *foie gras,* despite the fact that it means exactly the same thing.

After the Norman aristocracy took over the island and its kitchens, what appeared on banquet tables was no longer *cow, calf, sheep,* or *swine*—old Germanic names all—but *beef, veal, mutton,* or *pork,* each an adaptation of the French *boeuf, veau, mouton,* and *porc.* The animals that grazed out in the meadows or were harnessed to yokes, on the other hand, kept the names they bore before any Norman arrived on the shores of England. *Oxa, bula, cu, scæp, gat, swin* (oxen, bulls, cows, sheep, goats, swine) they remain, with no kinship whatsoever to *taureau, vache, mouton, chèvre,* and *cochon.* Ever since Sir Walter Scott's *Ivanhoe,* it has been commonplace to note that although live beasts are called by their Old English names, they become French after they've been slaughtered, jointed, and roasted. Early in the novel the serf Wamba informs the swineherd Gurth that his pigs will be "converted into Normans before morning."

> "The swine turned Normans to my comfort!" quoth Gurth; "expound that to me, Wamba, for my brain is too dull and my mind too vexed to read riddles."
>
> "Why, how call you those grunting brutes running about on their four legs?" demanded Wamba.
>
> "Swine, fool—swine," said the herd; "every fool knows that."
>
> "And swine is good Saxon," said the Jester; "but how call you the sow when she is flayed, and drawn, and quartered, and hung up by the heels, like a traitor?"
>
> "Pork," answered the swineherd.
>
> "I am very glad every fool knows that too," said Wamba, "and pork, I think, is good Norman-French; and so when the brute lives, and is in the charge of a Saxon slave, she goes by her Saxon name; but becomes a Norman, and is called pork, when she is carried to the castle hall to feast among the nobles . . .
>
> "Nay, I can tell you more," said Wamba in the same tone: "there is an old Alderman Ox continues to hold his Saxon epithet while he is under the charge of serfs and bondsmen such as thou, but becomes Beef, a fiery French gallant, when he arrives before the worshipful jaws that are destined to consume him. Mynherr Calf, too, becomes Monsieur de Veau in the like manner: he is Saxon when he requires tendance, and takes a Norman name when he becomes matter of enjoyment."[9]

Considering how many meaty words were ousted by their refined Norman counterparts, it seems noteworthy that *flæsc* alone wasn't replaced by the French *viande*. Instead, it was the indigenous word for food in general—*meat*—that came to refer primarily to edible animal protein, as though English speakers were insisting that meat was what food was all about. While it's possible, I suppose, to argue that the semantic shift was motivated by Norman culinary sophistication and by an attempt to downplay flesh's violent tearing of tissue from bone, it seems unlikely that the Angles and Saxons were much troubled by our modern ethical dilemma about the killing and eating of animals. It's far more probable that they were completely undisturbed by the slaughter, blood, and gore required to bring their spit-roasted haunches of flesh to the table. Maximinus the Thracian once again comes to mind. Disdaining vegetables entirely, he reveled in enormous quantities of meat as his only food, happily killing both men and animals for the sheer pleasure of it.

Maximinus was Thracian, though, not English. Nonetheless, he had at least three things in common with Anglo-Saxon meat eaters. He was not Roman; he ate flesh with impunity; and our view of him is filtered through a foreign lens.

ON THE MEDITERRANEAN DIET

By the fourth century, when Rome had attained the height of its empire and the *Historia Augusta* was being written, it had become almost a convention for Greeks and Romans to describe barbarians, whether Thracian, Scythian, Mongol, Celtic, or German, as insatiable meat eaters. As early as the second century BC, the Greek philosopher, geographer, historian, and traveler Posidonius had written about the eating habits of the Celts in Gaul. They sat on the ground, he began, and ate their meat in a cleanly but leonine fashion, raising up whole limbs in both hands and biting off the meat, while any part that is hard to tear off they cut through with a small dagger which hangs attached to their sword-sheath in its own scabbard. . . . Beside them are hearths blazing with fire, with cauldrons and spits containing large pieces of meat. Brave warriors they honour with the finest portions of the meat.[10]

Tacitus similarly reported on the carnivorous habits of the Germans and of the people his father-in-law Agricola sought to govern in what was then called Britannia. True Romans, on the other hand, ate vegetables, even the emperors who could have feasted on anything their hearts desired. "According to report," the *Historia* tells us of the second-century emperor Didius Julianus, "even when there was no religious reason, he was content to dine on cabbages and beans without meat." Of Septimius Severus, the emperor who first introduced our Maximinus to the Roman tribune, it reports, "he was very sparing in his diet, was fond of his native beans, liked wine at times, and often went without meat." True Romans preferred the products of their gardens, planted and cultivated according to the advice of agriculturalists like Columella and Varro. No wonder they were so appalled by the diet of the barbarians. Whether those barbarians really ate as much meat as is claimed, we can't know for sure; most of what we know about them was written by Romans who delighted in expressing their revulsion at the carnivorous appetites of virtually the rest of the known world and descriptions like the one I quoted from Posidonius a moment ago became an almost stock feature of travelogues.

None of this is to maintain, however, that the Romans were vegetarians. They enjoyed meat, especially of sheep, goats, and pig (beef was a decidedly non-Roman preference), but it was not, as food historian Florence Dupont has noted, "the *only* food eaten by Roman citizens, which is to say, by civilized men."[11] And civilized is certainly how they liked to conceive of themselves, not as savages who crammed down their throats chunks of badly roasted meats torn from animals hunted in the wild. Read for yourself the description of an eminently civilized first-century Roman banquet in which guests were ushered into their host's home by "slave boys from Alexandria [who] poured water cooled with snow upon our hands, while others following, attended to our feet and removed the hangnails with wonderful dexterity." The description is by the emperor Nero's advisor in all matters of luxury and extravagance, Gaius Petronius, and it's about as far removed from those leonine Celts raising up whole limbs of beasts as it's possible to imagine.

Trays of delicacies appeared before the astonished guests. On one such "stood a donkey made of Corinthian bronze, bearing panniers containing olives, white in one and black in the other." On another platter "was served a wild boar of immense size. . . . Around it hung little suckling pigs made from pastry, signifying that this was a brood-sow with her pigs at suck." On yet a third rested an enormous whole hog, still uncarved. When Trimalchio called in the cook to upbraid him for having forgotten to gut and bowel the beast, the guilty man "snatched up a carving knife, with a trembling hand, and slashed the hog's belly in several places. Sausages and meat-puddings, widening the apertures, by their own weight, immediately tumbled out."[12]

Obviously, Petronius's description of the banquet—from the *Satyricon,* which means "satire"—is as much an exaggeration as was the account of Maximinus's gargantuan appetite. But the first century produced many other such accounts of banquets and stories of gourmets such as Apicius, who is said to have poisoned himself when he realized that he could no longer afford the feasts for which he had become legendary. Exaggerations perhaps, but just as there was something behind the myth of Maximinus's carnivory, so too something gave rise to these Roman extravaganzas. Who hasn't heard of such Roman delicacies as peacock brains and flamingo tongues?

And yet most Roman meals didn't include meat at all, but instead were humble affairs consisting of bread, olives, onions, wine, and vegetables—exactly the ingredients comprising the Mediterranean diet so highly touted today for its emphasis on olive oil, legumes, unrefined cereals, fruits and vegetables and its downplaying of meat. It was only at banquets that meat was served, but even then no self-respecting Roman host would have served up flesh from an animal summarily hunted, slaughtered, and roasted with a bare minimum of culinary skill. In the first place, he wouldn't have *killed* so much as *sacrificed* the animal; and in the second, he would have subjected the resulting meat to the most lavish culinary preparation imaginable. Thus would he have transformed animal flesh into edible meat. Barbarian hunters killed and ate; civilized Romans sacrificed and dined.

The Greeks too, big meat eaters that they were, sacrificed before indulging. The lusty suitors who took over Odysseus's home and attempted to woo his wife Penelope didn't simply kill, but "sacrific[ed] great-sized sheep, and fat goats, and . . . an ox of the herd, and fattened porkers."[13] Even the bad guys knew to sacrifice; they might have been lecherous sponges, but they were still human, whether god-fearing or not. Only monsters like the one-eyed Cyclops ate without sacrificing; but then he didn't know the difference between flesh and meat anyway. "He sprang up and reached for my companions," Odysseus reports,

caught up two together and slapped them, like killing
   puppies,
against the ground, and the brains ran all over the floor,
   soaking
the ground. Then he cut them up limb by limb and got
   supper ready,
and like a lion reared in the hills, without leaving anything,
ate them, entrails, flesh, and the marrowy bones alike.[14]

In distinguishing between meat and flesh, the Mediterranean culture drew clear lines of contrast between civilized and noncivilized carnivorous diets. In fact, that such preeminent classical philosophers and mathematicians as Socrates, Plato, and Pythagoras were vegetarians suggests that the most civilized minds of all chose to abstain from meat entirely. Even myths of the Golden Age, in which "the fruitful grainland yielded its harvest," make it clear that meat never featured in the Mediterranean idea of life as it was meant to be.[15] And it was this vegetable-loving culture that sought to expand its borders by taking over lands inhabited by meat-eating barbarians. Their Mediterranean repugnance filled volumes. How different were the northern barbarians who ate in "leonine fashion" from Homer's Cyclops, who ate civilized men "like a lion"?

We've already seen that the Romans brought their grafted fruits and cultivated vegetables with them as they sojourned north, and the same holds true for their carefully tended meat. They introduced the first rabbits to Britain, keeping them in *leporia*, or hare gardens, attached to villas. All manner of poultry was introduced by the Romans—geese, pheasants, and even the chicken—as well as their beloved dormice, which they stuffed with acorns and chestnuts while alive and with minced meat when served at banquets. Snails were fattened on milk and spelt until they could no longer fit back into their shells, at which point they were fried in oil and served with a wine sauce. But of all the animal products the Romans brought with them, what they didn't bring was beef.

It had never been a favorite meat back in Rome—it's noticeably absent from the detailed descriptions of those lavish banquets—but when they arrived in Britannia, that soon changed. Although they ate sheep, goats, and pig as well, it was beef that became their favorite meat. The island was already known for its meat eating and was famous for the salted hams it exported to Rome. Most of all, it was known for a distinctive breed of cattle. In his account of the region, Julius Caesar noted that a "species of wild animal lives there which is not found anywhere else."

> They are slightly smaller than elephants, and in appearance, colour, and shape they resemble bulls. They are extremely fierce and swift-footed, and attack people and animals on sight. The Germans carefully trap them in pits, and then slaughter them. . . . The oxen cannot grow accustomed to people, or become tame, even if they are caught when young.[16]

This creature—Caesar called it an *uri*, or "ur-ox," which was his way of referring to what's more commonly known as an aurochs—was nothing like the domestic animals he was familiar with back home. The beast of the north was the animal counterpart to the northern hunter-gatherer: savage, barbarian, and untameable.

In fact, it might be descendants of those native cows that graze today in the enclosed park surrounding Chillingham Castle in Northumbria. The famed pure white cattle, according to the official Web site of the Chillingham Wild Cattle Association, might be the very same breed that once "roamed the great forest which extended from the North Sea coast to the Clyde estuary."

> As to their ancestors, the shape of the skull and the manner in which the horns grow out from it are similar to the Aurochs (*Bos primogenius*) and quite different from the skull of the Roman importation. . . . It is thought by many therefore that the Chillingham Wild Cattle are the direct descendants of the original ox which roamed these islands before the dawn of history.[17]

Whether this history is strictly true, I won't venture to say. On the one hand, the Chillingham Cattle Association has a vested interest in promoting the purity of its cattle; tourists come from far and wide to see the wild cattle from which they must maintain a respectful distance—they're feral, after all, and will attack humans who venture too close to the unusual-looking white beasts. On the other hand, scientific literature doesn't bear out the association's claims, insisting that the only reason the Chillingham cattle look different from any other cows is that they were never selectively bred for beef or milk; left to their own devices to graze in Northumbria, they reverted to ancestral type and thus came to resemble the ancient aurochs from which all contemporary breeds evolved.

I am no zoologist, so I can't hope to weigh in on the mystery of the snow-white cows of Chillingham. I am struck, though, by the intensity of the desire to believe in a special northern breed of cattle, a desire so great it throws genetics to the wind. The English want to believe that there are distinctive cows up north because they have always been identified with their cattle, both by themselves and by others. In an article called "Race, Breed, and Myths of Origin: Chillingham Cattle as Ancient Britons," Harriet Ritvo locates the source of this belief in a special strain of cattle: national pride. Since the snow-white cattle have been symbolically identified with their British owners for so long, to question their indigenous nature is to question the lineage of their owners as well.[18]

"IT IS GOOD TO NOT ETE FLEISH"

At the same time that Rome was conquering Germania, Britannia, and the fearsome aurochs, it had its hands full at the eastern end of its empire, where a new religion was beginning to take shape. It was that religion that was going to succeed in taming the northern meat-eating barbarians in a way the Roman Empire had never been able to do, and it did so, appropriately in this context, by transforming flesh into spirit.

It had already transformed another culture that was devoted to the killing of animals. For centuries the Temple in Jerusalem had been the center of a vast sacrificial system, with hundreds of priests slaughtering thousands of beasts every day. On one occasion alone, the Bible tells us, King Solomon "offered as sacrifices of well-being to the Lord twenty-two thousand oxen and one hundred twenty thousand sheep" (1 Kings 8:63). The priests who slaughtered those thousands of oxen and sheep would have dashed the blood around the base of the sacrificial altar for they were forbidden to drink it, and they would have burned the fat that the ancient world believed to be God's favorite part of the animal, but they would have kept the choice cuts of meat for themselves, doling out the less desirable bits to everyone else. When the emperor Titus and his legions sacked Jerusalem in 70 CE, the ancient Israelite practice of sacrificing animals came to an abrupt end. In one fell swoop, the whole building—with its altars, basins, pots, shovels, and snuffers—was burned to the ground and sacrifice was no more. Or perhaps it would be more accurate to say that sacrifice had been *transformed*. It was a sacrifice that had kicked off Christianity some forty years before the destruction of the Temple: the sacrifice not of an ox or a sheep, but of the Lamb of God. "Christ has no need to offer sacrifices day after day," the New Testament told its followers, "this he did once for all when he offered himself" (Hebrews 7:27).

Now, it's one thing to replace an ox or a sheep with the Son of God, but how does one go about eating the sacrificed flesh? It's easy to sympathize with skeptics both ancient and modern who have been horrified by the implications of what they call Christian cannibalism. Clearly the body of Christ had to be transformed into a substance more acceptable to the civilized Mediterranean people who comprised the target audience of the new religion. Thus, it was no longer literal flesh that was to be eaten, but a cereal substitute. "I am the living bread that came down from heaven," Jesus announces in the Gospel of John, "Whoever eats of this bread will live forever; and the bread that I will give for the life of the world is my flesh." Not many Christians like to think of themselves as cannibals, even though *spiritual* cannibalism—or perhaps *farinaceous* cannibalism—might be an apt way to describe the sacrament in which believers ingest the bread that stands in for the flesh of Christ. Mediterranean people never having been big meat eaters, it makes sense that the new religion of the area should have transformed animal sacrifice into a cereal celebration. But this new and improved cereal commemoration of the Christian sacrifice was bound to run into trouble when it traveled up to the meat-eating barbarians.

The Angles and Saxons might have been quite keen on some of the food stories in the book the Christians brought with them: they might have enjoyed, for instance, God's telling Noah that "Every living thing that moves shall be food for you"; or his later command to Peter: "Get up, Peter; kill and eat." But what would they have made of a line like "You shall not eat flesh with its life, that is, its blood"? They had no such qualms and regularly drank the blood of slain beasts, believing that doing so would imbue them with power and virility. In fact, as Alan Davidson noted in his *Penguin Companion to Food*, "the introduction of Christianity did not make the Nordic peoples give up their traditional blood dishes (black soup, black pudding, paltbread—a kind of black rye bread made with blood, dark beer, and spices)."[19] How were such barbarians to understand Paul's well-meant advice, "It is good to not ete fleish"?

As we've seen before, the Christians had much greater success exporting their spiritual beliefs than they did their food preferences to the hardy meat-eating and blood-drinking people of northern Europe.

PEOPLE OF THE FLESH

Animal sacrifice never featured in the Christian tradition, but it certainly was a big part of life among northern peoples. The Celts regularly offered up cattle, horses, dogs, sheep, pigs, and even occasionally people, according to Caesar and the Greek geographers Strabo and Diodorus. Eating was another matter. No evidence suggests that the Celtic people of early Britain felt the need to transform animal flesh into edible meat through the civilized and civilizing ritual of sacrifice.

Nor, apparently, did the Anglo-Saxons who also sacrificed regularly and were profoundly carnivorous as well. In his *British Food: An Extraordinary Thousand Years of History,* Colin Spencer envisions what a typical feast might have looked like in the hallowed halls of the chieftains and thanes of yore: "drunken warriors [would have thrown] large animal bones at each other in the hall. The inference is that whole ox or mutton carcasses had been roasted then presented well nigh whole to the table for the warriors to hack and carve themselves."[20] Northern mythology even includes an account of a meat-eating competition that would give today's Gentleman Joe Menchetti a run for his money.

A trencher was fetched and brought into the hall and filled with chopped-up meat. Loki sat down at one end and Logi at the other; and each of them ate as fast as he could. They met in the middle of the trencher and by then Loki had left only the bones of his meat, but Logi had eaten all his meat, bones, and trencher into the bargain, so everyone thought that Loki had lost the contest.[21]

Turns out the contest was rigged: *Logi* meant "wildfire," which explains how he managed to burn his way through meat, bones, and trencher at lightning speed.

All of a sudden these meat-loving northerners were being implored to give up their roasted haunches and carcasses—not to mention many other favorite foods. Both the gospels and epistles in the New Testament had often resorted to food imagery in their attempt to win over nonbelievers down in the Mediterranean: the kingdom of heaven was like a mustard seed or like yeast; Jesus fed the five thousand with loaves and fishes; infants in Christ were given milk until they were ready for solid food. We've already seen how difficult it was for a lactose-loving people to wean themselves of their favorite beverage. The situation was similar with flesh. Many of Paul's metaphors for the unenlightened—his exact words were "the people of the flesh"—used the indispensable staples of the northern diet to make their point: *mylk* and *flæsc*. Just as the northerners felt no pressing need to give over their traditional drink, nor did they feel any great urgency to spiritualize the flesh they were notorious for eating.

It would be foolish to argue that England resisted the Christian missionaries for very long. Historical records make it abundantly clear that within a very few generations of their arrival in Britain in the late sixth century, almost all of the English kings and their courts had been converted to the imported Mediterranean religion. A monastery was founded at Canterbury in the early seventh century and the cornerstone of Saint Paul's Cathedral in London dates to the same period. Nor am I arguing that the religion was practiced differently up north, although it's notable that it's only in Germanic-speaking countries that the holiday commemorating Christ's birth is referred to as Yule, from the pagan midwinter festival *Geol* (pronounced "yule"), and that the day marking his ascension into heaven is named after *Eostre,* the Germanic goddess of the dawn (in all other countries, its name derives from the Latin *Pascha*, Passover). I am suggesting, though, that the new religion, based in Mediterranean attitudes about food, had its work cut out for it when it transplanted itself in the far harsher soil of the north where there was no reason in the world to equate milk drinking with infancy (spiritual or otherwise) and meat eating with sin, human weakness, and cruelty.

It's no coincidence that the people who rebelled against the Roman Church centuries later were from the milk-drinking, meat-eating countries of the north. Not a single country of the Mediterranean where Christianity was born—and where bread, oil, and wine were commonplace—joined in the Protestant Reformation. Attitudes toward foods proved to be even more deeply rooted than religious beliefs and, consequently, to change at a glacial pace, if at all. Yes, England was thoroughly converted, but its food preferences were not. Nor were its names for the foods that were both religious symbols and dietary staples. We still call many of our most everyday foods by old Anglo-Saxon names and we're still famous—or infamous, depending on the perspective— for our meat-eating propensities, despite the triumph of the southern religion of the olive and grape. Despite our undeniable love for Mediterranean food as well.

ON *CHEBOLACE* AND HUMBLE PIE

From the time the Romans first landed on the island and introduced a produce-deprived people to fruits and vegetables that had never been seen so far north, the British fell in love with Italian food. Who wouldn't salivate at the sight of streams of golden polenta (then called *puls* or *pulmentus*) or at the scent of freshly baked focaccia (then called *panis focacius*)? Who wouldn't relish all those grapes, figs, plums, cherries, apricots, peaches, and almonds that the Romans brought with them? But it's one thing to love exotic new foods and quite another to make them one's own. Most of the Mediterranean imports vanished from the landscape when the Romans abandoned the island, and luxuries such as fruits, nuts, wines, and spices weren't to be seen again until the invasion of another people whose language—and many of whose foods—hailed from the south. Their food too was the stuff that dreams are made of: French food. To this day, when it comes to a matter of fine dining, few things can compete with an *entrecôte à point* and a glass of Bordeaux—certainly not beer and a burger.

When William the Conqueror and his supporters arrived on the shores of Hastings in 1066 they, like the Romans before them, brought new foods with such foreign-sounding names as *chebolace, tredure, mounchelet,* and *charlet*—not to mention early versions of the sauces for which the French are still legendary: *civey, gravey, egerdouce,* and *bukkenade.* For a brief period, they renamed familiar foodstuffs they found in England, turning *applys* into *pommys, bread* into *payn,* and *flesh* into *viande.* Yet the new names didn't stick. Our apples are still apples, our bread still bread, and very few of us know what the French dishes *chebolace* and *charlet* are (the former is a sort of onion soup and the latter, minced pork in a saffron-flavored milk sauce).

On the other hand, as we've seen, we still call most of our meats by the French names they received after the Conquest. Our earliest English cookbooks are jam-packed with the heavily sauced and exotically spiced meat dishes preferred by the country's French-speaking upper classes. A favorite dish called *mawme-nee*, for instance, consisted of minced *capouns*, from the Latin *caponem* (rather than *chicken*, from the Old English *cicen*), poached in wine and flavored with cloves and fried almonds. Minced *veal* (rather than *calf*), was simmered in almond milk and scented with galingale (a rhizome related to ginger), cinnamon, and sugar to produce a dish with the unusual name of *haucegeme*. Balls of minced *pork* (rather than *swine*) bound with egg yolk were poached in stock, then roasted, rolled in egg white, and coated in sugar in a recipe by the fanciful name of *oranges*. It goes without saying that such elaborate recipes would have been prepared exclusively for the refined palates of the nobility and the wealthy. No mere Saxon serf would have returned from the fields or forest to sit down to a repast of rose pottage or *Fylett in Galyntyne*.

Mawmenee

Take a potell of wyne greke and ii pounde of sugur; take and claryfye the sugur with a quantite of wyne & drawe it thrugh a straynour in to a pot of erthe. Take flour of rys and medle with sum of the wyne & cast togydre. Take pynes with dates and frye hem a litell in grece oþer in oyle and cast hem togydre. Take clowes & flour of canel hool and cast þerto. Take powdour ginger, canel, clowes; colour it with saundres a lytel yf hit be need. Cast salt þerto, and lat it seeþ warly with a slowe fyre and not to thyk. Take brawn of capouns yteysed oþer of fesauntes teysed small and cast þerto.

Mawmenee

Take a pottel of Greek wine and two pounds of sugar; take and clarify the sugar with some wine and put it through a strainer into an earthen pot. Take rice flour and mix with some of the wine and add it. Take pine nuts and dates and fry them in a little grease or oil and add them. Take whole cloves and cassia buds and add them. Take powdered ginger, cinnamon, cloves, color it with a little saunders if need be. Add salt and let it simmer gently over a slow fire—not too thick. Take the shredded breast meat of roasted capons or pheasants and add thereto.[22]

Note: A *pottel* was equivalent to a half gallon; *saunders* was a dried and powdered wood used as a red food coloring.

The Old English names used by the serfs, shepherds, and swineherds weren't vanquished entirely, and *swine, shepe, deer,* and *kydde* still dot the pages of the early cookbooks. They do so, however, only in recipes that sound much less appetizing than *veel in buknade* or *sawse noyre for capouns yrosted.* Then as now, to translate an animal product into French was to transform flesh into meat.

Take the dish called *corat,* a word that sometimes referred to the heart (think *coeur*), but more often was used as a euphemism for organ meats or entrails. The French-sounding dish with the refined name of *corat* turns out to be no more than humble pie, once called *umble pie,* umbles being the English mispronunciation of *noumbles,* another French term referring to the liver, heart, and other innards that went into the dish destined for the inferior lower classes. When the animals from which these umbles, or *noumbles*, were taken were named specifically, however, no euphemism disguised the living, breathing reality of what had once been a *calf, swyne,* or *shepe.*

It's a sign of our times that we prefer beef filets to pigs' feet, tenderloins to entrails, and entrecôtes to offal. Only a wealthy society like ours can afford to slaughter a twelve-hundred-pound cow and throw out most of the carcass for a six-pound tenderloin

Corat

Take the noumbles of calf, swyne, or of shepe; perboile hem and kerue hem to dyce. Cast hem in gode broth and do þerto erbes, grene chybolles smale yhewe; seeþ it tendre, and lye it with yolkes of eyren. Do þerto verious safroun, powdour douce and salt, and serue it forth.

Corat

Take the innards of calf, swine, or of sheep. Parboil them, skim and dice. Put them in good broth and add herbs. Mince spring onions; seethe until tender and layer with egg yolks. Add verjuice, saffron, sweet powder, and salt. Serve it forth.[23]

and a few other choice cuts. In past centuries and in countries where food is much harder to come by, far more of the animal was (and is) eaten than the average American supermarket-goer today would ever know existed, judging from the cellophane-wrapped packages of top and bottom roasts, sirloins, rib eyes, and chops in the freezer cases that separate us from the bloody-aproned butcher who goes about his unsightly business behind closed doors. Yet even during a time when people were grateful to eat meat—no matter where on the animal it came from—they nonetheless called their filets and sirloins by French names, keeping the Old English ones for the less desirable and bloodier cuts that never managed to lose the stink of the slaughterhouse. *Offal*, our general word for entrails and internal organs, traces back to those bits that fell off the butcher's table for the dogs to wolf down; it has no cognate in French, where kidneys, tripe, and the like are collectively referred to as *les abats*. Old English names were reserved as well for those parts of the animal that were recognizable body parts—tongues, lungs, and kidneys, for instance. The dishes

might have been made to sound more appetizing with French titles, but such euphemistic foreignness was restricted to recipe
names. Thus *Longue de buf* instructed the cook to scald the "tonge
of the rether" (*rether* was an old name for a young ox or cow),
while a version of *mawmenee* was thickened with the "blod of a
goot or of a pygg."

However much these early cookbooks seesawed between
languages, on one point they remained fixed. Meat was never
anything but good Old English flesh. Unsettling to our stomachs
though they may be, recipes for such dishes as *gele of flessh* and
pecys of flessh fill the cookery books that translated and euphe-
mized so much else. An exotically spiced pork pie enriched with
bits of fowl and rabbit bears the not particularly appetizing name
tartes of flessh.

Tartes of Flessh

*Take pork ysode and grynde it smale. Take harde eyren isode &
ygronde and do þereto with chese ygronde. Take gode powdours and
hool spices, sugur, safroun, and salt, & do þereto. Make a coffyn as
tofore sayde & do þis þerinne, & plaunt it with smale briddes istyued
& connynges, & hewe hem to smale gobettes, & bake it as tofore. &
serue it forth.*

Flesh Tarts

Take boiled pork and grind it small. Take hard-boiled eggs
and grind them; mix with ground cheese. Take good powder,
whole spices, sugar, saffron, and salt and add. Make a tart shell
as heretofore said, and put it in; add small stewed birds and
rabbit, cut into small pieces. Bake as directed and serve it
forth.[24]

No modern cookbook could possibly include a recipe called Flesh Tart; our reaction to the word is simply too visceral. We are not flesh eaters, but—in the words of Shakespeare—"great eaters of beef." Thus in Mrs. Beeton's *Book of Household Management,* we find a chapter called "Various Modes of Cooking *Meat*" and it includes numerous recipes for "*Beef*-steak Pie," "*Mutton* Pie," "Raised *Pork* Pie," and a "Savoury Jelly for *Meat* Pies"—but not a single Flesh Tart is to be found in the thousand-page compendium.

Linguists will be the first to admit that we can never know exactly why words undergo such semantic shifts, but that doesn't stop us from wondering. In the case of the shift from flesh to meat, two circumstances in particular stand out. In the first place, just as the word *meat* was taking on its modern sense, the substance meat was all of a sudden more abundant and available than ever before. The laws of supply and demand operated then as now: when the bubonic plague descended on Europe in the mid-fourteenth century and killed off somewhere between one- and two-thirds of the entire population, the supply of meat for the first time exceeded demand. The lucky few who somehow managed to survive the Black Death would have had a whole lot more to eat in the nearly deserted towns and villages. This is the grisly explanation of why it was suddenly easier than ever before to lay one's hands on meat: no need to distinguish between meat and food if most of what one eats happens to be meat.

The second circumstance is less grisly, and has more to do with a change in attitude. From as far back as written records take us, British cooks had been looked down on as unskilled hacks: "Little exquisite can be expected from a people so extremely barbarous"; "the notoriously bad cooking of England"; "You can't trust people who cook as badly as that." As long as the flesh was roasted or boiled long enough to break down its stringy fibers, no one complained. In a dialogue included in the tenth-century *Colloquy* by the monk known to us as Aelfric, a cook actually has to defend himself to a teacher who wonders why the profession even exists:

> TEACHER: What can we say about you, cook? Do we have need of any of your skills?
> COOK: If you drive me away from your community you would eat your vegetables raw and your meat rare; and, moreover, without my skill, you would be unable to have good rich broth.
> TEACHER: We do not care about your skill, it is of no importance to us, since we can cook what needs to be cooked and eat what needs to be eaten.

From all accounts, the Angles and Saxons were content enough with their simply roasted haunches, but when the trained chefs of the Normans arrived, highly seasoned and minutely minced pieces of *porc* and *boeuf* were simmered, boiled, and puréed into "strange and heterogeneous compositions," as the eighteenth-century editor of *The Forme of Cury* noted. Whereas one country's custom, Samuel Pegge continued, was to serve up "entire joints of meat," the other "seldom brought [anything] to table whole, but hacked and hewed, and cut in pieces and gobbets." To this day, England is known for its great slabs of roast beef, whereas France boasts of the culinary skill that lies behind its *boeuf en daube* and *coq au vin*.

There's a family resemblance between the cooking of ancient Rome and of Norman France, both preferring "to make of a thousand flavors, one flavor," as the Roman statesman Cicero so memorably observed almost two thousand years ago. The *mawmenies, haucegemes, oranges,* and other dishes prepared from the pages of late medieval cookbooks would have been right at home in feasts prepared by Apicius or at a gustatory extravaganza designed to amaze Trimalchio's guests. The spices, wines, raisins, and almonds needed for such dishes would have come from the Mediterranean as well, brought back by returning Crusaders, who found the sugar, lemons, and pomegranates of the faithless a lot more palatable than their religious beliefs. The Normans were closer in spirit to the Romans than they knew: both brought to England a complex Mediterranean cuisine; both used Latin (or Latinate) names for their foods; and both looked down on the primitive manner of cooking indigenous foodstuffs that the natives called by barbaric names. Both also provoked a defensive attitude. The early inhabitants of Britain had refused to abandon either their language or their meat, and the medieval Anglo-Saxons were similarly resistant.

Ultimately, though, the English seem to have settled on a savvy compromise, realizing centuries before Madison Avenue that to rename a food goes a long way toward making it more appetizing. They transformed those fleshy haunches into what we know as *meat*—but, and here's the twist, they didn't do so by translating them into French.

Viande never became anglicized, but the native word that replaced *flesh* was nonetheless part of the change in attitude toward food that began after the Conquest, when more polite (read: French) names were substituted for things that people would rather not think too closely about. *Meat* is much better than *flesh* at hiding the bloody corporeality of the animal that needed to be slaughtered and butchered to produce the fricassees, daubes, ragouts, and casseroles that had begun to replace the straightforwardly spit-roasted joints of yore. Derived from the Proto-Indo-European root that expressed unctuous oozing wetness, *meat* is more like breast milk than it is like *flesh*. *Meat* would have allowed refined diners—even English ones—to ignore the flayed carcasses they would have had to walk by at markets such as the famous one in Smithfield, established as early as 1174. Until it was finally enclosed from public view in the mid-nineteenth century, the Smithfield meat market was an open-air slaughterhouse, with blood, guts, and entrails on display for all the world to see. "London has always been celebrated for the excellence of its meat," the influential *Quarterly Review* announced in 1854, before admitting that if one were to look "for a national exposition of our greatness in the chief market dedicated to that British beef," what one would find would not be meat, but instead an "enormous aggregation of edible quadrupeds."[25]

What Londoners and visitors alike would have found in the slaughterhouses, triperies, bone-boiling houses, and gut-scaperies they couldn't help but see was nothing if not flesh. What they wanted to eat, however, was meat.

ON ROAST BEEF AND MEATHEADS

It may seem odd that the meat most associated with England should have a name derived from French. Roast beef has long been dear to the British, who, according to *The Forme of Cury*, "well knew how to make the best use of the cow." It's still served on festive occasions with the inevitable accompaniment of Yorkshire pudding, and its name has even become a slang way for the French to refer to the English people: *les rosbifs*. And yet, beef comes from *boeuf,* as roast does from *rôtir.* Wouldn't it be more appropriate if the iconic dish were called *Lendenbraten* instead, as it is in Germany even when it's prepared *englischer Art,* "in the English style," rubbed with softened butter, seared on all sides in a hot oven, and then roasted until medium rare?

Before the Norman Conquest, there was no Old English name for roast beef. Meat was simply known by the name of the animal from which it had been cut. A medieval medical treatise, for instance, advised pregnant women to abstain from "bull's flesh or ram's or buck's or boar's or cock's or gander's" (the flesh of male animals was believed to pose a threat to both mother and fetus).[26] Roast beef was first mentioned in print in the seventeenth-century play *Hey for Honesty*—"My nose smells the delicious odour of roast-beef"—and a hundred years later, the novelist Henry Fielding declared "mighty roast beef" to be both the source of English manliness and the iconic food of the nation.

> *When mighty roast beef was the Englishman's food,*
> *It ennobled our hearts, and enriched our blood,*
> *Our soldiers were brave,*
> *Our courtiers were good*
> *Oh the roast beef of England*
> *And old England's roast beef!*

The name of the dish is modern, but the love of roast beef is anything but. The British have always had a legendary infatuation with meat, and above all with beef. From Caesar to the Christian missionaries to the Norman *chefs de cuisine*, virtually everyone who commented on them took a perverse delight in their carnivorous appetites, seeing their infatuation with flesh as a sign of their barbarism.

When those barbaric English began to speak up for themselves, though, the same terms that had been used negatively for so long were turned inside out, and what had been held against them became effusive praise. If Maximinus the Thracian had ever been able to get a word in edgewise, he would have boasted, just as his Roman biographer did, of the forty to sixty pounds of meat he consumed daily, but he would have been proud of the excess, rather than disgusted by it, and he would have vaunted the virility that made such carnivory possible. The same could be

said of the latter-day Maximinus: John Bull. By the time he became the star of James Gillray's eighteenth-century caricatures,
the brawny Saxon-featured, beef-eating John Bull was to the
effete, foppish, scrawny-limbed, salad-eating Frenchmen what
Maximinus had been to the vegetable-eating Romans: the manly
counterpart. The "frogs," as they came to be mockingly called
for their love of frogs' legs, had looked down on *les rosbifs* for long
enough; the time had come for the English to go on the offensive. The centuries-long preference for French food turns out to
have been but a temperory infatuation with the cuisine that began during the "days of Rich. II. [when] our ancestors lived
much after the French fashion . . . [stuffing themselves with]
soups, potages, ragout, hashes, and the like hotche-potches."[27]
What were the French, though, but an emasculated nation of
prancing ragout eaters? Such was the conclusion Fielding drew in
the final stanzas of his "Ode to Roast Beef":

> *But since we have learnt from all conquering France*
> *To eat their ragouts as well as to dance,*
> *Oh what a fine figure we make in romance!*
> *Oh the roast beef of England*
> *And old England's roast beef!*
>
> *Then, Britons, from all nice dainties refrain,*
> *Which effeminate Italy, France, and Spain*
> *And mighty roast beef shall command on the main*
> *Oh the roast beef of England*
> *And Old England's roast beef!*

Even a serious writer like the novelist George Eliot wasn't above
drawing upon the stereotyped contrast of the meat-eating English and the French who "ne'er ate a bit o' beef i' their lives.
Mostly sallet, I reckon."[28]

The reaction against all things French dominated the cookery books of the period. The first chapter of Hannah Glasse's *Art of Cookery* opens with a recipe for how to roast beef and it insists that the meat be served "with nothing but Horse-raddish"—a clear dig against the vogue of French sauces. In a later chapter, called "Read this Chapter, and you will find how expensive a French Cook's Sauce is," Glasse instructs her readers how to make the dishes she knew they would find impressive—"The French Way of Dressing Partridges" and "A Cullis for all Sorts of Butcher's Meat"—but she also warns against such wasteful frivolity:

> It would be needless to name any more; though they have much more expensive Sauces than this.—However, I think here is enough to shew the Folly of these fine French Cooks. In their own Country, they will make a grand Entertainment with the Expence of one of these Dishes; but here they want the little petty Profit; and by this Sort of legerdemain Sum, fine Estates are juggled into France.[29]

Such staunch advocacy of the simply roasted meats of England was to become a commonplace that lasted into the twentieth century. In the words of the Anglophile American poet Robert P. Tristram Coffin, "No wonder the French have invented the world's most elaborate sauces. They had to, to hide the inferiority of their meats."

Nonetheless, the most English of all dishes remains known by its French name as though the impulse that long ago converted flesh into meat were with us still. And who's to say it isn't? Only to Hannibal Lecter would a Sunday dinner of *roast flesh* sound appealing, and no fast-food restaurant would be suicidal enough to advertise its billions and billions of *charbroiled ground cow flesh burgers*.

"Meat has ceased to have any connection with animals," Dorothy Hartley wryly observed in her *Food in England*.[30] The communal culinary split personality that makes us ashamed to drink milk in public is even more fractured in our attitude about meat. We can't live without our meat—our roast beef, our hamburgers, our lamb chops and pork tenderloins—but we don't want to be reminded where it came from either. And so we have an elaborate vocabulary in which we are *carnivores*, rather than *flesh eaters*, and meat is anything but what it once was: animal flesh.

The communal forgetting that meat is the flesh of animals is precisely the point of a new generation of blatantly carnivorous British cookbooks spearheaded by Fergus Henderson's *The Whole Beast: Nose to Tail Eating* and Hugh Fearnley-Whittingstall's *The River Cottage Meat Book*. This latter book includes graphic photos that follow a wide-eyed cow as it's led into the back of the truck to its delivery at the slaughterhouse, where its throat is slit and its carcass hung, flayed, and butchered—a photo essay that refuses to ignore the flesh in the meat. The pictures that accompany the recipes—of a pig's head and ears, a sheep's lungs and tail, a cow's tongue, and a bull's testicles—only emphasize the point. By the same token, the slogan of the trendy chef and restaurant owner Fergus Henderson is "If you're going to kill the animal it seems only polite to use the whole thing," and he delights in offering up dishes such as "Rolled Pig's Spleen," "Crispy Pig Tails," "Warm Pig's Head," and "Soft Roes on Toast" (the author helpfully explains to mystified readers that "soft roes are in fact herring semen"). There's simply no way to ignore the fact that you're dealing with what was once a living, breathing animal in a recipe for "Crispy Pig Tails," especially when you're advised: "By the by, dealing with any slightly hairy extremities of pig, I recommend a throwaway Bic razor." Nor is it possible to forget that you're dealing with flesh in a recipe like this one:

Pig's Cheek and Tongue (to feed two)

A brine
1 pig's head
stock vegetables (carrots, leeks, onion, celery)
a bundle of herbs tied together
black peppercorns
a splash of red wine vinegar

Brine your pig's head for 3 days, rinse it, and place it in a large pot with the stock vegetables, herbs, peppercorns, and vinegar. Cover with water and bring to a boil. Reduce to a gentle simmer and cook for 2½ to 3 hours. The cheeks should come away easily from the skull; keep these warm in the broth. Open the pig's jaw and pull out the tongue. Peel it while still warm and slice in half lengthwise, so each diner gets a cheek and half a tongue. Serve with mashed potatoes and Green Sauce.[31]

This unapologetic celebration of carnivorousness has found a home here in the United States as well, in the land of two-all-beef-patties-special-sauce-lettuce-cheese-pickles-onions-on-a-sesame-seed-bun that could almost make you forget the cow in your Big Mac. In the words of Bill Buford, "It's finally cool to be a carnivore." TV chef Emeril Lagasse's mantra "Pork fat rules!" never fails to draw thunderous applause, and even former vegetarian Mollie Katzen of Moosewood fame has begun to eat meat. *New York* magazine's Grub Street blog has dubbed the new style of cooking "The Refined Meathead School." Meatheads, it explains, are "mostly male, pork- and offal-obsessed cooks who disdain classical (read "French") haute cuisine in favor of an earthier brand of cuisine." Their king is Iron Chef Mario Batali, whose repeated dismissal of traditional haute cuisine is "fagotty

French"—a contemporary version of Fielding's "effeminate Italy, France, and Spain." Another king of the meatheads, the New York restaurateur David Chang, announced proudly on an early menu of his Momofuku Ssäm Bar Café: "We do not serve vegetarian-friendly items"; since the restaurant's opening in 2007, its Web site now answers the question of whether there are vegetarian alternatives to the bo ssäm: "No, but vegetarians can enjoy the bo ssäm without the pork or they may order items from the regular ssäm bar menu." Good publicity move, but last I checked, there were no vegetarian entrées on the bar menu.

And so we come full circle. How different are these Meat-heads from Maximinus the Thracian with his forty to sixty pounds of meat a day? After years of French cuisine, whether *haute* or *nouvelle,* we English speakers seem at last to have rediscovered our no-holds-barred meat-eating heritage and are flocking to restaurants with names like The Spotted Pig and Quality Meats. Granted, there are still plenty of refined people who prefer the attitude of the barbarian emperor's vegetable-loving biographer, but even in them, the nausea induced by the recent renaissance of our carnal appetites and our irrepressibly base desire for flesh is tinged, however faintly and however involuntarily, with titillation.

CHAPTER FIVE

Bread

"Give Us This Day Our Daily Bread"

Berme, otherwise clepid goddisgood . . . hath frely be goven or delyvered for brede . . bicause it cometh of the grete grace of God.

Barm, otherwise called "God-is-good," has been freely given or delivered for bread because it comes from the great grace of God.

—*Norwich Brewer's Book* (1468–1469)

Bread is the fruit of the earth, yet is blessed by the heavenly light.

—Friedrich Hölderlin, *Bread and Wine*

This is the most frustrating and ultimately satisfying thing I discovered: Bread is alive.

—Nancy Silverton, *Breads from the La Brea Bakery*

Proto-Indo-European: *bhreu, pa*

GERMANIC: **breuwan**   CELTIC: **bara**   LATIN: **panis**   GREEK: *artos*

Norwegian: *brød*	Irish: *arán*	Italian: *pane*
Swedish: *brød*	Scottish: *aran*	French: *pain*
Danish: *brød*	Welsh: *bara*	Spanish: *pane*
Dutch: *Brood*	Cornish: *bara*	Romanian: *pîine*
German: *Brot*	Breton: *bara*	
Old English: *hlaf*		
English: *bread*		

A MOST UNNATURAL FOOD

There's an obvious difference between bread and the other foods whose stories I've been tracing: unlike fruits, vegetables, and animals, bread is *not* found in nature. Apples grew in the wilds of Central Asia, leeks grew almost everywhere, and it goes without saying that milk and meat are biological facts of life. Bread, though, is in a class by itself, a testament to our ingenuity and resourcefulness in finding ever more sophisticated ways to feed ourselves from the earth's varied flora and fauna. The most primitive flatbreads, barely more than baked gruel, nonetheless represent an enormous imaginative and technological advancement on the part of our distant forebears. Wild grains that were scarcely distinguishable from grasses (which in fact all grains are botanically) had to be reaped, threshed, parched, hulled, ground, combined with liquid, shaped into flat rounds, and baked on stone slabs before they could be said to resemble anything that we would recognize as bread. Leavened bread, a much later innovation requiring a specific type of wheat, presupposed even greater control and an understanding of both agriculture and what today we call kitchen chemistry.

There's a second difference between bread and the other foods whose stories I've been telling. Because it's *produced* rather than found, bread has no one natural form, but instead can be made in a dizzying variety of ways depending on tradition and preference. The French and Italians often begin with a starter, which they call a *levain* or *biga,* whereas the English generally don't. The Tuscans are famous (or infamous) for not adding salt to their *pane sciocco.* Americans usually bake their breads in loaf pans (or at least they did until the artisanal craze took over), whereas *ciabatta,* the Italian "slipper bread," is baked directly on unglazed clay tiles. Bread can be made from wheat, rye, corn, bulgur, sorghum, oats, millet, teff, spelt, buckwheat, or almost any other grain that grows wherever the baking is being done. Last—but certainly not least, as we'll see when we consider the biases and prejudices attendant on the subject of leavening—the dough can be naturally fermented (as in San Francisco's famous sourdoughs), intentionally leavened by means of an added substance (as in most of the risen and presliced loaves we buy at the supermarket), or baked in its completely flat state (as in tortillas).

But difference is rarely as simple or as straightforward as one might think—certainly not when it comes to such an important matter as the staff of life. Wheat bread is almost always regarded as not just *different* from but *better* than millet or barley bread, both of which have a vaguely primitive feel to them, as though only those people eat them who haven't yet been exposed to the good stuff. Similarly, oat and rye bread are generally presumed to be the fallbacks of northern peoples whose colder climates don't allow wheat to grow. Why else, this reasoning holds, would the Scots have traditionally eaten dry little oatcakes and the Finns the flat barley bread they call *ohrarieska?* Because they didn't have white bread. And why, according to more developed countries, do less developed ones eat such flatbreads as Afghan *naan,* Indian *pappadam*, Bedouin *fatir*, Ethiopian *injeera*, Mexican *tortillas*, Armenian *lavash*, and eastern Mediterranean *pita*? Because they haven't mastered the art of leavening, are too nomadic to have standing brick ovens, or are too poor to afford the fuel required for baking towering loaves.[1] The leavening process—not simply natural or accidental fermentation, but deliberate leavening by means of an added agent—has almost invariably been seen as the more sophisticated way, the more civilized way, in short, the *better* way to make bread. When you think about it, leavening is to bread as grafting is to fruit trees, cultivation is to vegetables, cheese making is to milk, and saucing is to meat. People who eat flatbread, by this logic, are the same as those who eat hard little sour apples, weedlike leeks, curdled milk, and spit-roasted haunches of meat—the people who inherited neither the culinary skills nor the language that traveled up north from the shores of the Mediterranean so many centuries ago.

It does seem strange, all things considered, that our contemporary English word for bread has nothing whatsoever to do with the Latin word *panis* even though we, like the French, Italians, and Spanish, have so clearly inherited the Roman preference for intentionally and artisanally crafted loaves. Some of our favorite places to eat lunch have French and Italian names like Au Bon Pain and Panera, which, roughly speaking, translate to "at the place of good bread" and "bread baker"—or maybe "bread basket" (a made-up word along the lines of Häagen-Dazs, Panera is more evocative than it is specific). Would we frequent such cafés as often and as eagerly if they didn't have such names? Probably not, as Ken Rosenthal and Ronald Shaich, the founders of Panera rightly surmised. When Au Bon Pain bought the St. Louis Bread Company in 1993, it knew that in order to make it on the national stage, its bakery-café needed a less regional name. The popular Missouri eatery could have been renamed the

American Bread Company, which might have been abbreviated to the easy-to-remember ABC, but no such English name was even considered. Instead, the St. Louis Bread Company was re-christened Panera and its success was immediate. According to its Web site, by March 2010, there were 1,388 locations in the United States and Canada. Despite its Latin- or Italian-sounding name, every word in Panera's mission statement comes straight from Old English: "A loaf of bread in every arm." Our culinary split personality rears its head once again. We want our cafés to have impressive European names, but what we want to eat is *bread*—most especially at breakfast and lunch when we're not quite at our sophisticated best.

Bread. Despite our love affair with French and Italian loaves, the word we use to refer to them comes to us from those remote Germanic ancestors of ours, the ones who have gone down in history as having survived on milk, meat, and foraged wild fruits and vegetables. Seems unlikely that such simple and uncultured hunter-gatherers could have mastered the complex science of leavening, yet it's their word that we still use to refer to the risen loaves we eat day in and day out (or at least we did until the advent of the low-carbohydrate diet that advises us to avoid precisely the food that has sustained most of humanity for most of recorded history). When we want to clarify that what we're eating is unleavened, we have to specify *flatbread*, but when it's the leavened stuff we have in mind, we refer simply and succinctly to *bread.* Which is why Elizabeth David could call her majesterial tome *English Bread and Yeast Cookery,* while Jeffrey Alford and Naomi Duguid had to refine the title of their travelogue-cookbook *Flatbreads & Flavors.* The same situation, by the way, can be seen in an odd phrase used by the Portuguese to refer to the fresh version of their national staple, *bacalhau*—what we know as salt cod. The only way to refer to the unsalted fish is by adding a prefix to produce the strange phrase "fresh salt cod." To the Portuguese, dried salt cod is the default setting, so to speak, whether out of tradition or preference—just as leavened bread is to us. In each case, eating habits are reflected in word choice.

There are, of course, plenty of people with different habits and preferences, whether in the case of fish or bread. Ethiopians, Mexicans, and Arabs, for instance, might not just be used to eating their *injeera, tortillas,* and *pitas,* but actually *prefer* them to our risen white loaves, which goes to show once again that what we assume to be universals and absolutes are often more a matter of acquired cultural tastes and values. The famous two-kilogram *miche* of Parisian *boulanger* Lionel Poilâne is not inherently better than a corn tortilla slapped between a Mexican woman's palms and quickly browned on a cast-iron *comal*; it's just that we've been brought up to believe it's better—meaning, in this context, more refined, more sophisticated, more civilized. As with so many foods, our tastes and values have a lot to do with the food prejudices we inherited from the Romans and, centuries later, from the French, both of whom bequeathed to the peoples they conquered the belief that food is best when it's been transformed from its raw primitive state, not by the natural processes of spoilage that curdles milk and ferments dough, but by the deliberate human control that results in *parmigiano reggiano,* or, as the Italians call it, *il formaggio migliore nel mondo,* the world's greatest cheese, as well as in the classic French *baguette.*

ON AGRICULTURE, A FALLEN WORLD, AND SACRED GROVES

Isn't that what we've always sought to do, after all? Triumph over nature by improving on sour little wild crab apples, cultivating sweeter and meatier leeks, controlling the spoilage of milk by transforming it into cheese, and hemming round our animalistic

carnivorous appetites with civilizing sacrificial rituals? As Kath-
arine Hepburn so memorably and imperiously affirmed to Hum-
phrey Bogart in *The African Queen,* "Nature, Mr. Allnut, is what
we were put on this earth to rise above."

Or were we?

This is a question that has vexed us for centuries, certainly in the
case of bread. Leavened or not, bread requires work to produce, but
work hasn't always been understood in the same way. Sometimes
it's been seen as a sign of civilization, as it was in the classical world
of the Mediterranean. The many volumes of such Roman agricultural writers as Cato, Varro, and Columella speak to the high regard in which working the land was held. Columella's encyclopedic
De re rustica (On agriculture) opens by mocking the "leading men
of our state" who accepted the occasional "unfruitfulness of the
soil" as an inevitable part of nature's rhythms. The fault, he insisted, lay in human laziness. "I do not believe," he wrote, "that
such misfortunes come upon us as a result of the fury of the elements, but rather because of our own fault." It was against ignorance and slothfulness that classical agricultural knowledge pitted
itself, and the most esteemed Roman was he who worked his land
scientifically, intelligently, and manfully. In the words of the con-
summate statesman Cicero, "Of all the occupations by which gain
is secured, none is better than agriculture, none more profitable,
none more delightful, none more becoming to a freeman."

On the other hand, there have also been people for whom
work was the necessary evil of a fallen world in which nature had
been altered from its original pure state, obviously for the worse.
The Bible, for instance, is no great friend to agriculture, empha-
sizing instead the sinfulness that made labor necessary in the first
place. "Cursed is the ground because of you," God admonishes
Adam as he banishes him from Eden. According to Genesis, the
earth emerged from the days of creation covered in perpetually

ripe fruit trees and vegetation that needed only the barest minimum of tilling. One bite of the forbidden fruit and the landscape changed forever—and not for the better. From the moment of his exile, Adam had to work for his food, and it was no longer a matter of plucking fruit from trees or harvesting vegetables from the earth: "By the sweat of your face you shall eat bread," were God's exact words. Neither divinely created nor naturally occurring, bread is the Bible's food of exile, work, and struggle. It makes sense that the Hebrew word for bread, *lechem,* should be related to the word for war, *milchamah.* To feed oneself in a hostile postlapsarian world is a constant battle.

Still other people were afraid of agriculture. Pagans all over northern Europe, including the Celtic and Germanic peoples, venerated groves of trees as sacred—think of Merlin prophesying in his apple orchard or the northern origin of our Christmas trees—and since agriculture required the felling of those sacred forests, not to mention the plowing of the earth, it was viewed with deep fear and suspicion. One of the four great seasonal festivals in the Celtic year, Lughnasa, commemorated the beloved goddess of the earth and grain who cleared the land so that agriculture could come to Ireland and died of exhaustion in the process. For this reason, says H. E. Jacob in his book *Six Thousand Years of Bread,* "when [northern Europeans] tilled the soil, they did so with a bad conscience."[2]

These three distinct views converged when the Romans traveled from the land of the Bible, bringing their Mediterranean ideas, foods, and words to points as far north as Germany and as far west as Britain. We've already seen how they viewed the "barbarians"—as barely human milk drinkers and meat eaters who knew nothing of agriculture. Obviously, the northern peoples had a lot to learn from the Romans, and when they failed to heed their advice, they paid the price.

After the Romans abandoned Britain in the fifth century, their agricultural treatises were no longer studied, nor were their practices continued, and the Dark Ages that followed were consequently punctuated by frequent outbreaks of what was then known as St. Anthony's Fire, a disease in which victims suffered from hallucinations, insanity, vomiting, and gangrene of the hands and feet due to the constriction of blood flow to the extremities. Those afflicted felt as if they were being burned at the stake as their fingers and toes split open and dropped off, one by one. A late medieval chronicler wrote of an "invisible fire that separated the flesh from the bones and consumed it."[3] Today we know the disease by the name of ergotism or ergotoxicosis and understand that it is caused by the *Claviceps purpurea* fungus known as ergot, which affects rye, turning the predominantly northern grain black, waxy, and deceptively sweet-tasting. Ignorant of the results of ingesting the fungus, medieval northern Europeans threshed, ground, baked, and ate the grain that any naked eye could have seen looked different from what it was supposed to.[4] As early as the first century of the Common Era, though, Columella had already known of and described the fungus and warned against it. Because his work was no longer read, much less available, more than forty thousand northern Europeans died of ergotoxicosis in a single year—a steep price to pay for having been unable to consult those classical treatises and reference works.

Despite their later agricultural inferiority, those hardy northerners did have two advantages over the Romans early on. Their land grew grain easily and they were beer drinkers. It's entirely possible that the sophisticated Mediterranean people learned a thing or two about bread making from the barbarians they sought to subdue when they fought their way into Britain. Archaeological evidence shows that even before the Romans set foot on the island, the Celts already had clay domes in which they parched their grain and baked their bread, and rotary hand querns were used as early as the first century BC. The Celts even seem to have known how to leaven their bread with the yeasty froth that rises to the top of beer. Called *barm,* that froth was the primary way bread was leavened from before the start of the Iron Age (c. 800 BC) until as recently as the nineteenth century. Like other fermented foods—yogurt, for instance—leavened bread probably owes its existence to a fortuitous accident of antiquity. It may have happened in this way.

On a particularly warm day many hundreds, if not thousands, of years ago, an absentminded baker left some uncooked dough lying in the sun, perhaps to visit a nearby brewery. While he was quenching his thirst, the invisible yeast spores circulating in the air were attracted to the sugars in the wheat he'd used to make the dough and hungrily set to work digesting them, giving off as a waste product carbon dioxide bubbles that caused the warm wet mass to rise. The baker returned, saw the now swollen bubble-ridden dough, decided he had nothing to lose, and so baked it. To his surprised delight, the resulting golden-brown towering loaf not only tasted lighter but was more easily digested than the unfermented patty cakes he'd been baking since he'd entered his trade. Convinced he was onto something big, he tried to replicate what nature had taught him: perhaps he deliberately left future masses of dough to rest in sunny spots, perhaps he kneaded a bit of old dough into the new mixture, or perhaps he put two and two together and added the foamy barm which was so readily available at the brewery where he'd gone to quench his thirst. It's very likely that he recognized the close relationship between bubbling bread doughs and frothy brews.

Where did this absentminded baker live? Clearly in a beer-drinking land—perhaps Egypt, where clay figurines of women kneading bread and brewing beer were placed in the tombs of the pharaohs to ensure that the deceased royalty wouldn't go hungry in the afterlife. Or perhaps he lived in one of the beer-drinking barbarian lands of northern or western Europe, where leavened bread would have been seen as the happy collaboration between human labor and the natural forces of fermentation.

By contrast, wine, the drink of the Mediterranean, produces no barmy froth and could never have leavened much of anything. The Romans couldn't have known about the leavening powers of barm except through contact with beer-drinking people. As early as the first century, Pliny the Elder had commented that bread made in the barbarian lands was lighter than that baked elsewhere, and modern culinary historians often note that in the case of risen bread, it was the barbarians who had a thing or two to teach the Romans: "The Celts of Gaul and Spain deliberately encouraged fermentation by adding beer barm to their dough, so that they had a lighter bread than the Greeks and Romans; and we may believe that the Celts in Britain did the same"; "ultimately, the Romans did borrow the use of ale-barm or brewers' yeast . . . from subjected Germanic tribes."[5]

For more than two thousand years we've taken the Romans at their word and believed it was they who brought their superior technology to the barbarians. Certainly our fruits and vegetables wouldn't be what they are today had it not been for Roman agriculture, and our cheese owes quite a lot as well to their dairying techniques. In the case of bread, however, the situation isn't as clear-cut.

ON *PANIS, HLAFEN, AND BREAD*

Those northern barbarians might not have been the simple brutish and carnivorous hunter-gatherers the Latin writers were so fond of disparaging. Even Tacitus conceded that although they didn't plant orchards or irrigate gardens, they did demand their soil "produce a corn-crop" (that is, grain, not the corn that we Americans typically think of, which is maize introduced from the New World). Apparently they actually knew a thing or two about working the land and they don't seem to have been as eager to adapt new words and customs as their invaders could have wished. Despite the Roman historian's insistence that "instead of loathing the Latin language, they became eager to speak it effectively," after almost five hundred years of occupation, very few words stuck. The Celtic word for bread, for instance, hasn't changed at all over the centuries: it was *bara* then and it's *bara* to this day, as in the famous Welsh fruit bread still called *bara brith*. The word that ultimately replaced it on the island wasn't Latin at all, but the Germanic one that came over with the Angles and Saxons. Our contemporary English word for *bread,* thus, has no relationship whatsoever to the Latin *panis,* or for that matter to any of the modern bread words in the languages spoken by other peoples the Romans conquered. The French eat their *pain,* the Spanish *pan,* the Italians *pane,* and the Romanians *paine,* but the English insist on *bread*.

The Germans and the Dutch have similar names for their loaves—*Brot* and *brood*—but that's where the relationship ends. Northern through and through, the Germans store their bread and other essentials in a *Speisekammer,* work for *Gesellschaften,* and share their meals with *Freunden*. In English, though, we store our bread in a French *pan*try, work for com*pan*ies, and sit down to eat with com*pan*ions, literally, those with whom we break bread. In each case the *pan* reveals that the word in question entered the language with the French-speaking Norman conquerors, who called their staff of life *pain,* which had clearly evolved from the Latin *panis*. In Britain, though, neither *panis* nor *pain* had much staying power. *Bread*—the word, that is—has thus changed remarkably little over the centuries and is instantly recognizable in works written more than a millennium ago.

Yet although our modern word echoes the language of the Germanic peoples who inhabited the island, hunted for game, foraged for roots and weeds, and worshipped the Nordic gods of the wind and storms, the word used more often in Anglo-Saxon England was *hlaf*, the ancestor of our *loaf*, a word that has no equivalent in any of the Romance languages. In a seventh-century translation of Genesis, for instance, God told Adam that in the sweat of his brow he would *þinne hlaf etan,* "eat thine loaf." Seven hundred years later, *hlaf* had transmogrified into bread and the same passage appears as *In swoot of thi cheer thou schalt ete thi breed.* Somewhere in between the two translations, *hlaf* was replaced by *bread,* which had originally referred to a piece broken off from a whole loaf. This shift occurred at the same time that *flesh* was replaced by *meat*, in the centuries immediately following the Norman Conquest.

The two situations are similar. Generally speaking, when a new word entered the English language, it was the case of a French counterparts' taking over a native Germanic word. That's why today's Lord's Prayer asks God to forgive us our trespasses (from the French *trespasser*), whereas a thousand years ago, it was our *gyltas* (from the Germanic *gieldan*) we sought pardon for. In the same prayer still intoned the world over, however, *hlaf* was replaced not by *pain* but by *bread*. We don't ask for our daily loaves, but our "daily bread." Even though the substitution required a shift in meaning, English speakers seemed to prefer recycling their old words to relegating them to the dustbin of history. Perhaps they were too fond of those words to replace them so summarily. Perhaps those words reflected their speakers' attitudes, values, and preferences, just as *bacalhau* does the Portuguese love of salt cod. Perhaps *pain* and *bread* are not as synonymous as one might think.

To the Romans, *panis* was the child of the soil that they worked to produce grain. They derived their word from the same

Proto-Indo-European root that gave them *pastus,* pasture or field. We've already seen how the Romans felt about farming and agriculture: according to Cicero, working the land was what men were put on this earth to do. Bread fit into this model perfectly: it simply wouldn't exist without the work needed to produce it.

But in the north, bread words had different histories and evoked different attitudes. Most linguists trace our modern word back to the ancient *bhreue,* which encompassed the actions of *boiling, bubbling,* and *burning.* It's from this root that we derive many of our cooking terms—brew, broth, broil, and braise, for instance. *To breed* is a similarly related term, by the way, as are *breast* and *brisket,* all things that, when you think about it, increase in size or bubble up.[6] *Hlaf* was similarly effervescent, deriving from the Old English *hlifian,* "to rise high," "to tower"—which is exactly what wet doughy masses will do when yeast digests their carbohydrates and emits carbon dioxide. Both northern words were far more closely related to the natural processes of bubbling and fermenting than they were to any amber fields of grain waiting to be tilled.

The Latin word reflects its home in the Mediterranean; the Germanic ones their colder northern climate. The one derives from the earthiness of the pasture; the others suggest airy effervescence. The one stresses the human activity of the agriculturalist; the others point to forces that were seen as either natural or divine (since the two were scarcely distinguished until fairly recently, the distinction hardly matters). To the Romans, bread was first and foremost a manufactured *product*; in the north, it was primarily a natural *process.*

"I AM THE LIVING BREAD THAT CAME DOWN FROM HEAVEN"

The food historian Massimo Montanari has commented on the Mediterranean preference for nurture over nature. "The key factor," he concluded, "was the capacity to 'construct' one's food by domesticating and overcoming nature [which] in the Greco-Roman world, had a rather negative connotation."[7] Nature in all its wild glory wasn't something that was especially valued back then, and the Romans would have had a hard time understanding our contemporary fixation with getting "back to nature"—with all-natural vitamin and mineral supplements, cereals, iced teas, and even dog food. In the eyes of a true Roman, nature provided the raw materials to be shaped, controlled, transformed, and improved by hard-working civilized people. As far as food was concerned, the classical world thus distinguished between shepherds and farmers who diligently worked their land, and hunters and gatherers who merely lived off it. The former improved; the latter subsisted. In fact, the Greeks so identified manliness with agricultural skill that Homer could use the term "bread eaters" as a synonym for people in general: on his journey home from Troy, Odysseus "sent companions ahead, telling them to find out what men, eaters of bread, might live here in this country." By extension, those who didn't eat bread were considered to be more beasts than men. In Odysseus's world, what you ate defined who you were: the lotus eaters literally ate themselves into oblivion, the brutish Cyclops almost ate Odysseus, but only civilized people ate bread.

Like the Greeks before them, the Romans distinguished their bread from the foraged wild plant foods of non-Romans, whether Germanic, Celtic, or Numidian. Grain emerged from the fields, but it was their job to tend those fields, and it was by taming, controlling, and overcoming nature that they *produced*, rather than *found,* their food. Bread was thus not only an indispensable food-stuff but also a symbol of Roman superiority to the rest of the known world. Its evolution mirrored the progress of Rome itself. When it was no more than a minor city-state, Rome had eaten a porridge of parched cereals called *puls,* later renamed *pulmentum,* the ancestor of today's *polenta.* "It does not sound like particularly inspiring food," wrote Waverley Root in *The Food of Italy,* "but on it the Roman Legions conquered the world."[8] Gradually *pulmentum* became *maza,* a thick barley flatbread; still later, in the hands of trained bakers, *maza* was replaced by *panis,* which today we would recognize as leavened wheaten bread. By the time of Caesar Augustus and the vast empire over which he ruled at the dawn of the Common Era, 329 bakeries were in operation in Rome alone. Despite the enormous variety of breads, ranging from fine wheat loaves for the wealthy to coarse barley ones for the multitudes, purists insisted that no leavened bread be given as a sacrificial offering to the gods. Cato the Elder went so far as to provide a recipe for *libum,* the officially approved sacrificial bread, specifying that it be made with no more than a pound of flour, two pounds of cheese, and an egg. However tasty the Romans found their leavened bread, they viewed the fermentation required to produce it as an impurity. Among ancient peoples, as we'll see, they were hardly unique in this belief.

What kind of bread was it, then, that Jesus had in mind when he burst onto the scene not all that long after, announcing to the

Libum

Bray 2 pounds of cheese thoroughly in a mortar; when it is thoroughly macerated, add 1 pound of wheat flour, or, if you wish the cake to be more dainty, ½ pound of fine flour, and mix thoroughly with the cheese. Add 1 egg, and work the whole well. Pat out a loaf, place on leaves, and bake slowly on a warm hearth under a crock.[9]

world, "I am the living bread that came down from heaven. Whoever eats of this bread will live forever"? From the moment of his birth, this new god was associated with bread. Bethlehem, the city where he was born, means "house of bread." Combining in himself the human and the divine, he promised an end to the fallen world in which bread had to be procured by the sweat of one's brow, and he even managed to miraculously feed five thousand men (not to mention assorted women and children) with a mere five loaves of bread and a few fishes. The most casual reader of the New Testament can't help but notice how often Jesus likens himself to bread, feeds the crowds with bread, refers to sowing, reaping, and threshing, and uses the images of grain, wheat, and yeast in his parables. The end of time is the separation of wheat from chaff, and the kingdom of heaven is a field sown with good seed and weeds. "At harvest time," Jesus explains to his followers, "I will tell the reapers, Collect the weeds first and bind them in bundles to be burned, but gather the wheat into my barn" (Matthew 13:30).

Wheat and weeds are easy. The former is good and the latter bad. But what about yeast? Is it the spiritual, sacred, and divine ingredient in bread or, on the other hand, the agent of betrayal, corruption, and putrefaction? On this point, Jesus was less clear. Sometimes he told his disciples that "the kingdom of heaven is like yeast that a woman took and mixed in with three measures of flour until all of it was leavened" (Matthew 13:33). Invisible yet capable of transforming this world of exile into one of spiritual fulfillment, the kingdom of heaven was quite a lot like yeast, which, unseen by the naked eye, similarly aerates a stodgy mass into a beautifully risen loaf. At other times, though, Jesus wasn't too fond of fermentation, likening yeast to the teachings of the Pharisees and Sadducees he so often accused of corruption and hypocrisy. In these instances, yeast resembles nothing so much as a lot of hot air, and the authorities nothing so much as a bunch of gasbags.

> When the disciples reached the other side, they had for-
> gotten to bring any bread. Jesus said to them, "Watch
> out and beware of the yeast of the Pharisees and Saddu-
> cees." . . . Then they understood that he had not told
> them to beware of the yeast of bread, but of the teaching
> of the Pharisees and Sadducees. (Matthew 16:5–12).

Born Jewish, Jesus would have known the Old Testament's
strict prohibitions against leavening in the grain offerings that
were to be provided for God: "No grain offering that you bring
to the Lord shall be made with leaven" (Leviticus 2:11). Anything devoted to the Lord, whether animal, vegetable, or even
officiating priest, had to be perfect of its kind, and perfect was
understood to be exactly what God intended from the moment
of creation when he pronounced all that he had made good.
What kind of god would accept anything less than good? What
kind of god would be pleased by a rotten offering? And what is
leavening but a form of fermentation, which is just a euphemism,
after all, for decomposition—for rotting? Risen bread was bread
that had been changed from its original good state; leavening,
therefore, was as unacceptable an offering as rancid milk or a
maimed animal would have been. No bread is ever entirely natural, but one can at least insist that the loaves offered to God be
unfermented—sort of like the manna that God had caused to
rain down from the heavens, which the Bible describes as "like
wafers made with honey."

From both the Jewish and Roman perspectives, then, Jesus
was far more likely to have had the unleavened variety in mind
when he told his followers, "I am the bread of life."

Ancient peoples had very definite ideas about bread and leavening, but those ideas varied from location to location, just as
the substance itself did. Jesus' bread of life would have been as

different from a Germanic *hlaf,* as the Bedouin barley bread called *fatir* is from a German rye *Vollkornbrot.* When the new religion left the land of its birth where leavened bread was hailed as a triumph of human civilization but also as unfit for divine consumption, it voyaged to a northern land where *hlafen* were understood to be the result of natural—perhaps even divine—processes. Obviously there was bound to be friction. The Latin-speaking Christians told the hardy barbarians that if they ate the body of the bread god, they would see the light, become civilized men, and live forever. Like both the Jews and the Romans before them, the Christians were never entirely comfortable with leavened bread. The *panis* they ate for their eucharistic meal was in memory of the unleavened bread which Jesus had shared with his followers at the Last Supper, but because the Last Supper took place during the Festival of Unleavened Bread (today called Passover), the bread was necessarily flat. The hitch was that the northerners had bread of their own—*hlaf*—that was airy and effervescent and had nothing to do with manna, a Mediterranean Son of God, or a Festival of Unleavened Bread.

LOAF MASS?

"Clean out the old yeast so that you may be a new batch, as you really are unleavened," the Angles and Saxons were enjoined by the Christian missionaries. "Let us celebrate, not with the old yeast, the yeast of malice and evil, but with the unleavened bread of sincerity and truth" (1 Corinthians 5:6–8). Such a message would have fallen on the uncomprehending ears of people who had nothing whatsoever against leavening. Then as now, Germanic peoples were big beer drinkers and bread eaters, with distinct names for their loaves: in addition to *hlafen,* they had *peorfe,* or "low" bread, a term that clearly wouldn't have been needed if the unleavened variety had been the only bread they knew. In fact, the masters and mistresses of Anglo-Saxon manors even derived their titles from bread: *hlafweard* and *hlafdige,* the Old English ancestors of our lord and lady, literally, "loaf ward" and "loaf kneader."

The Germanic tribes didn't need the Christians to tell them about the wonders of bread. No one did. For as long as bread has been eaten, there have been gods and goddesses of grain: Egypt had Ab, the Greeks and Romans had Demeter and Ceres, and the Nordic peoples had their own goddess of the grain, Sif, the golden-haired wife of the thunder god Thor. Like the rest of the ancient world, the Germanic people celebrated the grain harvest as well, although it was after they invaded Britain that they began to observe a new holiday of which no previous record exists. Most historians believe that this new holiday was an adaptation of the Celtic festival of Lughnasa. Celebrated on August 1, Lughnasa, one of the four seasonal festivals of the Celtic year, marked the beginning of the grain harvest. It derived its name from the god Lugh, who, according to legend, instituted a funeral feast in honor of his foster-mother, the goddess of grain. The new Germanic holiday was also celebrated on August 1, although it was known as *Hlafmæsse,* or Loaf Mass. At first *Hlafmæsse*—or Lammas, as it gradually came to be abbreviated—was dedicated to pagan gods, but after they were converted to Christianity, the Germanic people easily enough shifted their veneration to the new deity and the holiday was observed throughout the Middle Ages; in the *Anglo-Saxon Chronicle,* it's referred to as the Feast of First Fruits. A Celtic agricultural festival before it was a Germanic holiday, Lammas became a Christian holy day, with Roman bread traditions grafted upon northern ones. Thus ripe grain was reaped and baked into a loaf which was blessed with Anglo-Saxon charms and then consecrated in a Roman church.

In the southern part of Spain stands a building commonly known as the Mezquita, Spanish for mosque. Today it is the

Cathedral of Córdoba—its official name, since the early thirteenth century, has been the Cathedral of Saint Mary of the Assumption—but as its popular name reveals, the building was designed by Islamic architects who built it as a mosque in the eighth century. The Islamic builders had no need to dig a foundation, though; one had already been dug by the Visigoths in the fifth century when they erected their church, called Saint Vincent of Saragossa. Even earlier, the site had been home to a Roman temple, fragments of which can still be seen in the more than one thousand columns of jasper, onyx, marble, and granite. As far as architecture is concerned, it has always been easier to accommodate and adapt than to raze to the ground and begin anew. The same can be said of religious beliefs and practices. What the Christians did with the religious customs they found in Britain is not all that different from what they did with the buildings they found in Spain. They adapted. Germanic holidays that were themselves built on Celtic foundations were Christianized, but as with the Mezquita of Córdoba, bits and pieces of the past can still be seen.

When Augustine, the future bishop of Canterbury, arrived in Britain in the year 597 to spearhead Pope Gregory's campaign of converting the northern heathens, he met with local bishops "at a place still known to the English as Augustine's Oak, which lies on the borders of the kingdoms of the Hwicce and the West Saxons."[10] He insisted upon conformity to Roman customs in essential matters, admitting, however, that "I am ready to countenance all your other customs, although they are contrary to our own." Thus Easter was henceforth celebrated in England according to the Roman calendar, but kept its native name, even though derived from the pagan goddess of the dawn, Eostre, to whom spring festivals had been dedicated in pre-Christian times.

Northern bread rituals were also "contrary to our own" customs and similarly required a compromise. Almost ten years after

Augustine met with the Celtic and English bishops at the oak tree, the pope was forced to send another emissary to "Romanize" the recalcitrant northerners, after which it was agreed that all bishops of the newly established church in England would meet annually under a central authority, obviously Roman. The date chosen was the day on which both Anglo-Saxons and Celts already gathered, August 1, marking as it did both Lughnasa and Lammas. Rather than outlawing or rejecting an originally pagan ritual, the Church appropriated it for its own purposes, reasoning that whether it's called *bara, hlaf, brot,* or *panis*, bread is a divine gift, even if its recipients attribute it to the wrong deity in the wrong way.

It's not entirely clear, though, which sort of bread the English church used to celebrate its eucharistic meals. Christianity had taken root in Britain centuries before Augustine's meeting with the bishops at the oak tree; otherwise there wouldn't have been any observances to have been deemed "at variance with the universal practice of the Church." Every reference to bread in the Old English gospels uses *hlaf,* the common term for the risen variety; nowhere does *peorfe,* "low bread," appear. Evidence certainly seems to suggest that the English church might have been using the risen bread northerners preferred, even though it had been viewed suspiciously for so long in the Mediterranean.

In fact it's not even all that clear what sort of bread Jesus wanted his followers to eat in memory of him. In three of the accounts of the Last Supper, Jesus and his disciples were celebrating the first night of the Festival of Unleavened Bread—during which anything fermented was strictly forbidden—and so it would have been unleavened bread he held up when he announced, "Take, eat; this is my body." According to this version of the story, Jesus couldn't possibly have held up a risen loaf. On the other hand, John's gospel tells the story differently. It wasn't during a Passover celebration that Jesus bid his followers "eat the living bread," and there's no compelling reason therefore it had to be flat. To this day, the Eastern Orthodox Church, which has always accepted John's chronology, does not require that its eucharistic offering be the dry wafer that Rome has traditionally insisted upon.

The question of which bread to use has long been a sticking point between the Western and Eastern churches, and there have been times when the question has mobilized people into warring camps. In eleventh-century Constantinople, for instance, those in favor of yeasted bread were known as "prozymites," and those opposed, "azymites" (*zymi* is Greek for leavening). The situation became so heated that in the year 1053, the Roman churches were closed, their monks expelled, and their unleavened but already consecrated Host unceremoniously trampled upon. Soon after, a leader of the Eastern church addressed a letter to the horrified Western bishops in which he argued that only leavened bread— *artos* in Greek—has the power "to elevate us from the earth to heaven as the leaven raises and warms the bread." He continued: "You call bread *panis*; we call it *artos*. This from *airoel* (*airo*), to raise, signifies a something elevated, lifted up, being raised and warmed by the ferment and salt; the *azym*, on the other hand, is lifeless as a stone or baked clay, fit only to symbolize affliction and suffering."[11]

In all likelihood, the etymology of the Greek *artos* from *airoel* was wishful thinking on the part of the Eastern bishop; authoritative sources state matter-of-factly that the history of the Greek word is unknown. But the bishop truly believed that "the living bread that came down from heaven" could have been nothing but a risen loaf. In this, he's no different from traditional Greek women, who to this day insist that "only the direct power of God can turn a mere flour batter into a leavening medium."[12] They thus mix their sourdough starters—called *prozymi*—on two specific days of the year: September 14, the date on which the Orthodox

Church celebrates the discovery of the crucifix; and the day before Easter, which marks Christ's ascension into heaven.

PAIN PERDU

The eleventh century marked not only the Great Schism that separated the Roman and Eastern churches but also the Norman Conquest of England. In fact, the two events were a mere twelve years apart and both had a consequence as far as bread is concerned.

The wine-drinking and fruit-eating Normans looked down on the beer-drinking, fruit-deprived Anglo-Saxons every bit as much as the Romans had looked down on the island's inhabitants a thousand years earlier, and they went to great lengths to procure the foodstuffs they needed to prepare their elaborate dishes rather than making do with mushy *porrays* and the occasional spit-roasted joint. A vast number of French names entered the English language, both for exotic new fruits, vegetables, and spices and for indigenous foods that had been called by Germanic names for hundreds of years. It was shortly after the Conquest that the older *hlaf* came to mean merely loaf, and that bread took on its modern meaning of risen wheaten loaves. We've never had an English form of *pain* though—other than in the antiquated *payndemayn* (from *pane dominis,* "the Lord's bread") or such derivative words as pantry, companion, and company. Despite their success in transforming the country and its language—not to mention its cuisine—the Normans were no more successful in getting their *pain* to take hold than the Romans had been with their *panis* a millennium earlier.

There have been many such times when a downtrodden people has refused to eat the bread of its oppressors. Who knows—maybe the Old Testament suspicions about leavened bread had more to do with the fact that the Egyptians—the Israelites' enslavers—were the acknowledged masters of leavening in the ancient world than they did with the belief that fermentation was a type of putrefaction? Throughout history, national solidarity has often been expressed in terms of food, and "bread rebellions" have been taking place from the time the Israelites fled their Egyptian taskmasters to the fateful day in prerevolutionary France when the people of Paris rioted for bread, eliciting the famously callous response from Marie Antoinette: "Let them eat cake" (her actual wording was "Let them eat brioche," but the point remains the same). Seen in this light, the Germanic people's refusal to adopt the *pain* of their conquerors takes on political overtones. Like the Spanish Jews who converted to Catholicism in name only in order to escape the Inquisition, the Anglo-Saxons converted to French cuisine in name only—or, to put the matter more precisely, in title only.

In the pages of our early cookbooks, thus, we find tarts and tartlets galore, but it was *bread* that chefs used to thicken their sauces and soups, as in a recipe for a saffron-colored, sweetly spiced soup that went by the French name of *tredure,* from *très dorée,* "very golden."

Tredure

Take brede and grate it; make a lyre of rawe ayren and do þerto saffroun and powdour douce, and lye it up with gode broth, and make it as a cawdel. And do þerto a lytel verious.

Tredure

Take bread and grate it. Make a thickener of raw eggs and add saffron and sweet spices. And use it to thicken up good broth and make it as a soup. Add a little verjuice.[13]

The story of one of our favorite contemporary breakfast dishes—known to us as french toast, though it's had many other names over the course of history—is illuminating in this context. No one quite knows when or where the dish originated. In Apicius's first-century *De re coquinaria*, there's a recipe for a sweet dish—called, simply, "Another Sweet Dish"—in which bread is broken into large pieces, soaked in milk and beaten eggs, fried in oil, and covered with honey. For all we know, resourceful cooks had been soaking their dry bread in some sort of liquid since they first discovered how to bake bread. After all, it's going to go stale sooner or later, and since thrift is the mother of invention, as they say, cooks have found many ways to turn their dried-out bread to good use. Sometimes they'd grate it into soups as a thickening agent; in fact, originally *soup* didn't refer to broth, but to the *sop* of bread soaking at the bottom of the bowl. Or they'd add bits of dry bread to such salads as Italy's *panzanella* or the Middle Eastern *fattoush,* not unlike the way we sprinkle our salads with croutons.

Another way to use up old bread is to soak it in some sort of liquid and fry it up in the manner of Apicius; the bread, the liquid, and the flavorings may change according to location, but the resulting dish is still something we'd recognize as french toast. In India, for instance, where they call it Bombay or masala toast, they dunk their bread into a mixture of eggs, milk, salt, green chili, and onion, and then deep fry it in butter or oil. In Spain, *torrijas* are made by soaking thick slices of bread in milk or wine, dipping them in egg, frying them, and then serving them with spiced honey. In Germany, *Arme Ritter,* "Poor Knights," are made from old bread that's been soaked in egg, coated with bread crumbs, fried in butter, and served with sautéed apple slices or plum jam; when the bread is soaked in wine instead of milk, the dish is called *Versoffene Jungfern oder Ritter,* "Drunken Maidens or Knights."

A similarly alcoholic version in England is known as "Poor Knights of Windsor," although the dish has gone by many other names over the centuries. In *The Forme of Cury*, we find a recipe for something called *Paynfoundew,* French for *melted bread.* Closer to a bread pudding than to what we serve today for breakfast, the stale bread was fried, soaked in red wine, ground to a paste with raisins and honey, bound with egg whites, boiled until firm, and then sliced, sprinkled with sugar and sweet spices, and browned in a hot oven. Such elaborate concoctions were, of course, the hallmark of Norman cuisine,

Paynfoundew

Take brede and frye it in grece oþer in oyle, take it up and lay it in rede wyne; grynde it with raisouns. Take hony and do it in a pot, and cast þerinne gleyre of ayren wiþ a litel water, and bete it wele togider with a sklyse. Set it ouere the fire and boile it, and whan the hatte arisith to goon ouere, take it adoun and kele it; whan hit is almost colde, take of þe wyte wyt a sclyse. And whan it is þes clarified, do it to the oþere, with sugur and spices; salt it and loke it be stondyng. Florissh it with white coliaundre in confyt.

Melted Bread

Take bread and fry it in grease or oil. Take it and lay it in red wine, grind it with raisins. Take honey and put it in a pot and add to it egg whites with a little water. Beat it well together with a spatula [or other stirring utensil]. Set it over the fire and boil it and when the bubbles arise, take it off the heat and let it cool. When it is almost cold, stir the whites with a spatula. And when it is clarified, add it to the other, along with sugar and spices. Salt it and make sure it's thick. Garnish it with candied white coriander seeds.[14]

as was the liberal use of raisins, saffron, *powdour douce,* and wine. None of these ingredients featured in Anglo-Saxon cooking, and so it's entirely to be expected that the dish would boast a French name.

As the dish evolved, it began to look less like a pudding and more like our modern breakfast special. Slices of bread were soaked—rather than grated—in liquid, fried in butter, and sprinkled with sugar; and the resulting dish was renamed *Payn Purdew,* or "lost bread," the "lost" alluding either to the bread's getting lost in the beaten eggs or, perhaps, to the leftover, or "lost," bits of bread that went into the recipe.

Payn pur~dew

Take fayre yolkys of Eyroun, & trye hem fro þe white, & draw hem þorw a straynoure, & take Salt and caste þer-to; þan take fayre brede, & kytte it as trounde rounde; þan take fayre Boter þat is claryfiyd, or ellys fayre Freysshe grece, & putte it on a potte, & make it hote; þan take & wete wyl þin troundes in þe yolkys, & putte hem in þe panne, an so frye hem uppe; but ware of cleuyng to the panne; & whan it is fryid, ley hem on a dysshe, & ley Sugre y-nowe þer-on, & þane serve it forth.

Lost Bread

Take egg yolks and separate them from the whites & draw them through a sieve. Add salt. Cut bread into rounds, then put either clarified butter or fresh oil in a pan and heat it. Soak the slices of bread in the yolks and fry them in the pan; be careful that they don't stick to the pan. When they are fried, lay them on a dish and sprinkle with enough sugar and then serve it forth.[15]

It was in Robert May's 1660 *The Accomplisht Cook, or, The Art & Mystery of Cookery* that french toast first received its name, no doubt because the bread often specified for the dish was the French wheat loaf known as a *manchet*.

French Toasts

Cut French Bread, and toast it in pretty thick toasts on a clean gridiron, and serve them steeped in claret, sack, or any wine, with sugar and juice of orange.[16]

Regardless of whether it was called *paynfoundew, payn purdew*, panperdy, as it was sometimes spelled, or French toast, the name of the dish has always had something French about it, even though the main ingredient has invariably been called for by its old Germanic name of *bread*. It was only in the United States that, for a short time, the dish lost its gallic connection, when Mary J. Lincoln included a recipe she called "Egg Toast, or Bread Sautéd" in her 1871 *Boston Cook Book*. She added a note of explanation: "It is called French, Spanish, German, and Nun's Toast; but Egg Toast seems to best indicate the character of the dish."[17]

Why, then, don't we serve *egg toast* to our families on leisurely Sunday mornings and why haven't Poor Knights or German toast ever featured on breakfast menus across the country? For the same reason that master chefs from the time of King Richard to that of Queen Victoria have called their stale bread concoctions *paynfoundew, payn per-dew, payn purdeuz*, or *panperdy*: because we think that anything French sounds better than anything English. Even though we Americans have vastly simplified the Norman version to suit our own tastes, replacing the clarified honey with maple syrup, and dispensing with the candied coriander seeds altogether, there's still something we find mysteriously evocative about french toast—or, even better, *pain perdu*—that all the straightforwardly named egg toasts in the world can never hope to match. Even when the House of Representatives, in a fit of pique, insisted on removing French toast from the menu, they never considered calling the perennial breakfast favorite German toast.

PANIFICATION

All these centuries later, bread is still the "staff of life," the food for which millions of people the world over pray every day in the familiar Anglo-Saxon words, "Give us this day our daily bread." Not too many of us, though, still believe that bread is literally the gift of a benevolent god (or gods). Today, thanks to Louis Pasteur's mid-nineteenth-century researches, we know that the air is filled with wild yeast spores, which, under the right circumstances, will feed on floury paste, converting complex carbohydrate molecules into simple sugars and giving off carbon dioxide that causes the dough to expand with gas bubbles held together by the gluten in certain types of wheat. We understand the process of fermentation and realize that the ancient custom of keeping bake houses close to breweries would have created the perfect environment for the leavening process. Much of the mystery has been solved and we no longer believe, as less scientifically educated people did for nearly five thousand years, that—in the words of biologist and wild yeast expert Ed Wood— "something divine created the bubbles in dough and made the loaves grow bigger and bigger."

Today, in fact, there's not a whole lot we don't know about leavening. Even before Pasteur published his findings detailing the chemical changes that occur during fermentation, it was from the brewery that bakers had traditionally gotten the yeast—or barm—they used to leaven their dough. Early household manuals generally followed their descriptions of home brewing with discussions of baking. In his 1615 book *The English Housewife,* Gervase Markham combined the two into one chapter: "Of the office of the brew-house, and the bake-house, and the necessary things belonging to the same."[18] Hannah Glasse advised her readers to leaven their home-baked breads with "a Pint and half of good Ale-yeast not bitter." And in his 1852 *Plain Cookery Book for the Working Classes,* Charles Elmé Francatelli similarly instructed home bakers to "put a bushel of flour into a trough, or a large pan; with your fist make a deep hole in the centre thereof; put a pint of good fresh yeast into this hollow."[19]

But there were two problems with the traditional reliance on what Francatelli clearly, if unpoetically, called the "scum" that rises to the surface of beer. First, in the words of Mrs. Beeton, "it is very bitter and, on that account, should be well washed." Second, it was inconsistent. Sometimes the dough rose, but other times it didn't. Bakers must have been delighted when a new form of yeast appeared on the market in the mid-nineteenth century, just about the time that Pasteur was publishing his findings. "The German yeast . . . is never bitter; it is therefore a valuable substitute for our own beer yeast," extolled Eliza Acton in her 1845 *Modern Cookery for Private Families.* As she noted in her *English Bread Book,* it also "ferments very easily." This was important. What home baker even today hasn't been frustrated by those capricious, stubborn, and invisible microorganisms that seem to obey a logic of their own? Who hasn't tried to jump-start the leavening process by adding organic grapes to their starters— or potatoes, cumin, or other ingredients touted as fermentation boosters? The food writer John Thorne tried almost everything and was almost brought to his knees. "In try after try," he confessed in "An Artisanal Loaf," "I activated starters with a chronic inability to leaven, producing, one after the other, flattish, dense, unappetizing loaves, no matter how much time they were allowed to proof."[20] Every honest bread baker who opts for natural leavening—instead of relying on the far more predictable active dry yeast marketed by Fleischmann's, Red Star, and the like—is sooner or later forced to admit to a degree of uncertainty and lack of control over the leavening process. Which is why so many bakers began using the new German yeast when it became available for home use in the 1860s. Scientists had discovered how to keep dormant yeast cells alive in a state of suspended animation at about forty degrees Fahrenheit; when released into the right temperature and environment, the yeast cells sprang hungrily into action. All of a sudden, baking became more controlled and reliable. For the first time in human history, consistent results were all but guaranteed.

At the same time that the baking process was more thoroughly understood and controlled than ever before, a new word entered the English vocabulary. Obviously borrowed from the French, it was as distant from the barmy breweries of yore as *pain* was from *bread*. Panification, as the process came to be known, was bread baking for the intelligent, the sophisticated, and the refined. "A general impression seems to exist amongst the intelligent orders of society," wrote Eliza Acton in her *English Bread Book,* "of the absolute necessity of a thorough reform in the old methods of 'panification,' or bread-making." Like the *panis* of the Roman conquerors and the *pain* of the Normans, panification was bread baking gone scientific, and for a while it was hailed as the way of the future.

The scientific technology and terminology went hand in glove with a new invention that promised to forever transform the way bread was produced. Hailed as a "revolution in the baking trade," the Appareil-Rolland was a kneading apparatus and oven rolled into one, the progenitor of today's bread machines. Conceived of on the Continent, the device was referred to by a French name and it seemed to mark the end of old-fashioned methods and labor-intensive kneading. *Bread baking* was far too outdated and germanic a term to describe the actions of this mechanical marvel. As Eliza Acton reported to her readers, "M. Rolland presented to the world a new and complete system of panification."[21] In one swift move, the scientifically named technique swept away the dusty old cobwebs of belief in the mysteries of bread. "See the blessed idea of Christian communion degraded into a mere act of divine panification!" wailed the conservative *Fraser's Magazine for Town and Country*.[22] Henceforth it was chemistry that was to rule the day. Acton went so far as to append a scientific report to her recipes for the benefit of her readers; it was titled "Chemistry Applied to Panification."

One of the most influential nineteenth-century panifiers of all was Dr. John Dauglish, a social reformer who earned his medical degree in Edinburgh and determined to use his scientific training to improve the disturbingly unhygienic process of bread baking, involving as it did potentially disease-causing bacteria, not to mention the dirty hands and sweat of the human kneader. The technique he patented in 1856 of producing risen loaves left nothing to the vagaries of natural fermentation, nor did it even require the human element. "Nothing but flour, water, a little salt and gas—no sweat!" In her *Book of Household Management*, Mrs. Beeton described the innovative new system implemented in the Aërated Bread Company that Dauglish incorporated in 1862: a precise weight of flour was deposited into a great iron ball, "common atmospheric air" was pumped out, and aerated water and carbonic acid gas pumped in (readers were assured that the dangerous-sounding carbonic acid gas was the source of the effervescence in the carbonated drinks they so enjoyed). Paddles began to knead and "it is not long before we have the dough, and very 'light' and nice it looks." The dough was then ejected into tins, which traveled down the "endless floor" of a vast oven, what today we would call a conveyer belt. "Done to a turn, the loaves emerge at the other end of the apartment—and the Aërated Bread is made." Nothing was left to chance. Some even claimed that the new aerated bread was not just easier to produce, but tastier and healthier than traditional coburgs, bloomers, farmhouse and cottage loaves. A scientific journal of the 1870s reported, "As to the perfect cleanliness of this mechanical process for making bread there can be no question; it is immeasurably superior to the barbarous and old, but as Dr. Richardson remarked, *not* 'time-honoured system of kneading dough by the hands and feet of the workman."[23]

The Continental Baking Company made similar claims in the 1920s when it introduced the product that was to permanently change the way Americans thought of bread: Wonder Bread. Advertised as completely lacking the air bubbles that resulted from natural fermentation and sold from the very start in its signature plastic bags festooned with the red, blue, and yellow balloons that inspired the company's vice president, Elmer Cline, to give the product its name, Wonder Bread was the first sliced loaf on the market. During World War II, the company enriched its dough with vitamins and minerals, all but eliminating such common diseases as beriberi and pellagra, which are caused by deficiencies of thiamine, niacin, and protein. When the value of dietary fiber was widely recognized, the company rose to the occasion once more, marketing new types of bread designed to give Americans both what they wanted—fluffy white loaves—and what they needed, dietary fiber. Thus was born Wonder's 100 percent whole-grain wheat bread for "White Bread fans," that "lets you have the soft, delicious taste you always loved about Wonder bread in a 100% whole grain bread." The company's motto says it all: "Go ahead and give 'em what they love—Wonder!"

Yet another revolution took place in the 1990s when the first bread machines for the modern home kitchen appeared on the U.S. market, having been introduced in Japan a decade earlier. Descended from the Appareil-Rolland and Dr. Dauglish's iron ball, bread machines are no more than metal boxes with stirring blades, timers, and heating elements. The ingredients are combined, allowed to rise for a set period at the right temperature, and then baked, all in the same compartment. The human element has only to measure ingredients (sometimes not even that if a premeasured bread machine mix is used), push a button on the control panel, and remove the bread when the cycle has run its course. No muss, no fuss, no sweat. The same results every time.

The box-shaped loaves taste the same every time too. And therein lies the problem. Somehow people just aren't happy with mechanized regularity when it comes to the staff of life. Despite the health-inducing claims of Dr. Dauglish's Aërated Bread and Elmer Cline's Wonder Bread and despite the undeniable convenience of bread machines, there have always been people who refuse to change their traditional ways and who long for the good old days of "natural leavening, slow by nature, [that] gives this more rustic loaf the time it needs to develop texture and flavor." The words are those of Nancy Silverton, founder of La Brea Bakery in Los Angeles. No rapid-rise instant yeast, bread machine, or panification for her, but instead a long slow process of natural fermentation that bakers must learn to accommodate themselves to rather than impose themselves on. In this regard, bread baking is not unlike childrearing: you have to feed the starter three times a day and watch over it "as a parent watches over a newborn." Most important, as new parents quickly realize, "If you try to be too controlling, the bread rebels." Unlike Dr. Dauglish and Elmer Cline, Silverton not only acknowledged but positively celebrated the time-consuming process that has resisted human control for millennia. Her recipe for a basic country white loaf takes up fifteen pages of her *Breads from La Brea Bakery*—not including the previous nine pages devoted to growing the starter needed to bake the loaf and the following five pages dedicated to "Making Your Own Bread Schedule"—fully justifying her claim that when at last you tear off a piece of the finished product, "You taste the time and sweat it took to make this loaf."[24]

As the twentieth century wound down, the reaction against panification, bread-baking technology, and rapid-rise dry active yeast grew stronger than ever and the vogue for artisanal loaves created enormous interest in traditional leavening processes. The finest breads were no longer the most sophisticated ones but the most natural ones, and the most accomplished bakers were not those who controlled every aspect but instead those who were willing to relinquish control and let nature follow its own course. "Why, then, would anyone prefer a natural leavening?" asked the food writer John Thorne.

> It might be argued that at the very center of the artisanal process is not so much insistence on fine ingredients nor mastery of any particular method, but rather a willingness to assume personal responsibility for the thing made. Paradoxically, this means surrendering control, for there can be no responsibility without risk of failure.[25]

Mastering a method versus surrendering control—we come full circle. Centuries ago it was the Romans who attempted to conquer both the barbarian world and nature itself, in both cases by taming, domesticating, overcoming, and subduing. They grafted wild fruit onto trees. They cultivated weeds into vegetables in their enclosed gardens. They transformed raw milk into cheese. They civilized meat eating. And they mastered the science of baking bread. Their *panis* was to evolve into some of the greatest culinary triumphs the world has ever known: French and Italian bread. Who hasn't stood before a *boulangerie* or a *panetteria*, greedily gazing at the *baguettes, michettes, pains de campagne, pains au levain, pains sur poolish,* and *pains de mie* or the *pane toscano, pane all'olio, schiacciatas, ciabattas,* and *focaccia*?

And yet we call them loaves of bread.

ABC: AËRATED BREAD COMPANY OR ACME BREAD COMPANY?

So the pendulum has swung and continues to swing between the Mediterranean and northern understanding of that most unnatural of foods. Because it can be made in so many different ways, it is. In the United States today, Wonder Bread, the child of panification, outsells all other sliced bread—or so claims its official Web site: "It's no surprise Wonder is America's favorite brand of white bread. So soft, so delicious, so fresh." *Consumer Reports'* top-rated Zojirushi bread machines bring Dr. Dauglish's panification technology into the home of anyone who wants fresh loaves without the fuss and bother of getting one's hands dirty.

And yet in 2004, the Interstate Bakeries Corporation (which had acquired the Continental Baking Company, maker of Wonder Bread, about a decade earlier) filed for bankruptcy. In August 2007 it announced that it would no longer make or sell bread in southern California, where buyers seemed to prefer whole-grain and other "premium" loaves. Not coincidentally, southern California has a lot of people who were raised eating tortillas instead of risen white bread and who continue to prefer them. "Tortillas are taking over for bread, I guess," is how one blogger responded to the closing of the factories that put more than thirteen hundred people out of work.[26]

Neither is it a coincidence that California—northern California, in this case—is home to the so-called bread revolution. Since the days of the 1849 Gold Rush, tourists have flocked to Fisherman's Wharf in San Francisco for two foods in particular: the chocolate created by the failed miner but hugely successful confectioner, Domingo Ghirardelli, who had emigrated from Italy via Uruguay and Peru; and sourdough bread. It was another immigrant similarly drawn to the Bay Area by dreams of sudden wealth, the Frenchman Isadore Boudin, who applied his traditional baking techniques to the loaves that fermented so easily in the region; scientists have even named the local wild yeast *Lactobacillus sanfranciscensis*. Thus was born the famous San Francisco sourdough loaves, a marriage of French tradition and American ingredients.

Fast forward more than a hundred years and the story repeats itself, albeit with a twist. A university student earning extra money as a busboy at Alice Waters's Chez Panisse, Steve Sullivan spent the summer of 1977 cycling through Europe. While in England, he bought a copy of Elizabeth David's newly published *English Bread and Yeast Cookery,* but it was the breads of Paris that he was determined to re-create when he returned home to California. Several years later, with the backing of the Doobie Brothers' guitarist Patrick Simmons, he opened the Acme Bread Company. Since its inception in 1983, Acme has leavened all its breads with a natural starter made with unsulfured Cabernet Sauvignon and Zinfandel grapes, a technique Sullivan learned while honeymooning with his wife in Provence. Although wine will never produce the frothy barm that beer does—as the Romans discovered so many centuries ago—the wild yeast on the skins of grapes turns out to be a big help in jump-starting the fermenting process. The rest is history. Acme Bread Company's success was instant and huge. Area restaurants advertised that their bread was supplied by Acme; three other locations soon opened, each producing more than sixty thousand loaves every week. Nancy Silverton dedicated her bread book to Steve Sullivan, and, in a nod to his technique, her instructions for a starter call for a pound of pesticide-free organically grown black or red grapes.

There are a number of ironies in Steve Sullivan's success story, just as there are in our attitude toward the loaves we eat. When it comes to bread we can't seem to make up our minds what to call things and we can't seem to decide what we're most comfortable with. That an American student should read an English bread book yet resolve to bake French bread seems a bit odd. That despite its "slight sour flavor characteristic of San Francisco sourdough," as a recent review has described Acme's specialty bread, it's sold as *pain au levain,* rather than sourdough bread, is also striking. That Sullivan's claims to fame are his *baguettes, bâtards, pains de mie,* and *croissants,* yet he nonetheless chose to call his business the Acme *Bread* Company is perhaps the most ironic of all.

We'll never give up our bread. When we're down and out, it's breadlines we stand on; we can't imagine doing without our bread and butter; we insist on knowing which side our bread is buttered on; we look up to the upper crust and to the breadwinners of the world who make a whole lot of dough. And yet still we prefer the panache of a *pain au levain.*

Apparently, much as we can't do without it, we do not want to live on bread alone.

The Return of the Native

"Who Killed "Gourmet" Magazine?"

> In short, *Gourmet* will speak that Esperanto of the palate that
> makes the whole world kin . . . good food, good drink, fine liv-
> ing . . . the universal language of the gourmet.
>
> —*Gourmet,* January 1941

In October 2009, the *New York Times* stunned the world with
its report that "a magazine of almost biblical status" was closing up shop. The November issue of *Gourmet: The Magazine of
Good Living* was to be its last. "Slain at 68, RIP," read the headline of Gawker.com, a New York City blog devoted to Manhattan media news. Immediately, investigators went to work rounding
up the usual suspects. Was the guilty party the flagging economy,
which had resulted in lower circulation rates and one of the
worst declines in advertising of any popular periodical? In the
second quarter of 2009 alone, *Gourmet*'s ad pages were down by
50 percent, prompting Condé Nast, the publisher of the magazine since 1983, to stop the bleeding and cut its losses.

Or was the blame to be pinned instead on "the mass of un-
regulated internet chat about food," as Chris Kimball, founder
and editor-in-chief of *Cook's Illustrated,* suggested in his article
"Gourmet to All That," printed in the *Times* shortly after the

shocking news had been made known to the world? "The shut-tering of Gourmet," he wrote, "reminds us that in a click-or-die advertising marketplace, one ruled by a million instant pundits, where an anonymous Twitter comment might be seen to pack more resonance and useful content than an article that reflects a lifetime of experience, experts are not created from the top down but from the bottom up." Although Kimball insists that "the world needs fewer opinions and more thoughtful expertise," all evidence suggests that most of us identify with food bloggers who live ordinary lives and cook in ordinary kitchens more than we do with trained chefs. According to Foodblogblog.com, a blog about food blogs, there are currently almost two thousand sites on which people just like us post their culinary thoughts and musings, not to mention the recipes they've prepared at home rather than under the controlled circumstances of a pro-fessional test kitchen. "Go ahead and make that broccoli casse-role off your Google search and see how you like it!" Kimball warns us: "In cooking, as in all things, there is a right way and a wrong way. Very little in life is truly relative."[1] Such finger-pointing inspired MediaShift, PBS's online guide to the digital media revolution, to cleverly—and not wholly unsympathetically—summarize Kimball's closing argument in the language of the board game Clue: "The murder happened in the kitchen with a laptop."

Then again, maybe it wasn't a homicide at all. Maybe it was death by natural causes. The day after the announcement, the *Boston Globe* ran an obituary of the nation's oldest food magazine under the title "Gourmet Magazine, 1941–2009: A recipe for obso-lescence." Whisk together "culinary excellence," "gorgeous photog-raphy," and "big-name bylines," the mock recipe instructs; freeze the resulting magazine in "mid-20th-century high-end lifestyle" and "serve as symbol of bygone vision of gourmet life in

America."[2] Perhaps, the *Globe* was stating with all the subtlety of a brass band, *Gourmet* had simply outlived its time. In the year the magazine was born, after all, 1941, the Great Depression hadn't yet ended. Franklin Delano Roosevelt was sworn in for his third term as president. Charles Lindbergh testified before Congress, advising a neutrality pact with Hitler. Orson Welles's *Citizen Kane* premiered in New York. Joe DiMaggio's fifty-six-game hitting streak began in a game against the Chicago White Sox. And on June 19, General Mills introduced a new breakfast cereal called Cheeri Oats.

If recipes are signs of their times, then the 1940s were as different from the first decade of the twenty-first century as a Nut Crust Ham Slice is from an Indonesian pork satay, both made with pig and peanut butter, but that's about where the resemblance ends. The former is a tribute to the ingenuity of the thrifty housewife who could stretch a slice of ham into a sweet-and-salty supper for her family; the latter is evidence of our contemporary preference for international flavors and our spirit of culinary adventure.

Could a magazine born during an age that relied on processed

Nut Crust Ham Slice for 4

Don't be frightened by the peanut butter in this recipe—the best pigs are peanut-fed.

One slice ham
½ cup peanut butter
brown sugar
1 cup soft white bread crumbs
¼ cup margarine, melted
1 cup milk

Place the ham, large enough to serve 4, in a well-greased flat baking dish, spread the top of the slice with peanut butter, being sure it reaches all edges of the slice. On top of the peanut butter press in about ½ cup of brown sugar. On top of the sugar, strew about 1 cup of soft white bread crumbs. Sprinkle the melted margarine on top of the crumbs. Pour the cup of milk over the whole. Bake about 45 minutes to 1 hour in a moderate oven (350 degrees F.). When done, it has a crusty top, golden brown. The peanut butter gives a delicious flavor and the milk gravy tastes splendid on mashed potatoes.[3]

Indonesian Pork Satay with Spicy Peanut Sauce

1 pound boneless pork loin, sliced very thin

Marinade:
½ cup coconut milk
1 tsp fish sauce
1 tsp jaggery (or brown sugar)
½ tsp ground cumin
½ tsp ground coriander
½ tsp ground turmeric

Sauce:
½ cup coconut milk
1–2 tsp red curry paste
½ cup chunky peanut butter
½ cup chicken stock
3 tbsp jaggery (or brown sugar)
2 tbsp tamarind concentrate (or lime juice)
1 tbsp fish sauce
½ tsp salt

To make meat: Combine all marinade ingredients and add thinly sliced pork. Toss to coat, cover, and let stand for 1 hour or refrigerate for up to 24 hours. Thread meat onto soaked bamboo skewers. Grill until just done and serve with peanut sauce.

To make sauce: Warm coconut milk over medium heat for 5 minutes. Add curry paste and stir for 3 minutes. Add peanut butter, stock, and jaggery (or brown sugar). Heat for 5 minutes. Remove from heat and add tamarind concentrate (or lime juice), fish sauce, and salt. Let cool.[4]

American foods, was sublimely oblivious to nutritional concerns, served Nut Crust Ham Slice for supper, and felt obliged to reassure its readers that it was okay to cook with peanut butter, adapt itself to our current taste for natural ingredients, global influences, and Indonesian pork satays—not to mention our insistence that what we eat be as low in sodium, cholesterol, transfats, and calories as possible?

Certainly *Gourmet* did all it could to lead its readers "on explorations into new bypaths of culinary delights, to whet their appetites and excite their senses so that they will strive for broader horizons in their dining and wining adventures." Obviously it had in mind a different sort of reader from the one who subscribed to the leading women's magazines of the day, *American Cookery, Good Housekeeping,* and *Ladies Home Journal*—all of which had been around since the nineteenth century. *Gourmet,* on the other hand, was never intended for housewives who had to make ends meet. The passage quoted at the beginning of this chapter is from the opening issue's letter of introduction, in which founding editor Pearl V. Metzelthin, chef Louis P. De Gouy, and publisher Earl R. MacAusland explained how they had come to choose the title *Gourmet: The Magazine of Good Living.* Addressing themselves "To You—A Lover of Good Food," they justified their choice: "The name *Gourmet* is selected for this publication because it typifies the acme of appreciation of food perfection. In a broader sense, however, the word *gourmet* signifies far more than just food perfection. It is a synonym for the honest seeker of the *summum bonnum* of living."

With the prospect of Nut Crust Ham Slice for dinner, lovers of good food might be excused for having sought "food perfection," but today, when our choice of what to eat for dinner is almost limitless, the phrase is bound to strike us as narrowly provincial. What food perfection did the founding triumvirate have in mind? Certainly not Thai, Filipino, Algerian, Ethiopian, Peruvian, Lebanese, or Mexican, and probably not even American. In 1941, it went without saying that "perfect food" was food prepared for and eaten by those who knew what both *gourmet* and *summum bonnum* meant in the first place. In other words, it was not the food of barbarians, understood in its original sense of people who spoke a language other than Greek or Latin—or, to extend the term into the twentieth century, people who spoke a language other than French, whether English, German, Indonesian, or Gujarati.

The forty-eight pages of *Gourmet*'s premier issue were nothing if not Francophile through and through. Its features included "Burgundy at a Snail's Pace," the first of many articles by Samuel Chamberlain, the artist and photographer who had lived in France and was to go on to write the popular series about his family's Burgundian cook Clementine, later published as *Clementine in the Kitchen*. Other articles were "*Le Gourmet,*" "*Gastronomie sans Argent,*" and "*Specialités de la Maison.*" The "Meal of the Month" was an eleven-course Christmas dinner conceived by Georges Gonneau, executive chef at the Hotel Pierre; it began with *Potage Pierre le Grand,* wended its way through *Merlans À La Pluche Verte, Dinde Rôtie Des Artistes (Avec tous Ses Maquillages et*

HOLIDAY ISSUE · JANUARY 1941 · 25 CENTS

The cover of the first issue of
Gourmet magazine from 1941.

Arrangements), and *Salade Verte Tendre À L'Estragon*, and closed with *Charlotte Glacée Pierrette Au Curaçao*. Its hand-painted cover featured the clove-studded head of a wild boar on a silver platter lavishly adorned with boughs of holly. No mere suckling pig or splayed-open carcass à la North Carolinian pig-pickin', the boar's head has been tamed by the civilized and civilizing agriculturalist: its menacing eyes and horns are intact, but sheaves of wheat spray out of its ears, a juicy apple is set in its mouth, and a glass of red wine accompanies this testament to the transformative skills of the gourmet.

The letter of introduction closed with a promise to lovers of good food wherever they might be: "In short, *Gourmet* will speak that Esperanto of the palate that makes the whole world kin . . . good food, good drink, fine living . . . the universal language of the gourmet."

Esperanto. The late-nineteenth-century dream of a universal second language that could promote peace and international co-operation by putting an end to the confusion of tongues that has separated the world's people since the Tower of Babel. A beautiful dream, but like most dreams, it fades in the light of day. Often accused of being Eurocentric, Esperanto uses the Latin alphabet and derives both its syntax and two-thirds of its vocabulary from the Romance languages, giving Western Europeans a decided advantage over the almost two and a half billion people who live in India and China, not to mention another billion people who live in Africa.

Today it's almost painfully obvious that *Gourmet*'s dream of an "Esperanto of the palate" was similarly Eurocentric—and, above all, Francophile, as its very title indicates. The "good life" it featured was a wealthy, privileged, and elegant one of fine dining and luxury travel; and the "lovers of good food" for whom it was intended were the educated men and women with discriminating palates who had been trained to appreciate the oozy unctuousness of *escargots à la persillade,* the acrid pungency of an *epoisses de Bourgogne*, and the mouth-puckering bitterness of a bloodred Amer Picon. "The universal language of the gourmet" turns out to have been spoken by a very few people: the French and those who wished they were.

None of this is to say that *Gourmet* didn't change with the times. By the late 1990s, when *New York Times* restaurant critic Ruth Reichl took over the editorship, the magazine was regularly publishing pieces on food politics, sustainability issues, and bioethics, and articles were devoted to such nongourmet topics as "What's Your Favorite Hot Dog," "Kiss My Grits," and "Dandelion Wine." The number of Italian offerings equaled—if not surpassed—French ones as readers demanded recipes for the likes of *gnocchetti all'amatriciana, bollito di manzo e vitellone*, and *gianduia gelato*. Such relevant exposés, populist articles, and non–haute cuisine notwithstanding, the magazine simply wasn't able to shed the aura of sophistication that, back in the 1940s, had earned it legions of devoted readers.

"So who killed *Gourmet*?" asked Craig "Meathead" Goldwyn, in the *Huffington Post*. His verdict acquitted no one.

A thorough post-mortem shows that, like Julius Caesar, *Gourmet* was surrounded and knifed from all sides. Clearly Brutus was Condé Nast, but conspirators were numerous: The recession, advertisers, Google AdWords, Google Search, Bon Appetit, Epicurious.com, printers, the US Postal Service, perceived elitism, Web sites like mine, and You.[5]

The same year in which Reichl took over the editorial helm of the not-yet-moribund *Gourmet* saw the birth of a revolutionary new food movement in France. No *nouvelle cuisine* or *cuisine minceur*, the new movement celebrates casual cooking, messy eating, and gigantic picnic-style events. The brainchild of gastronomic journalists Alexandre Cammas and Emmanuel Rubin, it even required the invention of a new word for its title and was daring enough to venture outside the French language for its inspiration. Rebelling against the gastronomical discipline of *la cuisine classique, Le Fooding,* as Cammas explains, is "a mélange of 'food' and 'feeling.'" "I like the provocation of using an English word within the context of French cuisine," he adds.[6] Fed up with haute cuisine and the rigor mortis that had calcified French food culture, Cammas and Rubin call for "the beginning of a new taste of one's time." They publish an anti-Michelin restaurant guide that omits such traditional three-star greats as Alain Passard's L'Arpège and Jean-François Piège's Les Ambassadeurs at L'Hôtel de Crillon, and instead recommends Bob's Juice Bar (Paris 10e), Pizza 104 (Paris 19e), and British Sandwich (Paris 17e). Cammas even admits to a fondness for Chipotle Mexican Grill and McDonald's. In September 2009, *Le Fooding* came to New York and hosted a two-day charity benefit at Long Island City's PS 1. Six New York chefs—including Momofuku's David Chang and The Spotted Pig's April Bloomfield—worked with an equal number of Paris chefs to feed up to a thousand people each night, with proceeds benefiting the global humanitarian organization, Action Against Hunger.

A third blow was delivered to the unquestioned belief in French culinary hegemony when the lifestyle magazine *Le Figaro Madame* and the BBC food magazine *Olive* published the results of a survey they'd conducted jointly, during which they interviewed more than three thousand French and British people about their cooking and eating habits. The findings were shocking. "Official: British are better at cooking than the French."

It is one of the pillars of the French "exception culturelle": haute cuisine so lofty that the president, Nicolas Sarkozy, wanted the United Nations to declare it a "world treasure." Those perfidious Rosbifs could attack their language and buy up half the Dordogne but they could never compete in the kitchen, declared the Gallic gods of gastronomy.

But a poll has undermined France's reputation as the home of unrivalled culinary excellence. . . . As the French television station TF1 put it: "They trounced us at Trafalgar. They whipped us at Waterloo. Now the English have scored their ultimate victory: they are better at cooking than us."[7]

Who could be surprised at the comments that were posted in response to the unexpected results of the poll? On the one hand, sheer disbelief: "Maybe the British are just bigger liars than the French." "Fish & Chips, Sausage & Chips, Chicken & Chips, Curry & Chips, Gravy & Chips, Burger & Chips, Pie & Chips." "The British eat food that the French would not even use as fertilizer."[8]

On the other hand, pride—at least on the Dover side of the Channel—that the Brits no longer had to be embarrassed by their traditional food: "Roast beef with Yorkshire pudding, roast potatoes, veg and gravy . . . I mean, that is a great meal." "Give me rosbif over steak tartare any day of the week. ANY day. made me laugh out loud."

A final commenter took comfort in the knowledge that however bad either English or French cooking might be, it could always be worse: "Well at least we can both look down on German cuisine—tut mir lied deutsche Freunden" [sic].

Logically we have to admit that German food is no more necessarily bad than French and Italian food are necessarily good, or English and American necessarily indifferent. The bratwurst-eating German, the crêpe suzette–eating French, the pasta-eating Italian, the roast beef and Yorkshire pudding–eating Brit, and the hamburger-eating American: each is a cultural stereotype and each stereotype comes to us from the pages of history that I've tried to illuminate. My aim in telling the stories of our foods and their names was in no way to dethrone French or Italian food— the world would be a poorer place, and I a hungrier person, without the glories of haute cuisine, *cuisine à la bonne femme,* not to mention the Mediterranean diet. Nor was my aim to crown any other nation's cooking in its place—English, German, or American. What I've tried to demonstrate is that when it comes to the important matter of food, our prejudice in favor of all things French and Italian is neither natural nor inevitable, but instead historically determined. The attitudes that we have about food today are the legacy of a very powerful people who lived many centuries ago and who bequeathed to the world their unwavering belief in what civilized people should put into their mouths, as well as what sounds should come out of them.

Viewed through the telephoto lens of contemporary food trends, the age-old conflict between the barbarian hunter-gatherers and the sophisticated agriculturalists becomes surprisingly relevant. From the time of Julius Caesar, through the days of the early Christian missionaries, the Norman conquerors, and the French chefs, the inhabitants of Britain have been looked down on as subsisting on milk, meat, and wild food, when anyone who mattered knew that civilized people transformed such natural ingredients into the sophisticated dishes their palates had been trained to appreciate. By the same token, seen through the wide-angle lens of history, our contemporary trends take on larger contours. The death of *Gourmet,* the popularity of foodie blogs, the birth of *Le Fooding,* magazine surveys about the relative culinary abilities of the Brits and the French: all point to a changing of the guard that has stood before the palace of good taste for more than two millennia.

But the guard turns out to have been not so much a person—or even a people—as an attitude. An attitude that's captured in the belief that certain foods and words are inherently better than others. An attitude that holds a *tarte aux pommes* to be more refined than an apple pie, a *soupe a l'oignon* more sophisticated than a cock-a-leekie, a *bleu d'Auvergne* preferable to a glass of milk, a *boeuf à la bourgignon* superior to a beef stew, and a *pain au levain* better than a sourdough loaf. An attitude that's plagued us, the descendants of those long-ago barbarians, who still eat the foods they did, calling them by the names they did as well. An attitude that's forced us to squelch our appetites for what our heads have told us we shouldn't hunger for. An attitude that's resulted in what I've diagnosed as the collective culinary split personality of us English speakers.

Looks like our barbarian appetites are at long last coming out of the closet. The prognosis is good for at least a partial recovery.

Notable Events in the History
of English Food Words

55–54 BC: Julius Caesar's two expeditions to Britain. Caesar writes *The Gallic Wars,* in which he comments on the diet of the native Celts: "*lacte et carne vivunt,*" "they live on milk and meat."

43 CE: Roman conquest of Britain under Emperor Claudius. The Romans introduce Mediterranean foods—including vines, pheasants, and guinea fowl, such fruit and nut-bearing trees as walnut, chestnut, medlar, and mulberry; such herbs as parsley, dill, fennel, mint, thyme, rosemary, and sage—as well as cultivating such vegetables as cabbage, lettuce, turnips, and leeks. They also bring Latin to the island. Few traces of the language or the culinary traditions remain when the Romans abandon Britain four hundred years later.

1ST CENTURY CE: Apicius's *De re coquinaria,* first known cookbook. Birth of Christianity in Roman-occupied Judea; the new religion adopts the culinary trinity of the empire: bread, wine, oil. Although medieval legend holds that Joseph of Arimathea brought the Holy Grail (and Christianity) to Glastonbury in the south of England, no definite records exist concerning the arrival of Christianity in Celtic Britain.

98 CE: *Agricola* and *Germania*, in which the Roman historian Tacitus observes of Britannia, "the climate is wretched."

173–238 CE: Maximinus the Thracian, the first barbarian Roman emperor, wears the imperial purple from 235 to 238 and is reputed to eat between forty and sixty pounds of meat daily.

410 CE: Romans abandon Britain to save their capital from being sacked by the Visigoths; the emperor Honorius writes to the cities of Britain when they beg for Roman help in fighting off the invading Germanic tribes, "Fend for yourselves."

450 CE: *Adventus Saxonum*: traditional date of the arrival of the Saxons, Angles, and Jutes from northern Germany. They push the Celtic-speaking people as far north and west as possible—hence the Celtic fringe of Britain (Cornwall, Wales, Scotland, and Ireland)—and establish their west Germanic dialect as the language of the island.

450–518: Alcimus Ecdicius Avitus, bishop of Gaul, writes *De spiritualis historiae gestis,* including *The Fall of Man,* in which he identifies Eden's forbidden fruit as the apple.

597: Pope Gregory the Great sends St. Augustine (later of Canterbury) to England on a missionary campaign. Augustine accuses Celtic bishops of acting contrary to Rome's teachings, and successfully converts the English kingdoms of Kent, Essex, East Anglia, and Northumbria.

5th–6TH CENTURIES: The pagan Celtic seasonal festival Lughnasa is transformed into the Christian Anglo-Saxon *Hlafmæsse* (Loaf Mass) or Lammas, the Feast of the First Fruits.

6TH CENTURY: The pagan Celtic spring festival Imbolc (*In-Milk*), which had already been transformed into the Irish St.

Brigid's Day, now becomes the Christian holiday of Candlemas, commemorating the presentation of the baby Jesus in the Temple; St. Brigid is identified as Jesus' wet nurse.

664: Synod of Whitby: Celtic and English bishops discuss whether to comply with the doctrines of Rome or to observe Irish practices: bishops in favor of Rome triumph over Celtic faction.

731: The Venerable Bede's *Ecclesiastical History of the English People.*

793: The Vikings (aka Northmen, Norsemen, Danes) raid the Lindisfarne monastery in Northumbria. Next few centuries are marked by frequent raids.

911: King Charles the Simple gives the northwest part of France (today's Normandy) to the Viking raiders in an attempt to placate the fearsome marauders.

1054: The Great Schism between Western and Eastern churches. Among the many liturgical differences is the question of what type of bread should be offered during communion. The Western azymites insist on unleavened bread, while the Eastern prozymites demand leavened bread.

1066: Duke William of Normandy defeats and kills King Harold of England at Apuldre, "Apple Tree," in Hastings. The Normans reintroduce rabbits, pheasants, fallow deer, and pears; their chefs are known for their sauces, including *civey, gravey,* and *egerdouce*; meats are given French names (beef, veal, pork, and mutton). Over the next few centuries, French words and syntax gradually transform Anglo-Saxon (also called Old English) into Middle English.

11TH–12TH CENTURIES: Returning crusaders bring fruits, spices, and other foods from the East, including lemons, oranges, melons, rhubarb, dates, apricots, sugar, ginger, rice, and coffee.

1388: First complete English Bible is translated by John Wycliffe.

1390: First English cookbook, *The Forme of Cury,* is assembled by French-speaking master chefs of King Richard II.

1517: Protestant Reformation in which milk-drinking and meat-eating northern countries break away from oil- and wine-based Church of Rome.

1545–1563: Council of Trent at which it was decreed that the mass must be celebrated exclusively with wine from the grape, not with fermented cider or perry.

1640s: To escape Cromwell's Commonwealth, John Evelyn travels on the Continent, bringing new vegetables to England when he returns with the restoration of the monarchy. Encourages his countrymen to eat *artichaux,* cucumbers, fennel, *sellery,* and *scorzonera*—not to mention the more than seventy possible salad ingredients listed in his *Acetaria: A Discourse of Sallets.*

1651: "Roast beef" appears in print for the first time in Thomas Randolph's 1651 *Hey for Honesty.*

1747: Hannah Glasse publishes *The Art of Cookery Made Plain & Easy,* in which she complains that, "So much is the blind Folly of this Age, that they would rather be impos'd on by a French Booby, than give Encouragement to a good English Cook!"

1862: Louis Pasteur invents a process in which milk is heated to kill bacteria and molds; the process is known as pasteurization. Dr. John Dauglish's Aëreated Bread Company (ABC) is incorporated: "Nothing but flour, water, a little salt and gas—no sweat!"

1941–2009: *Gourmet: The Magazine of Good Living.*

Acknowledgments

All a writer has at her disposal is words, but there are times when words just aren't up to the task of expressing what she wants to convey. Now is one of those times. That said, many many thanks go to my agent, Farley Chase of the Waxman Literary Agency, who, from our very first conversation, made it abundantly clear that he shared my fixation with the connections between food and words. Thank you, Farley, for believing in this project and for all your hard work in shepherding it along its way. Many thanks go as well to my editor at St. Martin's Press, Daniela Rapp, whose close reading, incisive questions, and sure instincts—not to mention her love of languages and foods of all sorts—have made this book infinitely tighter and stronger than it would otherwise have been. I wish you many delicious meals with your new smoker.

Thanks of a different sort go to my wonderful family, who have listened, read, commented, and encouraged me during the writing of this book: to my parents, who introduced me to the pleasure of good food (despite my absurdly self-imposed and blessedly short-lived childhood eating restrictions) and to the pleasure of ideas as well; to my sister, who first taught me to read and whose calm and untroubled carnivorousness used to put me to shame; and to my brother, another reluctant eater and himself a writer, who has been one of my most careful readers.

Finally, my biggest thanks go to my children, Natt and Camilla, who love me enough to not only put up with my ramblings about apples and leeks, but who actually egg me on with questions like "I wonder why it's called a clementine" and "Is flour related to flower?" (answers: after the French missionary Father Clément Rodier who reputedly created and named the hybrid in 1902 ; and yes, *flour*—in the sense of "the finest part of the meal"—was spelled *flower* until as late as the early nineteenth century); to Noah and Dylan whose jaw-dropping ability to eat is rivaled only by their bottomless curiosity; and—last but never least—to Gary, my partner in food, words, and everything else, who has been my greatest support and who never stopped reminding me that "a spoonful of sugar makes the medicine go down." I love you all.

Notes

Introduction: Pig-Pickin's, Prunes, and Häagen-Dazs

1. Frank Bruni, "Fat, Glorious Fat, Moves to the Center of the Plate," *New York Times,* June 13, 2007, D1. Emphasis added.

2. Ibid., D5.

3. Edward Behr, "A Multiplicity of Apples," *The Artful Eater: A Gourmet Investigates the Ingredients of Great Food* (New York: Atlantic Monthly Press, 1992), 165.

Chapter 1: Fruit and Apples

1. The subtitle for this chapter comes from Rainer Maria Rilke's *Sonnets to Orpheus,* I: 13.

2. Charlotte Zolotow, *Mr. Rabbit and the Lovely Present* (New York: Harper & Row, 1962), n.p.

3. The story of Popeye and his muscle-building spinach is an illuminating one in this context. Because of a misprint, a 1920s study attributed to spinach ten times its actual iron content. This is why Popeye, created in 1931, downs cans of spinach when he needs the strength to defend his lady love Olive Oyl from the clutches of the villainous Bluto. The nutritional error was discovered in the 1930s, but Popeye continued to eat his spinach nonetheless—and to help parents in their campaign to get their children to eat the iron-rich vegetable, even if not quite as iron-rich as it was once believed to be.

4. To be absolutely precise, the Roman gourmet Marcus Gavius Apicius lived during the first century under the Emperor Tiberius; it was his name that

was later given to the compendium of recipes known as *Apicius: De re coquinaria*, believed to have been compiled in the late fourth and early fifth centuries.

5. John Ayto, *The Diner's Dictionary: Food and Drink from A to Z* (New York: Oxford University Press, 1993), 9.

6. Cornelius Tacitus, *The Agricola and the Germania*, trans. H. Mattingly (98 CE; New York: Penguin Books, 1977), 62.

7. Ibid., 123.

8. Behr, *The Artful Eater*, 160.

9. The myth most associated with Pomona is her seduction by Vertumnus, the god of the seasons and plant growth, whom the Roman writer Varro identified with a major Etruscan god. In the fourteenth book of Ovid's *Metamorphoses*, Vertumnus tricked Pomona into talking to him by disguising himself as an old woman. Thus did he gain entry to both her orchard and her affections.

10. As Alan Davidson describes in *The Penguin Companion to Food* (originally published in hardcover as *The Oxford Companion to Food*), the same confusion between specific and general characterizes the history of the word *tomato*. "The Aztec word *tomatl* meant simply plump fruit. For them, our edible tomato was *xitomatl*, while the husk tomato (*tomatillo*) was *miltomatl*. Spaniards, not understanding the importance of the suffix in each name, used *tomatl*, which they turned into *tomate*, for both. As a result, it is often difficult, when reading early Spanish sources about Aztec use of the tomato, to know which fruit is meant" (New York: Penguin Books, 2002), 962.

11. Tacitus, *The Agricola and the Germania*, 102, 73.

12. In fact, German has two words that are translated as *fruit*: *Obst* and *Frucht*. The latter obviously derives from the Latin *fructus*, whereas the former, which is more commonly used, evolved from the Old German *obez*, and appears to have meant something like "food that is more than merely edible"—food that is not merely edible, but palatable. In other words, food that tastes good.

13. Apicius, *De re coquinaria,* ed. and trans. Joseph Dommers Vehling (4th–5th century CE; New York: Dover Publications, 1977), 115. The *matianum*, or Matian apple, was named after Matius, a friend of Caesar, who was also a cookbook author. In the course of time, *matianum* evolved into the Gallo-Roman *matiana*, which on the Iberian peninsula was pronounced *manzana*, today's Spanish word for apple.

14. Snorri Sturluson, *The Prose Edda*, trans. Jean I. Young (13th century CE; Berkeley: University of California Press, 1954), 54.

15. I am indebted to Stewart Lee Allen for calling my attention to Avitus's role in identifying the forbidden fruit as the apple. See his discussion in *In the Devil's Garden: A Sinful History of Forbidden Food* (New York: Ballantine Books, 2002), 7–16.

16. *The Poems of Alcimus Ecdicius Avitus,* trans. George W. Shea (5th century CE; Tempe, AZ: Medieval & Renaissance Texts & Studies, 1997), 85.

17. *The Caedmon Poems,* trans. Charles W. Kennedy (7th century CE; New York: Dutton, 1916), 37; II: 925–938.

18. John Milton, *Paradise Lost,* IX: 584–586.

19. *Cautels of the Mass,* http://anglicanhistory.org/liturgy/sarum_cautels.html (accessed May 14, 2010).

20. *The Anglo-Saxon Chronicle,* trans. James Ingram (9th–12th century CE; El Paso, TX: El Paso Norte Press, 2005), 154.

21. *Curye on Inglysch: English Culinary Manuscripts of the Fourteenth Century (Including the Forme of Cury),* eds. Constance B. Hieatt and Sharon Butler (1390; New York: Oxford University Press, 1985), 137. Translation by author.

22. Ibid., 69. Translation by author.

23. Ibid., 74–75. Translation by author.

24. "Apple Pye," *The Poetical Works of Dr. William King,* vol. 2 (1781; Adamant Media Corporation, 2001), 139.

25. Hannah Glasse, *The Art of Cookery Made Plain & Easy* (1747; Devon, UK: Prospect Books Ltd., 1995), 81.

26. Eliza Acton, *Modern Cookery for Private Families* (1845; London: Southover Press, 1993), 3.

27. Ibid., 400.

28. Jane Grigson, *English Food* (London: Penguin Books, 1977), 7.

29. Acton, *Modern Cookery,* 37.

30. Florence White, *Good Things in England: A Practical Cookery Book for Everyday Use, Containing Traditional and Regional Recipes Suited to Modern Tastes Contributed by English Men and Women Between 1399 and 1932* (1932; London: Persephone Books, 2003), 226.

31. Dorothy Hartley, *Food in England* (1954; London: Little, Brown, 2003), 28.

32. Ibid., 416.

33. Jane Grigson, *English Food,* 2.

34. Isabella Beeton, *Beeton's Book of Household Management: A First Edition Facsimile* (1861; New York: Farrar, Straus and Giroux, 1969), 622.

Chapter 2: Leeks: Weeds or Vegetables?

1. Jane Grigson, *Vegetable Book* (London: Penguin Books, 1980), 451. Alphabetically speaking, it would be neat if Grigson's book proceeded from artichokes to zucchini, but since she was English, she referred to what we Americans call zucchini as *courgette*, thus making *yam* her final entry.

2. John Evelyn, *Acetaria: A Discourse of Sallets,* ed. Christopher Driver (1699; Devon, UK: Prospect Books, 2005), 21.

3. Darina Allen, *The Complete Book of Irish Country Cooking: Traditional and Wholesome Recipes from Ireland* (New York: Book-of-the-Month Club/ Trafalgar Square, 1995), 168.

4. Although the Italian word for the vegetable is *carciofo,* according to John Ayto, "The word artichoke itself was borrowed in the sixteenth century from northern Italian *articiocco.*" *The Diner's Dictionary,* 10.

5. True yams, as we're often told, are grown neither in England nor in America, but in Africa and the Caribbean. What we call *yams* are in fact *sweet potatoes,* a botanically distinct species, but since I'm discussing names at the moment, rather than things, and since so many people think of them as *yams,* so will I call them.

6. Karl Philipp Moritz, *Travels in England in 1782* (Bremen, Germany: Salzwasser-Verlag, 2010), 15.

7. Robert P. Tristram Coffin, "British Breakfast," *Gourmet: The Magazine of Good Living,* October 1948.

8. Davidson, *The Penguin Companion to Food,* 295.

9. Elizabeth David, *A Book of Mediterranean Food* (New York: Penguin Books, 1983), preface to the 1955 edition.

10. Ibid., 126.

11. D. H. Lawrence, *Sea and Sardinia.* Quoted in Elizabeth David, *A Book of Mediterranean Food,* 127.

12. David, *A Book of Mediterranean Food,* preface to the Penguin edition (unnumbered page).

13. Grigson, *Vegetable Book,* 451.

14. Allen, *Irish Country Cooking,* 168.

15. Carol Field, *In Nonna's Kitchen: Recipes and Traditions from Italy's Grandmothers* (New York: HarperCollins, 1997), 30.

16. Quoted in R. J. Apple's "Ah, the Sweet Smell of Spring," http:// query.nytimes.com/gst/fullpage.html?res=9805E5DD113DF933 A05757C0A9659C8B63 (accessed January 15, 2009).

17. Yoshi Yamada, "Ravenous for Ramps," *Gourmet: A Magazine of Good Living*, April 2008.

18. Christie Matheson, "In the Weeds," *Boston Globe Magazine*, July 15, 2007, 17.

19. Allen, *Irish Country Cooking*, 175.

20. Maria C. Hunt, "Backstory: Haute Cuisine's Hunter-Gatherer," *Christian Science Monitor*, May 3, 2006, http://www.csmonitor.com/2006/0503/p20s01-lifo.html.

21. Stephen Brill, www.wildmanstevebrill.com/clippings.folder/Fracas OverParkTours.html (accessed October 25, 2010).

22. Tacitus, *The Agricola and the Germania*, 123.

23. Jane Renfrew, *Food and Cooking in Roman Britain* (UK: English Heritage, 1985), 23.

24. Our word *vegetable*, as I discussed in the previous chapter, evolved either from the Latin *vegetare*, to make lively, or from the closely related *vegere*, to be healthy. The Romans had no one single corresponding word, instead calling all green and leafy vegetables *holera* and all beans, peas, and other pod plants *legumina*.

25. Norway's name for the leek, *purre,* is the sole Latinate aberration among the Germanic-speaking Scandinavian countries. Histories of the language routinely point to the influence of Christian missionaries who introduced the Latin alphabet, as well as many Greek and Latin words, to the Norwegians around the year 1000; of course, the same missionaries were at work throughout Scandinavia, so the reason that Norway alone adopted the Latin name for the leek remains unclear.

26. Although *cainnenn* was the Irish word for leek, the traditional soup is known as *brotchán foltchep*, invariably translated "leek broth." *Foltchep* appears to have been a portmanteau word composed of *folt*, Irish for "hair of the head," and *chep*, from the Latin *cepa*, "onion." *A New History of Ireland* (Oxford University Press, 2005) thus concludes, on the basis of the description of its appearance, that *foltchep* "is certainly to be identified with the chive" (566), but it's worth remembering that the native Babington leek was as slender-leaved as today's chives. In her *Complete Book of Irish Country Cooking*, Darina Allen writes that the broth is called "*brotchán foltchep* after the main ingredients, leeks, possibly the perennial Babington leek, a vegetable frequently mentioned in old manuscripts." She further notes that "there is considerable debate about the translation of *foltchep* and it has been variously rendered as leek or onion" (18).

27. Claire Macdonald, *Scottish Cookery* (Hampshire, UK: Pitkin Guides, 1998), 6.

28. Allen, *Irish Country Cooking,* 18.

29. Patricia Solley, *An Exaltation of Soups: The Soul-Satisfying Story of Soup, As Told in More Than 100 Recipes* (New York: Three Rivers Press, 2004), 207–208.

30. Evelyn, *Acetaria: A Discourse of Sallets*, 27.

31. Davidson, *The Penguin Companion to Food*, 535.

32. Pliny the Elder, *Natural History of the World,* 1st century CE; http://penelope.uchicago.edu/holland/index.html (accessed May 21, 2010).

33. John Cooper, *Eat and Be Satisfied: A Social History of Jewish Food* (Northvale, NJ: Jason Aronson, 1993). See his discussion of vegetables mentioned in the Bible, 11–12.

34. The Venerable Bede, *The Life and Miracles of St. Cuthbert, Bishop of Lindesfarne*, 8th century CE; http://www.fordham.edu/halsall/basis/bede-cuthbert.html (accessed July 16, 2007).

35. *Curye on Inglysch,* 115.

36. Thomas Austin, ed., *Two Fifteenth-Century Cookery Books* (Whitefish, MT: Kessinger Publishing, 2007), 14.

37. Quoted in *An Etymological Dictionary of Modern English*, ed. Ernest Weekley (1921; New York: Dover Publications, 1967), II: 1125.

38. Acton, *Modern Cookery for Private Families*, 274; Beeton, *Beeton's Book of Household Management*, 71.

39. Grigson, *Vegetable Book*, 291.

40. For more on the Victorian view of the Irish, see L. Perry Curtis's 1971 *Apes and Angels: The Irishman in Victorian Caricature* (Washington, D.C.: Smithsonian Institution Press, 1971).

41. Jane Grigson, *Good Things: A Celebration of Fresh Daily Fare Lovingly Presented* (New York: Atheneum, 1984), 189–190.

42. Claire Macdonald, *Seasonal Cooking* (1983; London: Corgi Books, 1997).

43. Euell Gibbons, *Stalking the Wild Asparagus: Field Guide Edition* (New York: David McKay, 1972), 157.

44. Ibid., 159.

45. Quoted in Jane Grigson, *Good Things,* 186.

46. "Rampant Wild Leeks," http://forums.gardenweb.com/forums/load/weeds/msg0614523117119.html (accessed July 20, 2007).

47. Yamada, "Ravenous for Ramps," www.gourmet.com/food/2008/04/ramps (accessed October 25, 2010).

Chapter 3: Milk and Dairy

1. The Celtic languages of the British Isles are divided into two broad groups, known as Brythonic and Goidelic (from Brittonic and Gaelic). To the former belong Welsh, Cornish, and Breton; to the latter, Scottish, Irish, and Manx. Because it was the Brythonic languages that were spoken in the southern parts of Britain during the Roman period, there are more traces of Latin in Welsh, Cornish, and Breton than in the Gaelic languages of Ireland and Scotland, both of which lay beyond the heavily fortified borders built by the Romans. It is for this reason that we can see the Latin *lac* in the Welsh *llaeth*, Cornish *leath*, and Breton *laezh*, but not in the Irish and Scottish *bainne* or the Manx *bainney*.

2. In response to a letter asking why the pork industry has never capitalized on its dairy potential, the Illinois Pork Producers Association points out that while the average cow yields 65 pounds of milk per day, the average pig yields only 13 pounds per day. The response continues: "The biggest challenge facing the porcine dairy industry is collecting the product. Pigs on average have fourteen teats as opposed to cows that have four teats. Pigs also differ from cows in their milk ejection time, a cow's milk ejection is stimulated by the hormone oxytocin and can last ten minutes, whereas a pig's milk ejection time only lasts fifteen seconds as the suckling pigs stimulate the release of oxytocin. The technology of a 14-cupped mechanized milking machine that can milk a pig in 15 seconds is not available to pork producers."

3. http://joannagoddard.blogspot.com/2008/03/poll-do-you-drink-milk.html (accessed May 24, 2010).

4. Homer, *The Odyssey*, trans. Richmond Lattimore (New York: Harper Perennial, 1991), IX: 244–249.

5. *Curye on Inglysch,* iii–iv.

6. Ovid, *Metamorphoses*, trans. Rolfe Humphries (Bloomington: Indiana University Press, 1955), I: 108–111.

7. *Boston Globe*, February 4, 2003, C2.

8. C. Anne Wilson, *Food and Drink in Britain: From the Stone Age to the 19th Century* (Chicago: Academy Chicago Publishers, 1991), 151.

9. Harold McGee, *On Food and Cooking: The Science and Lore of the Kitchen* (New York: Charles Scribner's Sons, 1984), 39.

10. The Venerable Bede, *Ecclesiastical History of the English People*, trans. Leo Sherley-Price (731; New York: Penguin Books, 1990), 103.

11. Ronald Hutton, *The Stations of the Sun: A History of the Ritual Year in Britain* (Oxford, UK: Oxford University Press, 2001), 134–135.

12. Quoted in Ann Hagen, *A Handbook of Anglo-Saxon Food: Processing and Consumption* (Norfolk, UK: Anglo-Saxon Books, 2002), 28.

13. Quoted in Maguelonne Toussaint-Samat, *History of Food*, trans. Anthea Bell (Oxford, UK: Blackwell Publishers, 2001), 123.

14. Ibid.

15. Waverley Root, *The Food of France* (1958; New York: Vintage Books, 1992), 116.

16. Ibid., 119–120.

17. Wilson, *Food and Drink in Britain*, 156.

18. Quoted in *Two Fifteenth-Century Cookery Books: About 1430–1450*, Thomas Austin, ed. (Whitefish, MT: Kessinger Publishing, 2007), 8.

19. Marion Cunningham, *The Breakfast Book* (New York: Wings Books, 1997), 32–33.

20. Gervase Markham, *The English Housewife, containing the inward and outward virtues which ought to be in a complete woman; as her skill in physic, cookery, banqueting-stuff, distillation, perfumes, wool, hemp, flax, dairies, brewing, baking, and all other things belonging to a household*, ed. Michael R. Best (1615; Montreal: McGill-Queens University Press, 1994), 42.

21. Glasse, *The Art of Cookery Made Plain & Easy* (1747; Devon, UK: Prospect Books, Ltd., 1995), 121.

22. Beeton, *Beeton's Book of Household Management*, 893.

23. Ibid., 72–73.

24. Charles Elmé Francatelli, *A Plain Cookery Book for the Working Classes* (1852; London: Scolar Press, 1978), 10–11.

25. Ibid., 16.

Chapter 4: Meat

1. *Historia Augusta*, http://penelope.uchicago.edu/Theyer/E/Roman/Texts/Historia_Augusta/Maximini_duo*.html (accessed June 2, 2010).

2. Stendhal, *Memoirs of an Egotist*, trans. David Ellis (New York: Horizon Press, 1975), 94.

3. Patrick Barkham, "Chirac's Reheated Food Jokes Bring Blair to the Boil," *Guardian*, July 5, 2005, http://www.guardian.co.uk/guardianpolitics/story/0,,1521483,00.html (accessed June 13, 2007).

4. Ayto, *The Diner's Dictionary*, 214.

5. Mimi Sheraton, *The German Cookbook: A Complete Guide to Mastering Authentic German Cooking* (New York: Random House, 1993), 139.

6. Herman Melville, *Typee: A Peep at Polynesian Life* (1846; New York: Penguin Books, 1996), 25–26.

7. *Jungle Ways* (1930), http://en.wikipedia.org/wiki/William_Buehler_ Seabrook (accessed June 9, 2007).

8. St. Jerome, *Against Jovinianus* (c. 360 AD). In *The Principal Works of St. Jerome*, trans. W. H. Fremantle (New York: Christian Literature Company, 1893), 394.

9. Sir Walter Scott, *Ivanhoe* (1819; New York: Penguin Books, 1984), 14–15.

10. Posidonius, quoted in Wilson, *Food and Drink in Britain*, 68.

11. Florence Dupont, "The Grammar of Roman Dining," *Food: A Culinary History from Antiquity to the Present*, eds. Jean-Louis Flandrin and Massimo Montanari (New York: Penguin Books, 2000), 113.

12. Petronius, *The Satyricon*, 1st century CE; http://www.gutenberg.org/ dirs/5/2/1/5219/5219.txt (accessed June 1, 2007).

13. *The Odyssey of Homer*, trans. Richmond Lattimore. (New York: Harper Perennial, 1991), XX: 250–251.

14. Ibid., IX: 288–293.

15. Hesiod, *Works and Days*, trans. Richmond Lattimore (Ann Arbor: University of Michigan Press, 1959), line 121.

16. Caesar, *The Gallic War*, trans. Carolyn Hammond (58–56 BCE; Oxford: Oxford University Press, 1998), 132–133.

17. Chillingham Wild Cattle Association, http://www.chillingham -wildcattle.org.uk (accessed January 26, 2009).

18. Harriet Ritvo, "Race, Breed, and Myths of Origin: Chillingham Cattle as Ancient Britons," *Representations* 39 (Summer 1992): 1–22.

19. Davidson, *The Penguin Companion to Food*, 97.

20. Colin Spencer, *British Food: An Extraordinary Thousand Years of History* (New York: Columbia University Press, 2002), 23.

21. Snorri Sturluson, *The Prose Edda: Tales from Norse Mythology*, trans. Jean Young (Berkeley: University of California Press, 1954), 73–74.

22. *Curye on Inglysch*, 102.

23. Ibid., 100.

24. Ibid., 137.

25. Andrew Wynter, "The London Commissariat," *Quarterly Review*, vol. 95, no. 190, 1854.

26. Quoted in Ann Hagen, *A Second Handbook of Anglo-Saxon Food and*

Drink: Production and Distribution (Norfolk, VA: Anglo-Saxon Books, 2002), 72.

27. Samuel Pegge, "Preface to the Curious Antiquarian Reader," *The Forme of Cury*, included in http://www.gutenberg.org/dirs/etext05/8cury10 .txt.

28. George Eliot, *Adam Bede* (1859; New York: Penguin Books, 1985), 522.

29. Glasse, *The Art of Cookery Made Plain & Easy*, 54.

30. Hartley, *Food in England*, 60.

31. Fergus Henderson, *The Whole Beast: Nose to Tail Eating* (New York: HarperCollins, 2004), 80.

Chapter 5: Bread

1. Confusingly, perhaps, some flatbreads—such as Middle Eastern pitas and Indian naan—are in fact leavened, although they are significantly thinner than what we think of as risen bread. We are dealing here not so much with the difference between leavened and unleavened bread as we are with a vast economic divide. As Jeffrey Alford and Naomi Duguid explain in *Flatbreads and Flavors: A Baker's Atlas* (New York: William Morrow, 1995), "In many parts of the world, having sufficient fuel for cooking has been an ever-present problem. Flatbreads, unlike loaf breads, tend to cook very quickly, requiring only a limited amount of fuel to provide heat" (2).

2. H. E. Jacob, *Six Thousand Years of Bread: Its Holy and Unholy History*, trans. Richard and Clara Winston (1944; New York: Lyons Press, 1997), 116–117.

3. Quoted in Jacob, *Six Thousand Years of Bread*, 122.

4. It might be tempting to blame the frequent outbreaks of St. Anthony's Fire on the illiterate peasantry's ignorance of what had been fully understood hundreds of years earlier, but we should remember that another grain infected by a fungus is, to this day, considered a delicacy. *Huitlacoche*, the fungus that grows right from an ear of corn, has been prized in central Mexico since pre-Columbian days. Although it's considered a disease in the United States, the earthy-tasting black fungus is a rare and prized treasure in Mexico. We can't fully blame the medieval peasants for eating blackened rye, in other words, especially when it was so much sweeter than the unaffected grain—not to mention that it might very well have been the only edible grain available.

5. The first passage is from C. Anne Wilson, *Food and Drink in Britain*,

231. The second is from Alan Davidson, *The Penguin Companion to Food and Drink*, 115.

6. Another theory holds that our modern word *bread* derives from the Indo-European root *bhreu*, which signified the acts of cutting or breaking up. This explains how *bread* could have once referred to a piece broken off from a loaf rather than to the whole thing.

7. Flandrin and Montanari, eds., *Food: A Culinary History from Antiquity to the Present*, 72.

8. Waverley Root, *The Food of Italy* (1971; New York: Vintage Books, 1992), 4.

9. http://penelope.uchicago.edu/Thayer/E/Roman/Texts/Cato/De_ Agricultura/E*.html.

10. Bede, *Ecclesiastical History of the English People*, 104.

11. Catholic Encyclopedia, "Azymite," http://www.newadvent.org/ cathen/02172a.htm (accessed June 8, 2010).

12. Aglaia Kremezi, *The Food of the Greek Islands: Cooking and Culture at the Crossroads of the Mediterranean* (Boston: Houghton Mifflin, 2000), 207.

13. *Curye on Inglysch,* 101.

14. Ibid., 110–111.

15. Austin, ed., *Two Fifteenth-Century Cookery Books*, 42.

16. Robert May, *The Accomplisht Cook, or the Art & Mystery of Cookery* (London: Obadiah Blagrave, 1685), 176.

17. Mary J. Lincoln, *The Boston Cook Book: What to Do and What Not to Do in Cooking* (1871; Boston: Little, Brown, 1926), 76–77.

18. Markham, *The English Housewife,* 204.

19. Charles Elmé Francatelli, *A Plain Cookery Book for the Working Classes,* 68.

20. John Thorne, "An Artisanal Loaf," *Outlaw Cook* (New York: Farrar Straus and Giroux, 1992), 246.

21. Eliza Acton, *The English Bread Book* (1859; East Sussex, UK: Southover Press, 1990), 39, 46.

22. Quoted in the *Oxford English Dictionary*.

23. *Nature*, December 26, 1878, 174–175.

24. Nancy Silverton, *Breads from the La Brea Bakery* (New York: Villard Books, 1996), xxi.

25. Thorne, *Outlaw Cook*, 215.

26. Sign on San Diego, http://www.signonsandiego.com/news/business/ 20070828-1355-bn28bread.html (accessed September 5, 2007).

Epilogue: The Return of the Native

1. "Ship of Fools," http://christopherkimball.wordpress.com/2009/10/09/ship-of-fools/ (accessed June 15, 2010).

2. "Gourmet Magazine, 1941–2009: A recipe for obsolescence," *Boston Globe*, October 7, 2009, A16.

3. Lola Wyman, *Better Meals in Wartime* (New York: Crown Publishers, 1943), 55.

4. Author's personal recipe collection.

5. Craig "Meathead" Goldwyn, "Who Killed Gourmet Magazine?" http://www.huffingtonpost.com/craig-goldwyn/who-killed-gourmet-magazi_b_323745.html (accessed June 15, 2010).

6. Quoted in Adam Gopnik, "No Rules! Is *Le Fooding*, the French Culinary Movement, More than a Feeling?" *The New Yorker*, April 5, 2010, 38.

7. Kim Willsher, "Official: British are better at cooking than the French," http://www.guardian.co.uk/lifeandstyle/2010/mar/22/british-cook-better-than-french (accessed June 15, 2010).

8. Ibid. All comments were posted on March 22, 2010.

Index

PIE stands for Proto-Indo-European. Italic page numbers refer to illustrations.

Index

Recipe Credits

Chapter 1: Apples

Chaucer's Roast Apples: Extract from *Food in England* by Dorothy Hartley, published by Piatkus, an imprint of Little, Brown Book Group. Copyright © 1954 by Dorothy Hartley. Reproduced by permission of Sheil Land Associates Ltd.

Chapter 2: Leeks

Cock-a-Leekie: From Claire Macdonald's *Scottish Cookery*. By permission of Claire Macdonald.

Brotchán Roy: From Darina Allen's *The Complete Book of Irish Country Cooking*. By permission of Darina Allen.

Cawn Cennin: From *An Exaltation of Soups: The Soul-Satisfying Story of Soup, As Told in More Than 300 Recipes* by Patricia Solley, copyright © 2004 by Patricia Solley. Used by permission of Three Rivers Press, a division of Random House, Inc.

Cornish Leek Pie: Reprinted from *Good Things* by Jane Grigson. Copyright © 1971 by Jane Grigson. By permission of the University of Nebraska Press.

Chicken, Leek & Parsley Pie: From Claire Macdonald's *Seasonal Cooking*. By permission of Claire Macdonald.

Forager's French Onion Soup: Reprinted from *Stalking the Wild Asparagus* by Euell Gibbons. By permission of the publisher, Alan C. Hood & Co., Inc., Chambersburg, PA.

Chapter 3: Milk
Milk Toast: From *The Breakfast Book* by Marion Cunningham, copyright © 1987 by Marion Cunningham. Used by permission of Alfred A. Knopf, a division of Random House, Inc.

Chapter 4: Meat
Pig's Cheek and Tongue: Recipe for Pig's Cheek and Tongue (p. 80) from *The Whole Beast: Nose to Tail Eating* by Fergus Henderson. Copyright © 2004 by Fergus Henderson. Reprinted by permission of HarperCollins Publishers.

Epilogue:
Nut Crust Ham Slice: From Lola Wyman's *Better Meals in Wartime.*

Indonesian Pork Satay with Peanut Sauce: from author's recipe collection.

Illustration Credits

Indo-European Family of Languages: Copyright © 2000 by Houghton Mifflin Harcourt Publishing Company. Reproduced by permission from *The American Dictionary of Indo-European Roots*, Second Edition.

Hieronymus Bosch, detail from *The Garden of Earthly Delights*, 1490–1510. Courtesy of Museo Nacional del Prado, Madrid.

Hugo van der Goes, *The Fall of Man*, c. 1470. Courtesy of Kunsthistorisches Museum, Vienna.

Sea Kale at West Worthing Beach. Photo by Andy Potter.

Allium ampeloprasum. Photo by Graham Day for National Museums Northern Ireland.

Allium porrum. Photo by Kim Delaney for Hawthorn Farm Organic Seeds.

Irish-Iberian, Anglo-Teutonic, and Negro Physiognomy. Drawing by H. Strickland Constable for *Harper's Weekly*, 1899.

A hand-carved statue of Saint Brigid with her cow. Courtesy of Carlow County Museum, Ireland.

Caspar Milquetoast: 1930s Christmas card with Caspar Milquetoast by H. T. Webster.

James Gillray, *John Bull Taking a Luncheon*, 1798. Courtesy of © National Maritime Museum, Greenwich, London.

Henry Stahlhut's hand-drawn cover of the January 1, 1941, issue of *Gourmet: The Magazine of Good Living.* Stahlhut/Gourmet/Condé Nast Archive. Copyright © Condé Nast.